CARIBBEAN JOURNEYS

D1598558

CARIBBEAN JOURNEYS

AN ETHNOGRAPHY OF MIGRATION AND HOME

IN THREE FAMILY NETWORKS

KAREN FOG OLWIG

Duke University Press

Durham and London 2007

© 2007 Duke University Press

All rights reserved

Printed in the United States of America

on acid-free paper ∞

Designed by Katy Clove

Typeset in Bembo by Keystone Typesetting, Inc.

Library of Congress Cataloging-in-Publication

Data appear on the last printed page of this book.

CONTENTS

This study owes its greatest debt of thanks to the approximately 150 individuals in three family networks of Caribbean origins who made it possible. Their contributions ranged from participating in life-story interviews to extending generous hospitality in their homes, showing me around in their local communities, helping make contacts with other relatives included in the study, and reading and commenting on earlier writings. I am deeply grateful for their help, which not only enabled me to carry out the study, but also made the research process a pleasure. I have tried to safeguard individuals' anonymity by changing personal names as well as certain place names, just as I have attempted to respect people's sense of privacy by omitting many details concerning personal relationships. I hope that the family narratives in this book, built up around individuals' life stories, will resonate with their experiences and that my analysis will offer them an interesting perspective on their lives, even if they probably will not agree with it entirely. Most of all, I hope that they will think that I have done justice to the trust they showed me by sharing their life stories with me.

The book grew out of my research project "Constructing Lives in the Global Ecumene: A Study of West Indian Life Stories," which was part of a larger research project, "Livelihood, Identity and Organisation in Situations of Instability," funded by the Danish Council for Development Research. The larger project was a collaborative venture between the Center for Development Research (now part of the Danish Institute of International Studies), Roskilde University, and the University of Copenhagen and took place in 1996–2000. My project was based on life-story interviews with individuals in three extended family networks of Caribbean origins that had become dispersed through migration to North America, Great Britain, and the Caribbean. This research led to a number of articles in international edited volumes and journals that focused on different aspects of the Caribbean background and migration experiences of these dispersed family networks (see Olwig 1999a, 1999b, 2001, 2002a, 2002b, 2003a, 2003b, 2004, 2005). This volume is informed by these preliminary and partial works but offers a much more comprehensive, ethnographically rich, and complex analysis.

I acknowledge the constructive critique offered especially in the early stages of the work by members of the research group who formed the core in the larger research project of which this project was part. I also thank the many colleagues who discussed various aspects of the research with me, giving helpful comments and advice at different stages of the work. They include Jean Besson, Mary Chamberlain, Nancy Foner, Carla Freeman, Akhil Gupta, Lennox Honychurch, Antonio Lauria, Peggy Levitt, David and Mary Alice Lowenthal, Karsten Pærregaard, Dwaine Plazza, Connie Sutton, and Mary Waters, as well as the many participants at conferences and seminars in Denmark and abroad where I have presented papers on my work. I thank in particular Vered Amit, Kenneth Olwig, Nina Glick Schiller, and the two anonymous readers at Duke University Press, who read the manuscript and gave valuable critique that much improved the final product—though I am, of course, entirely responsible for its shortcomings. I also owe a great debt of thanks to Ken Wissoker at Duke University Press for believing in the book project and making it possible for me to do the necessary revisions.

The Department of Anthropology, University of Copenhagen, offered an academic home where I was able to present and discuss my research at lectures, seminars, and conferences, as well as in more informal discussions where I received many insightful comments. I thank especially Michael Whyte who, as chairperson during the late 1990s, allowed me to take breaks from the ordinary semester work to travel on intermittent fieldwork during the four years in which field research took place, and Vibeke Steffen who, as chairperson during the early 2000s, gave me a semester's leave, thus enabling me to write a good part of the monograph. I also thank the Norwegian Center of Child Research for giving me a friendly and helpful academic base in Trondheim, Norway, from 1998 to 2001.

Finally, I thank Kenneth and Mette for bearing with my many periods of absence from home and for accompanying me enthusiastically on trips to United States, the U.S. Virgin Islands, Jamaica, Dominica, and Great Britain. They helped make this a fun project and were living proof that family relations can be resilient and supportive, and can serve as an important source of belonging in a globalized world.

Caribana, the Caribbean Carnival, was just beginning when I arrived in Toronto in August 1997. The city was full of Caribbean music, food, and arts and crafts, and the huge parade, in which thousands of people would take to the streets dressed in fantastic costumes and dancing to live calypso, soca, steel-pan, and reggae bands, was only days away. It was no coincidence that my trip to Toronto coincided with Caribana. I was doing fieldwork on Caribbean migration by studying three Caribbean family networks that had become dispersed in the United States, Canada, Great Britain, and diverse Caribbean islands. A central element in this research was life-story interviews with family members in different migration destinations, and I had timed my fieldwork in the Toronto area so that it took place during Caribana. In this way I would be able to experience this important Caribbean cultural festival and get an impression of the way in which the family members—and the Caribbean community in Toronto—celebrated their cultural heritage.

CARIBBEAN BELONGING

When I discovered that the first person that I interviewed, Matthew, was a professional musician and acoustic engineer with a recording studio, I praised my luck. He would certainly be an eager participant at Caribana, and I imagined that he might take me along to some of the musical events. Great was my surprise when he explained that he had no plans at all to attend Caribana. He did not care for calypso, he explained, and therefore did not see the point of going. But he added that he would he happy to introduce me to his Filipino girlfriend. She would be participating in the Carnival because she liked to walk on stilts—the stilt-walking "moko jumbies" being traditional figures in West Indian Carnivals—and she would probably be willing to take me along to some of the events.

As I interviewed other members of Matthew's family in Toronto, it became clear that many of them did not have a special interest in Caribana. This did not mean that they were indifferent to their Caribbean background—or that they had anything against Caribana, for that matter. They were quite interested in contributing to my study and keen to tell me about their life experiences in relation to their particular background. To these family members, their Caribbeanness was an ordinary part of their family background that had shaped their everyday life, not something they necessarily wanted to celebrate in the wider society to assert an ethnic identity. This understanding of Caribbean belonging as grounded in individual life experiences, yet embedded in collective family histories, was a central theme in the life-story interviews that I carried out in the three dispersed family networks of Caribbean origin. This is illustrated by the life stories related by Matthew, Susanna, and Shelly. They raise important questions concerning what it means to be Caribbean, or to have an immigrant identity more generally.

Matthew It was almost 11 o'clock on a hot August night when I met with Matthew at one of the big hotels in downtown Toronto. We took the elevator to an outdoor café located on the roof and ordered coffee so that our minds could be as fresh as possible. Matthew was groggy after a long day and evening's hard work in the recording studio that he operated, and I was tired, having just arrived from a nearby town, where I had visited, and interviewed, Matthew's elder sister. This was the best time for Matthew to meet with me because of his busy schedule.

As we began to drink our coffee, I explained that I wanted to do a life-story interview with him as part of my research on three Caribbean family networks that have become dispersed through migration. I said that it would be great if we could just begin with his relating his life story to me as he remembered it. Matthew nodded, and as the night wore on, he recounted that he was born on the outskirts of London but had moved to Toronto with his family when he was eight. The family was encouraged to do this by his mother's sister, who was already living in Toronto and who thought Canada offered better opportunities than Great Britain. In Toronto, Matthew had become "basically a Canadian," with an interest in sports and writing, and in his youth he developed an interest in music. After earning a degree in acoustic engineering, performing and recording music became his career. He added that he was thinking about moving back to London because he thought that London offered better opportunities for the kind of music that he performed. He ended his life story by noting that he belonged to a family with close relations, and he liked to visit Dominica—the family's Caribbean island of origin—where his parents now were living after their retirement.

When Matthew finished his brief life story, I asked him to elaborate on each point in the story. In this way I learned more about his early childhood recollections from England, where his parents had migrated from Dominica during the 1950s. I also learned about the move onward to Toronto, where he felt both like he was a foreigner, being one of the few black kids who spoke with a British accent, and like he was at home, being surrounded by other members of the Gaston family who had settled in Canada. He noted his parents' disappointment that he had not opted for an education in a profession like law or medicine and explained that acoustic engineering was a compromise between his parents' educational ambitions for their children and his own passion for music.

When, toward the end of the interview, I asked Matthew how he identified himself, he said that he regarded himself as "British West Indian," since he was born in Britain of West Indian background, but his African heritage was also important to him. Mostly, however, he identified with the avant-garde music scene in which he worked with white as well as black people who were interested in the blending of widely different music styles. He had recently been in London, where there was a great deal of interest in his type of music and where he had felt at home immediately. He was hoping to move "back to London" to further his music career—and to prove to his parents that his decision to become a musician had been a good one.

Susanna   At the time I interviewed Susanna on the Leeward island of Nevis, I had known her since the summer of 1982, when my husband and I drove up from London to visit her family in Chapeltown, the West Indian section of Leeds, England. While doing research in the Caribbean in the 1970s and 1980s, I had become friendly with the family's relatives in the U.S. Virgin Islands and British Virgin Islands, as well as those in Nevis, and was curious to meet the only family member who had gone to England, Susanna's father, Edwin. When my husband and I arrived at Edwin's home, we were welcomed as if we were family. After a great West Indian meal of well-spiced chicken with rice and peas, we were taken to a West Indian party where we soon found ourselves in a crowded living room full of people from Nevis and St. Kitts, drinking rum and dancing to the latest calypso and soca music.

I do not have strong recollections of Susanna from my first visit in Leeds, but during the late 1980s, when I did research among Nevisians in Leeds, I got to know her as a very friendly and helpful teenager who cooked an impressive English meal—spiced up with her mother's West Indian gravy—when we were invited for Sunday dinner. She was then on the verge of entering college to train as a chef. When I later began to do interviews on Nevis with members of the Smith family, as part of this study of three dispersed Caribbean families, I was surprised to discover that Susanna was living on Nevis. As she related her life story to me, she explained that, after having worked as a chef at the same restaurant in Leeds for nine years, she became fed up with her job—and with life in England. While visiting Nevis in connection with a family reunion organized by her mother's family, she realized that she did not want to go back to work in cold and depressing England. She therefore stayed only long enough in Leeds to pack her things and return to Nevis. She related that she was enjoying life in Nevis, working as a chef at one of the upscale hotels and living with her boyfriend—another second-generation Nevisian returnee from Leeds, with whom she was expecting a baby. She had applied for citizenship in St. Kitts-Nevis and planned to stay on the island.

Three years later, when I paid another visit to the Smiths in Leeds, Susanna surprised me again. She had moved back to Leeds and was living in an apartment in Chapeltown with her two-year-old daughter. She told me that she was happy to be with her family and friends again. Nevis had been a great experience, but things had not worked out in the long run, and she realized that she would never be accepted as a real Nevisian. England might not be a perfect place, but it seemed to be where she belonged—at least for now.

Shelly In November 1996, I arrived in a small regional airport in rural northern California to meet Shelly, who could be identified as a "second-generation Jamaican immigrant." I did not easily identify Shelly in the small crowd waiting for passengers because, with her light-skinned complexion, she did not stand out from others at the airport. On the way to the rural community where she made her home, we stopped briefly at a casino owned by a Native American tribe to pick up her husband, who maintained the gambling videos. He explained that he was of Native American origins but that this was not documented. He therefore had no privileges as a Native American but was just an ordinary employee at the casino. As we approached the area where Shelly and her husband were living, Shelly told me not to blink when we drove through the town or I might miss seeing the tiny settlement. Outside the town, we turned to the right and began to drive up an unpaved mountain road to the family's home, which was located in the middle of woods overlooking the valley.

Over the next days I stayed with Shelly and her family, enjoying their generous hospitality, partaking in their lives in the small, environmentally conscious local community, and chatting with Shelly and recording the life story that she related to me. She told me about her childhood in New York City, where she had grown up surrounded by Jamaican relatives, and she recounted the experiences of her several extended childhood stays in Jamaica with her grandmother; her move as a young adult to live with an aunt in San Francisco; her employment with a major airline, which allowed her to visit Jamaica often; her move to northern California after a work accident; her involvement in an interfaith gospel choir that attracted a wide variety of people; her marriage, after two divorces, to her third husband in a Native American–inspired wedding ceremony; the birth of her son when she was in her forties; and the family's purchase of the small house on the mountainside, which they had made their home a few months before I came. Shelly noted that her relatives had been very pleased that she had "finally settled down with a husband, child, and home."

THREE FAMILY NETWORKS

My trips to interview Matthew, Susanna, and Shelly circumscribed a field site that stretched from North America to Britain and the Caribbean and encompassed the disparate places where individuals in three family networks of Caribbean origin were living under widely different social and economic circumstances. This diversity of lives, the result of many different Caribbean journeys away from home, is often referred to as the "Caribbean diaspora" and described as consisting of "transnational communities" or a hybridity of Caribbean and other cultural elements. The concepts of "diaspora," "transnational," and "hybridity" may seem to capture the lives of these people well. It is, of course, possible to describe Matthew's, Susanna's, and Shelly's lives in terms of transnational engagement, longing for a diasporic homeland and an interest in different cultural traditions. Yet I shall argue here that such notions of transcendence, exile, and mixing do not take us far enough if we want to understand how these people perceive their origins in another place, their families' journeys and dwellings in different destinations, and the ways in which this has affected their lives and identity. This is because these notions are defined in contrast to an implicit norm of stable life in a culturally homogeneous homeland that is often assumed to be coterminous with a nation-state (cf. Wimmer and Glick Schiller 2003: 595; see also Khan 2004). I argue, however, that migrants' lives cannot be interpreted in such contrastive terms. Rather, they must be understood within more specific contexts of interpersonal relations that stimulate and inform their mobile life trajectories and shape their attachments to a shared place of origin. This book seeks to do so by focusing on three Caribbean networks of family relations that have provided a central context of migratory moves, as well as continued relations with particular places of origin in the Caribbean. In this way it seeks to develop an interpretive framework informed by migrants' ways of thinking and acting rather than by the national culture and ideology of the sending and receiving societies.

Life stories are not just accounts of individual trajectories, within the framework of family relations, but also histories of specific periods and places as these have been experienced by the narrators. This work is therefore also an ethnography of people creating their own lives within the global migratory regime that migrants and their descendants, from the Caribbean and elsewhere, have encountered—the world system of unequal social and economic relations that transforms physical movement into possibilities for socioeconomic mobility. It does not deal directly, however, with the international political order of nation-states that seeks to regulate migratory flows and the ethnic politics of the sending and receiving countries that have come to set important parameters for sociocultural identification and mobilization among immigrants. This would be the subject of another kind of study.[1] The migratory regime therefore is examined not in terms of sociological abstractions, but from the ethnographic perspective of three concrete Caribbean families evolving through extensive networks of relations, touching down in North America, Europe, and various parts of the Caribbean. Notions of family relations, improvement, and belonging, which are vital to the migrants, are therefore at the center stage of this analysis.

By investigating the intimate context of family relations and their modes of expression and forms of self-understanding, this study departs from a recent tendency in migration research to investigate cultural expression and identity formation among migrants in the public arena, whether in the form of ethnic festivals, cultural politics, or hybrid artistic expression. This book builds on earlier ethnographic studies that have pointed to the significance of family networks in migration processes, but it also incorporates new anthropological approaches that examine kinship and place as social constructions that are shaped and given meaning in the course of everyday social life.

THE THEORETICAL CONTEXT

Social Fields and Networks "Roots," "ethnic origins," "transnational relations" and "diasporic homelands" are some of the buzzwords that became prominent in migration studies toward the end of the second millennium. The terms emerged at the same time that people became aware of the increasing global mobility and interconnectedness that characterize contemporary human life. The more interrelated and fluid the world became, the more concerned people appeared to become with identifying local places of origin and corresponding cultural identities. These concerns have had an impact on migration research. Thus, during the past decades a number of migration studies have explored the interrelationship between global contexts of mobility and interconnectedness and local sources of rooting and demarcation. This has resulted in the development of theoretical frameworks emphasizing the significance of disaporic homelands and transnational identities among migrants and their descendants. Indeed, it has become common to refer to migrants and their descendants as "transmigrants" or as forming "diasporas" that remain oriented toward a place of origin, even several generations after migration took place.

The strong emphasis on migrants' continued ties to their country of origin represents a radical departure from the approach that has long predominated within migration research. Until the 1980s, migration studies were carried out by what the British sociologist Robin Cohen (1998: 21) has termed "a rather conservative breed of sociologists, historians, demographers and geographers" who documented population movements in time and space and were largely concerned with immigrants' integration into their new place of residence. This field of migration research emphasized such aspects of the migration process as the push–pull factors that induced people to leave for various migration destinations and the processes of incorporation that migrants underwent in their new place of residence.

These research issues reflect, to a great extent, concerns of the receiving countries—the causes and patterns of migration flows that shape the influx of people, the processes of incorporation whereby the newly arrived are turned into proper citizens, and the kind of identities that they develop in their new country. This perspective has prevailed in most Western social sciences (Brettell 2003: 1). Sociology has thus been most interested in *immigration*, the impact of immigration on the receiving society and various aspects of migrants' integration in the receiving societies. Because of its traditional focus on peripheral non-Western societies that provide the place of origin of many migrants, the discipline of anthropology, however, has generally studied migration ethnographically from the vantage point of the migrants. It has therefore investigated *migration processes* more broadly. Ethnographic migrant-focused research thus has involved investigating the meaning and purpose of migration to migrants and those left behind, the impact of migration on sending as well as receiving societies, the concrete relations that migrants maintain with people in their place of origin, and the ways in which these relations may influence patterns of adaptation in the migration destination.

Ethnographic studies have maintained a migrant point of view by making migrants' social field of relations the main empirical object of study. The notion of networks has been central in the conceptualization of these fields. Network analysis entered anthropological migration studies during the 1940s and 1950s in the context of ethnographic fieldwork among rural-urban migrants in Central Africa. In these studies, anthropologists realized that migrants from tribal areas to the new urban developments did not operate within a tribal social framework; nor did they become modern urban dwellers. Rather, they developed social networks of relations that included friends and relatives from the place of origin as well as neighbors, workmates, and others encountered in the migration destination. By examining migrants' networks of relations, anthropologists were able to study how individuals in the migration destination renegotiated earlier tribal relations within the new context of their migration destination at the same time that they developed new relations that crosscut tribal affiliations. The concept of social networks therefore allowed for the study of local as well as translocal relations; individual agency as well as social structure; change as well as continuity (Barnes 1969; Epstein 1969; Gluckman 1963 [1961]).

The focus on social networks among migrants was extended to studies of migration to destinations in the Western world when Stuart Philpott, during the 1960s, studied Caribbean migration to Great Britain on the basis of fieldwork on the small British West Indian island of Montserrat as well as among Montserratsian migrants in London. In a 1968 article he suggested that the most promising approach to the study of this migration was to be found in "the pursuit of the migrants themselves, in the study of the networks of relations in which they are involved in their overseas environment and of the relations which they maintain with their home societies" (Philpott 1968: 465; see also Philpott 1973). In the next decades, a host of ethnographic studies followed that also examined migration within the wider context of the social relations that frame migrants' lives (Brettell 2000: 97–98).

When examined within the context of networks, migration involves neither rupture nor continuity in social life. Rather, it involves the extending, developing, negotiating, and redefining of relations. There is an extending of locally developed social relations over long distances as well as the gradual development of new relations in the migration destination; there is a negotiation of local and translocal relations in the light of obligations, opportunities, and constraints in both the migration destination and the place of origin; and there is a constant redefining of the significance of these relations in the light of experiences gained in the migration destination and in return visits in the place of origin.

One of the reasons social networks have become a useful framework of study in ethnographic migration research is that they, at their most fundamental level of operation, consist of relations between individuals, not between institutions, corporate structures, or other collectivities. For this reason, networks are not confined to circumscribed social contexts or localities but can be extended and reshaped as individuals move and form new relations. Migration networks, Caroline Brettell emphasizes, "must be conceived as facilitating rather than encapsulating, as permeable, expanding, and fluid rather than as correlating with a metaphor of a rigid and bounded structure" (Brettell 2000: 107; see also Tilly 1990). Furthermore, networks "can become self-perpetuating to migration because 'each act of migration itself creates the social structure needed to sustain it,' " creating what has been called "network-mediated migration" (Brettell 2000: 107, quoting Wilson 1994).

"Network-mediated migration" involves individuals moving along the lines of personal relationships that extend from their place of origin to a migration destination. For many migrants, it is often through those networks of relationships that they obtain knowledge about possible migration destinations, the social and economic opportunities that they offer, and the best modes of access to these places. It is therefore insufficient to describe such migration as the movement from one country or nation-state to another. This may be a correct description from an official, legal, and political point of view, but it says little about the pathways of interpersonal relations by which the move actually takes place. These relations may, for example, extend from a particular point of departure, such as a remote village, to a specific destination—for example, a certain neighborhood in a distant city. Furthermore, when examined from the vantage point of networks, it becomes apparent that migratory moves are not necessarily directed toward one major migration destination. Rather, they are oriented toward those destinations that become available and attractive to migrants (Brettell 2000:107).

Networks are particularly relevant and illuminating contexts within which to do migration research because they are, by nature, cross-categorical and cross-institutional (Amit 2002b: 22–25; Boissevain 1974). As noted by J. Edwards and M. Strathern (2000: 162), heterogeneity is "written into . . . theorising on networks." Networks thus "have become, definitively, links between the disparate. In this view, they are found in those contexts where one makes a passage from one domain of materiality to another" (Edwards and Strahern 2000: 162)—in the case of migration, from one place to another. An important principle behind networking is the creating and maintaining of connections between people in different social, economic, and political positions. This means that these people will have different things to offer and therefore be interesting partners in the various transactions that form the basis of the relations in the network. Networks are thus incorporative by nature, and they may involve complex, often asymmetrical interpersonal transactions. Networks have therefore been described as integrative patterns of transactions that connect individual relations and the social system, the local and the national (Boissevain 1974: 25). In the context of international migration, their integrative function involves an even more complicated interstitial system linking people located in different parts of the world. This means that networks are based on quite another logic than nation-states, with their clearly demarcated borders, exclusive memberships based on birthrights, and strong ideology of shared common identity.

While the networks of relations that link individual migrants with people in the migration destination, as well as in the country of origin, are interstitial, they are not defined—at least initially—in relation to the more permanent structures that they connect or circumnavigate through these interpersonal ties. Thus, if migrants develop networks that can be characterized as transnational, diasporic, or even hybrid, this is not necessarily because migrants consciously seek to transcend nations, maintain ties with a distant homeland, or blend different cultural forms. It is, rather, because migrants' networks consist of a variety of ties to a range of individuals they know both from their country of origin and from the different social, economic, and political contexts that they have experienced as migrants. Important topics in research on migrant networks therefore are the formation of particular constellations of relations in individuals' networks, the significance of these sets of relationships, and the ways in which networks change in form and content through time in the course of individual life trajectories.[2]

Relatedness and Place Making   So far I have emphasized that a central element of networks is their flexibility and inclusiveness because individuals, rather than institutions or corporate structures of various kinds, constitute the focal points in the web of relations that constitutes a network. It is apparent, however, that individuals act not just on their own, but within wider contexts of social relations. These contexts have been described as social fields of interpersonal relations involving complex sets of moral obligations and rights extending among migrants and between migrants and those left behind (see, for example, Philpott 1968). Migration studies have shown that family relations often play a central role in migrant networks (Baud 1994; Brettell 2000; Philpott 1968). From a network point of view, close family consists of those people who share a certain set of moral values and expectations that impel them to engage in intensive exchange relations involving, for example, various kinds of help, visits, recollection of memories, or communication, whether face to face or by letter, phone, or electronic means. Thus, family networks—with their systems of exchanges—should not be reduced to adaptations to particular conditions of social and economic inequality. Instead, as Edwards and Strathern (2000: 160–61) point out, family closeness "summons affective ties, the obligations and duties such ties entail, and the warmth and mutual care with which relationships are sustained" in contrast to "distance, and 'distant relatives' [who] are those with whom interaction is infrequent, with whom obligations are at a minimum and with whom confidences are unlikely to be shared." Thus, when individuals' expectations of the nature of specific relations are disappointed, because, for example, certain relations of exchange fail to materialize, family feelings, and notions of kinship, will tend to fade.

Just as individuals are perceived and defined according to their concrete engagement in a field of social relations, the places involved in the migratory moves will be viewed through the lens of social relations making up the migrants' social field. And just as networks of relationships provide potential migrants with knowledge about and access to various destinations, they help actual migrants maintain contact with their place of origin. Thus, this place will remain an important site of personal belonging as long as migrants maintain close relations to people in this site, but it may become a more abstract place of identification if the center of migrants' social relations, and sociability, shifts to the migration destination. From the point of view of the logic of social fields, family and kinship as well as places—regarded as the bedrock of social life—therefore do not exist in and of themselves. Rather, they become defined and attain meaning as individuals' lives take social form and place within specific networks of social relations.

The theoretical concepts of *relatedness* and *place making* are useful in migration research because they draw attention to the fact that notions of kinship and place emerge and acquire meaning in the context of social life. Thus, kinship and place are constructed as people, through "statements and practices," give specific substance and meaning to certain kinds of relationships (Carsten 2000:24) and physical environments or localities (Kahn 1996). It is therefore necessary to examine what kind of relations and places migrants construct as "natural" and the significance that they attribute to them in their particular situation. In the case of this study, the focus is on place making in relation to a self-identified or imputed place of origin. This focus, in turn, is of relevance to the process of constructing place identities in the different destination locations—a complex issue that, given the variety of locations under study, can only be touched on here. The central topics of investigation in this book are thus the notions of relatedness that individuals create within a social network, defined as family, who share common origins in a particular place, and how this in turn may create various sources of belonging and identification for the migrants.

The concepts of relatedness and place making are central to the analysis of this book because they draw attention to the fact that family and place are cultural phenomena created in the course of social life. This is important when studying immigrants and their descendants, because they are often categorized matter-of-factly in terms of ethnic groups according to their foreign place of origin. An important reason that this understanding of immigrants prevails, as Baumann (1997: 213) has noted, is that "ethnos" seems to designate "a biological fact" that cannot be disputed because it rests on the idea that migrants have a natural tie to their site of origin by virtue of having been born there, a tie that is believed to be passed by biological descent through the generations. Ethnicity therefore becomes an identity that is ascribed to people on the basis of natural characteristics, not something that is necessarily actively chosen and defined by individuals depending on their particular situation. For this reason, Vered Amit argues, "The rhetorical emphases on descent and continuity which are a feature in most ethnic charters provides for an affiliation which, in principle, precedes actual interaction and performance" (Amit-Talai 1995:131). Caribbean people have generally been associated, in the receiving societies in North America and Europe, with the natural characteristic of being blacks of primarily African origin. By this definition, people like Shelly, who are light-skinned, may be regarded as only peripherally Caribbean even if they identify strongly with their Caribbean background.

The ascription of ethnic identity to "visible" immigrants is related to the dominant understanding, in Western society, that notions of family and place cohere in the concept of belonging and are associated with a positive sense of community and sociability (Edwards and Strathern 2000:152). Naturalistic metaphors apply at the local level of village life at the same time as they operate in the form of larger units of belonging, most notably in the form of national communities, even if such communities can only be imagined, as Benedict Anderson (1991[1983]) has argued. This power of imagination rests, to a great extent, on metaphors that seem to give a material, natural basis to the national community. As Deborah Bryceson and Ulla Vuorela (2002:10) point out, "When the family is taken as a parallel and central metaphor for the nation, it remains unproblematized, assumed to be a natural community." With this understanding of communities of belonging as based on "natural" ties of blood and soil, immigrants will be identified with their place of origin. Furthermore, their descendants will continue to be associated with their parents' community, especially if they, for some reason, are perceived as being different—for example, because of their racial appearance.

Few, if any, anthropologists would seriously suggest that ethnicity is biologically determined. But by making an a priori categorization of people according to their place of birth, or the place of birth of their immigrant ancestors, they nevertheless end up lending unintended support to such views. This conceptualization of ethnicity as grounded in nature is quite far removed from the understanding of ethnicity that Fredrik Barth (1969) put forward and that has become widely accepted within the general field of anthropology. According to Barth, ethnicity is constructed in specific situations as social groups demarcate themselves as culturally different in relation to others. Ethnicity, in other words, designates a dynamic form of cultural attachment that may be defined according to changing criteria and attributed with varying meanings in different social, historical, and geographical contexts. It therefore behooves us to examine through careful ethnographic analysis how blood and soil are socially constructed in specific situations as the "natural facts" (cf. Strathern 1992: 17) forming the basis of ethnicity. There is, in other words, a need to examine how migrants and their descendants understand and practice relations to family and place, and how—and if—they connect these personal experiences of identity with the social categories of ethnicity that they are expected to share (cf. Campbell and Rew

1999: ix). An important aim of this study is to determine what kind of relatedness individuals create as members of a group of people sharing common origins in a particular family home in the Caribbean and how this, in turn, influences the ways in which they construct this "home" as a place of belonging and identification.[3]

Steven Feld and Keith Basso (1996: 5) claim that there has been a tendency for ethnographic writing on place to focus on "contestation" and to describe places as "sites of power struggles" or "displacement as histories of annexation, absorption, and resistance." This is certainly the case in migration research. Here place has largely figured in the form of a homeland celebrated by a minority population who resist absorption into the hegemonic nationstates of migration destinations (see, for example, Basch et al. 1994). Alternatively, it has figured as a place of origin that allows a majority population to categorize immigrant populations as ethnic minorities. However, places are much more than powerful referents that can be used in the political power struggles between minority and majority populations in immigrant countries. They emerge and attain meaning in the course of everyday life, as people develop communities of social relations that are grounded in certain physical localities (Olwig 1997). The very notion of different communities of people, defined in relation to specific places, therefore can only be understood by exploring the concrete social practices and cultural values that have given meaning to particular concepts of place and the people associated with them (cf. Amit 2002a, 2000b).[4] Place making never happens in a vacuum; it occurs within a larger framework that may involve widely different social, economic, and political interests, especially in situations of unequal power relations. In the Caribbean, places were created in a European-dominated colonial setting where race, gender, and class were important parameters of control. This is reflected in complex ways in African Caribbean places, because they can be seen to constitute sites of adaptation as well as resistance to these structures of domination (Olwig 1985). Places, furthermore, are constructed at many different levels of abstraction, ranging from a home associated with an intimate community of relatives to a village or town linked with a close-knit local community of neighbors and friends to a country identified with a more diffuse, imagined national community of people.

When migrants arrive in a migration destination, they do not necessarily identify primarily with an ethnic community rooted in a country of origin.

Their sense of a place (Tuan 1974, 1980) is linked to the specific places within their country of origin with which they identify because of their particular background. Indeed, individual migrants from the Caribbean, where place making is shaped by systems of unequal race, class, and gender relations, may identify with very different places of origin. This means that immigrants from the same nation-state do not necessarily share an identity, except at a nominal level. Take the example of Shelly. Her particular notion of her Jamaican identity was closely related to her specific family background and the kind of ties to Jamaica that it had afforded her. Her parents were born in a British colony; she was born an American citizen but took Jamaican citizenship when the island became an independent nation-state, and she married a person who identifies with his Native American background. In the light of such complex sets of national identities, it becomes necessary to elucidate how the "natural" ties of family and place, in actual practice, are constructed as specific forms of relatedness among individuals who share a particular site of origin and the ways in which this, in turn, influences their definition of a place of origin and its possible role as a source of identification.

There may be a tendency, when seeing a book about Caribbean migration, to think that it is primarily about race, because the issue of race impinges to varying degrees on all members of Caribbean society in particular, and on the societies to which they have immigrated in general. Race, however, is only one facet in the complex of economic, class, gender, and ethnic factors that shape Caribbean migration experiences. The interpretation of this complex in any given context depends on the theoretical and methodological prisms through which one looks. While race does play an important role in the family narratives, the ways in which issues of race are represented and given meaning in life narratives must be placed within a broader framework that investigates understandings of family, migration, and belonging more broadly.

THE METHODOLOGICAL CONTEXT

The Relating of Life Stories   To fully examine social practices and cultural values in relation to place, it is necessary to shift ethnographic focus from the homelands represented in public manifestations of cultural politics to the places of belonging that emerge in the private, intersubjective context of migrants' and their descendants' lives. Varying understandings and forms of place making are ever emergent in the ongoing practice of social life. A place comes into being, according to Marc Augé (1995 [1992]: 43), when it is "discovered by those who claim it as their own." An important part of place making at a collective level thus is the creating of foundational narratives that validate the claim of a social group to a particular place (Augé 1995 [1992]: 43). Foundational narratives, however, do not only involve the validation of a place by people who discover it and "claim it as their own." As people claim a particular place through their foundational narratives, they also create a particular notion of relatedness as a group vis-à-vis the place in question. Foundational narratives are therefore narratives of relatedness, as well as of place.

I suggest that dispersed family networks, where individual family members have a common background in a particular place of origin, offer a highly relevant site in which to study place. Furthermore, I propose that life stories, narrated by individuals in these family networks, provide insight into the foundational narratives that give substance to, and define, the particular sites of origin and notions of relatedness that relatives in these networks claim for themselves. A life story entails an accounting of an individual's movements through life—geographical, as well as social, economic, or cultural—in such a way that it portrays a sense of coherence reflective of the narrator's sense of self (Bruner 1987; Langness and Frank 1981; Linde 1993; Ochs and Capps 1996; Peacock and Holland 1993). Life stories need to be created out of the welter of occurrences and relationships that characterize most lives, because they must conform to norms concerning the sort of life deemed to be credible and socially acceptable. Life stories are, of course, also personal, because they reflect individuals' particular cultural understanding of themselves. Life stories therefore shed light on the life courses people have lived, the sociocultural order that they establish in their life stories, and, hence, their understanding of this order from their particular vantage point. This means that while individuals in their life stories refer to and, to a certain extent, validate a specific foundational narrative defining their family network and linking it to a shared place of origin, they also interpret this narrative from their variously positioned vantage points and relate it to the lives that they have lived. This particular methodological approach thus gives insights into how individuals, through the act of *relating* their life stories to each other, and to outsiders, create a sense of *relatedness* demarcating cultural values and social norms associated with their family *relations*. To "relate" a life story is more than *telling* a life story. It involves the relating of one's life to that of others (cf. Somers 1994). The life-story approach also gives insight into how these notions are grounded in the shared origins linked with their particular place of identification in the Caribbean. Finally, it shows how these notions of relatedness and place are negotiated and changed in response to the various social, economic, geographic, and personal circumstances of the narrators. This raises questions concerning the significance of a place of origin as a source of belonging in relation to other sources of belonging developed by family members through their variegated life trajectories.

By investigating life stories, I focus on how individuals through accounts of their lives affirm and re-create the notions of relatedness that sustain and further develop the intimate family relations that link them to a distant place of origin. I therefore do not so much draw on narrative theories rooted in literary genres as on theory concerning the construction of relatedness and place through practice—here in the form of the relating of life experiences.[5] A key methodological tool in my research therefore was the life-story interview.

I began all of the interviews—as described in my interview with Matthew—by simply asking individuals to tell me their life story. Virtually everybody responded to this request by outlining the main events in their life, although the length of this account varied from a few minutes to more than an hour. In the remainder of the interview I asked interviewees to elaborate on various points in this life-story sketch and asked supplementary questions on issues that had come up in other interviews but that had not been touched on in the initial life story related by the interviewee. My idea was to give them an opportunity to introduce themselves in a way that corresponded to how they thought about themselves as individuals. Early in the research, some of the individuals appeared to be attempting to relate their life narratives in accordance with what they thought might be my research interests. Any self-representation involves a social relationship with another person, because narratives, as Elinor Ochs and Lisa Capps (1996:35) state, are "interactional achievements" where "the role of primary recipient can be highly consequential." As my research became a topic of conversation in the family, and individuals learned about me and my research from those who had already been interviewed, the social context of the life-story interviews became defined by the wider field of family relations as well as the social relationships that I gradually established with the individual family members I interviewed. As this occurred, individuals became less interested in my research agenda and more concerned about giving a "proper" impression of the family and their own position in it. The self-presentations of the people I interviewed therefore turned out to offer an important entrance to insights into notions of relatedness among people in the family networks.

The narrative aspect of the life-story interviews was particularly useful in this study of relatedness within family networks because, as Ochs and Capps (1996: 27) have observed, "Narrative activity attempts to resolve the discrepancy between what is expected and what has transpired." The "expected" that the family members were trying to account for was defined with reference to the family network that I was studying and the cultural norms and social conventions with which it identified. By presenting their life stories in relation to the expected ways of the family, individuals inscribed themselves within the family network. It was quite apparent that individuals did not just tell stories about themselves, and other family members, when a visiting anthropologist did a life-story interview. The maintaining and reshaping of family ways occurred, to a great extent, as individuals related stories—or gossiped—within the family network, whether by phone, letter, or e-mail or face to face when visiting. Talking with me about themselves, as with others in the family, therefore was part of the ongoing process of family conversation that constituted an important lifeline within the family. In this way, the life stories that individuals narrated to me, as I moved about in the family networks, reciprocally informed the cultural values and social conventions that were expected to define family relations. They were therefore highly revealing of the family members' sense of relatedness.

While the life-story interviews form the backbone of my research, they do not stand alone. Thus, most of them were related in the family members' homes, and I was therefore able to socialize informally with the family before and after the interviews and thereby gain an understanding of family dynamics through participant observation. Furthermore, many of the family members, like Shelly's family and Susanna's parents, invited me to stay with them in their homes when I traveled to their part of the world to interview them. Because of this generous hospitality, I usually spent several days with them, chatting informally with the family members, moving around in the local area with them, and meeting the people with whom they associated in their everyday life. This provided valuable knowledge about their daily lives as well as an important context for interpreting the life-story interviews that they related to me.

By employing life-story interviews as a primary mode of investigation and by drawing on the analytical concepts of place and relatedness, this work combines different strands of method and theory that have been recently invigorated and further developed in various areas of anthropological research. Furthermore, by pointing to the constructed nature of all relationships, the book calls for the need to investigate the ways in which certain relations are imbued with particular cultural significance and naturalized as ties of kinship or ancestral origins associated with a particular ethnic community. The life stories presented and analyzed here show that while all the narrators identified, to some degree, with their Caribbean background, their notions of relatedness and place of origin varied considerably. Thus, the three different family networks emphasized somewhat different ideas and practices of relatedness, and associated places of origin, just as individuals within the families held their own views on these matters. This suggests that an essential dimension of intimate family relations, and the places of belonging that they define, is the opportunity that they grant individuals to develop both collective and more personalized sources of identification and contexts of belonging. This is of particular importance to Caribbean migrants and their descendants when they live in societies where they tend to become "appropriated by" the more generalizing notions of "ethnic communities," "transnational relations," and "diasporic homelands."[6]

A Dispersed Field of Ethnographic Research   Migration research has primarily taken place in ethnic communities in major European and North American migration destinations. As a consequence, scholars tend to investigate, on the one hand, the push–pull factors that can be expected to lead people to migrate, and on the other, the processes leading them to settle in major gateway cities. Since cities with heavy concentrations of migrants often are characterized by ethnic organizations, the focus on these migration destinations, in turn, tends to lead to an emphasis on the identity politics of immigrants' relationship to their homeland and their gradual integration, or lack of integration, into the society and culture of the receiving country. If, however, one starts at the beginning of the migration process, with families living in a

variety of locations under different conditions, and if one follows these families to a multiplicity of destinations, then a much more complex picture of
migration experiences emerges. This is even more the case, if one follows this
fabric of migration movement through the life-story narratives of the actors
who, in their own understanding, respond less to external push–pull factors
than to the internal drives of personal and family ambition and measures of
achievement set by the society of their origin. From such an approach,
migration does not begin when individuals move to Western migration
destinations, but is part of a long family history of movement to improve the
family's position in society. Migration therefore becomes less a matter of
migrants who undergo processes of integration in a new destination than a
case of new places and destinations becoming integrated into the life stories
of striving human beings. It is also less the standard narrative of migrants
funneled into the immigrant areas of major metropoles than a diverse weave
of movement bringing people both to inner-city migrant communities and
to affluent suburbs; both to cities like New York, Toronto, and Leeds and to
the isolated reaches of rural communities in California, Nova Scotia, and
England.

The approach to migration adopted in this study required a change in field
method. The term "field" calls to mind an enclosed territory, be it that of a
rural Third World village or a Western urban ghetto, but the approach to
migration taken here forced me to explore a field that was more like a web of
extensive relations that connected people who had moved to different parts
of the world. My interviews with Matthew, Shelly, and Susanna represent
only a few of many stops on a long and extensive journey that took me to
many different people and places. I initiated field research in June 1996, when
I traveled to Great Britain, where I spent approximately one week in Leeds,
in northern England, interviewing four members of the Smith family, a
network of relatives who share origins in Nevis, one of the Leeward Islands
that is now part of the independent nation-state of St. Kitts-Nevis. Then I
went for a couple of days to metropolitan London and, finally, to the Oxford
area, where I stayed for another three to four days. In that part of the country, I interviewed other relatives in the Smith family network, as well as
several members of Shelly's family—the Muirs. In August, I journeyed to
Nevis, where I joined members of the Smith family of Leeds—among them
Susanna—in celebrating the wedding of a family member who worked in the

U.S. Virgin Islands but was marrying a woman living on Nevis. In November, I resumed fieldwork with the Muir family, traveling first to London, where I spent the day conducting an interview with a family member who had moved there recently, before flying on to the United States, where I first visited Shelly in northern California and then some of her cousins in southern California and Texas. From Texas, I moved onward to the Caribbean Windward Island of Dominica. There I spent about two weeks interviewing members of the Gaston family, the third network of relatives studied. From Dominica I went to the U.S. Virgin Islands and British Virgin Islands, where I spent close to three weeks interviewing members of the Smith family. Before returning to Denmark in January, I went back to Nevis, where I spent another two weeks interviewing members of the Smith family.

The next three years were less hectic. Nevertheless, I managed to travel to Ontario and Nova Scotia in Canada; to New York City and elsewhere in New York State, as well as to New Jersey and Florida in the United States; to Jamaica, Barbados, and—again—Dominica in the Caribbean. Finally, I returned to Great Britain twice, interviewing people living in various towns and villages in central and southern England. During the four years that the research lasted, I spent approximately six months visiting and interviewing 150 members of the three dispersed family networks originating in the Caribbean islands of Nevis, Jamaica, and Dominica.

Some anthropologists might shake their heads at this sort of fieldwork, dismissing it as shallow jet-set ethnography producing thin, if not useless, data. Yet I will here argue for the opposite point of view: that this kind of fieldwork can produce in-depth data that provide important, new insights into areas of study that have received little attention in anthropology. These areas are the non-local spheres of life that are not easily captured by traditional localized fieldwork methods, but that are of growing importance as people become more and more interconnected and mobile on a global scale. If we wish to capture these spheres of life, we need to develop field-research methods that can make them our object of study rather than merely the background, or wider context, of research. One can call this "multi-sited" ethnographic research in the sense that it entails fieldwork that takes place in many different geographic locations. However, my fieldwork entailed more than an attempt to "make connections through translations and tracings among distinctive discourses from site to site" (Marcus 1995: 101). It was ethnographic research in the extended field sites of three different family networks. This research has, in many ways, reversed usual fieldwork practices—it has produced limited data on the local sites where the research took place but rich data on the family relations that were the actual field site. Similarly, a methodological approach of this kind generates relatively little data on everyday life of the sort produced by participant observation. However, it produces a wealth of narrative data on lives lived. This reflects the main focus of the study. Thus, it is not primarily concerned with family members' everyday, ongoing lives in different migration destinations and the social relations and sense of place developed in the course of these local lives. Rather, the focus of analysis is on individuals' life trajectories within the context of dispersed, yet intimate family relations grounded in distant places of origin and the possible sites of belonging and identification developed within this context. It would be fascinating to follow this study up with one that concentrates less on the places of origins, and the theoretical and popular discourse of origins, and more on place making in the destination. Such a study, however, would require a different research trajectory, and it would be directed toward a somewhat different set of academic issues and discourses than this study. In this study, the field is not the migrants' place of origin or place of settlement, but the relations between the immigrants themselves through which a notion of their place of origin is generated. Akhil Gupta and James Ferguson (1997: 2) have argued that the "idea of 'the field,' although central to our intellectual and professional identities, remains a largely unexamined one in contemporary anthropology." Ethnographic fieldwork, they state, therefore has been regarded not as the study of the particular place where it is located, but as "a form of dwelling that legitimizes knowledge production by the familiarity that the fieldworker gains with the ways of life of a group of people" (Gupta and Ferguson 1997: 31). Gupta and Ferguson go on to argue that a "focus on *shifting locations*" rather than on "*bounded fields*" will produce interesting field data, and they call for anthropologists to be more aware of this. While I agree with Gupta and Ferguson that anthropologists need to consider the impact of their localizing practices, and different points of view within a local field site, I think that it is still important to consider anthropological fieldwork as a "form of dwelling." Such dwelling, however, does not have to revolve around a group of people who are confined to a particular location. Thus, by "dwelling" within an extensive field of social relations, I gained in-depth data on particular ways of life and forms of understanding at the same time that I examined the complexity of shifting locations that this field of social relations entailed. By making three families, and their journeys through time and space, my field sites, I therefore in essence continued the time-honored method of carrying out prolonged fieldwork in social communities of relevance to the people studied.

This, then, is not a descriptive ethnography of circumscribed locations, but a narrative ethnography of social fields of movement through which emerges a more cohesive understanding of migration as it is experienced by the active subjects, who make the decision to plunge into new worlds of hoped-for opportunity. Tracking down these far-flung adventures into geographic and social mobility is a daunting task for the jet-lagged anthropologist, who is used to working at the leisurely pace afforded by long residence in a well-demarcated field site. But the need to move through space to weave together the paths of a far-flung family helped lay the basis for a questioning of extant theory and for the development of new frameworks of interpretation. In this work I have built on my own prior fieldwork with Nevisian migrants in the Virgin Islands and Leeds and with their family relations in Nevis (Olwig 1993b). I have also drawn on earlier ethnographic research by other anthropologists who have followed Caribbean migrants from their place of origin to one or more destinations abroad, exploring the fields of relations that connect migrants in these various sites with those left behind (Basch et al. 1994; Foner 1979; Hendricks 1974; Philpott 1973). Unlike these ethnographic studies, however, I have not examined networks linked to a few major migration destinations. Rather, I have made my field site the very movements of a few families and the fields of social relations to different parts of the world that these movements generated. In this respect, the book can be regarded as a continuation of Mary Chamberlain's work on family networks of Barbadian origin, based on life-story interviews (Chamberlain 1997), and Nina Glick Schiller's and Georges Eugene Fouron's detailed study of a single family network of Haitian origin (Glick Schiller and Fouron 2001).[7]

When shifting perspective from immigrant communities to migrant lives, one uncovers a variety of paths of movement, and spaces of belonging, that do not necessarily conform to the more collective diasporic representations emanating from major migration settlements when ethnic organizations seek to further the interests of particular ethnic communities, typically by promoting an idealized version of their native culture, as, for example, through music, drama, Carnivals, and other cultural festivals that celebrate particular diasporic cultures.[8] From the perspective of individual migrants, who may only have a passing connection to the identity politics of ethnic communities, the relationship to culture connected with a place of origin has a much less performative character. My visit with Shelly was a good example of this. Shelly clearly identified with her Jamaican background. She emphasized the importance of her Jamaican family, with whom she had grown up on the East Coast of the United States, and she had made a point of visiting her aunt in New York when her aunt was terminally ill. Shelly noted that she maintained close ties with her cousin in southern California and always spoke "patois" with her on the phone. She recalled with fondness her many visits to Jamaica since her early childhood and explained that she had taken out Jamaican citizenship as an adult, when it became possible to have dual citizenship. She was hoping that her son would spend at least some of his childhood in Jamaica, and she dreamed of getting a small house on the island. Yet she lived in a small rural community in northern California, far from other Jamaicans, and she was keen to engage in a variety of cultural events, ranging from Native American ceremonies to concerts with black gospel music. For Shelly, being a Jamaican did not mean associating with an ethnic community or maintaining ongoing ties with Jamaica but, rather, living with the values and modes of life that she had learned through her intimate family relations—her mother's emphasis on dressing properly, her aunts' joking, the family's particular expressions and modes of speaking. In this respect, her Jamaicanness resembles the expressions of cultural identity that one is likely to meet in the Caribbean itself rather than in the culturally hyper-aware environments of the urban conurbations to which migrants have emigrated. In the Caribbean, it is primarily during the Carnival season, when many migrants return home expecting (and willing to pay for) a dose of genuine ethnic identity, that West Indians cultivate their cultural roots with any intensity. At other times of the year, Caribbean cultural life is characterized by a cosmopolitan mix of everything from American soul music to English brass-band music, from rap poetry to high art poetry, the caliber of Derek Walcott.

By studying how several generations, through "statements and practices," develop and transform their notion of relatedness in relation to a family network of Caribbean origin, this book examines what is involved in being

Caribbean at the intersubjective level of the intimate family relations that tie individuals to particular places of origin. This in itself involves a series of complex questions. How do individuals' understanding of their own life trajectories, and place(s) of origin and belonging, intersect with dominant family narratives of a shared past in a particular place of origin? How do these family stories articulate with the larger narratives of migration and national belonging that prevail in both the country of origin and the new countries of residence? More specifically, how can the varying forms of identification expressed in individuals' narratives be represented, and gain acceptance, in societies where immigrants and their descendants tend to be viewed in terms of externally defined ethnic categories that may bear little relation to individual migrants' understanding of themselves? This questioning has led to a critical examination of notions of diasporic and transnational identities, ethnic communities, and places of origin, concepts that have been of central importance in migration studies. At a more general level, it has also led to a critical analysis of categorizations resulting in certain people being labeled second- or third-generation ethnic "immigrants," while others have become "ordinary citizens." Thus, although this study focuses on migrants from the Caribbean, the conditions of their movement are not dissimilar to those of migrants from many other parts of the world. I will leave it to others, however, to log the necessary air miles to trace the narratives of the many other migrant groups who are now crisscrossing the world.

THE CARIBBEAN CONTEXT

A History of Movement   The following family narratives reflect a long history of movements that began in the post-emancipation period, when families sought to secure viable, socially accepted, and culturally valued livelihoods, providing respect in the communities with which they identified. The following analysis of these different Caribbean family legacies elucidates how they give meaning and purpose to individual family members' migratory moves, the lives that they have lived in different parts of the world and their Caribbean place of origin as a site of belonging. Finally, I explore the significance of this Caribbean past to later generations of family members who are born and reared in various migration destinations abroad. This is thus an ethnography of mobility, interrelations, and ties to place from the point of view of individuals who negotiate a variety of sociocultural frameworks that influence their notions of belonging and identity.

The Caribbean offers a particularly interesting context within which to study migration, because the area, as noted, is entirely the product of massive population movements due to its particular geopolitical past. The archipelago was settled first by several Indian groups from North America and South America who lived by fishing and horticulture. This population was virtually eradicated within fifty years of Columbus's discovery of the islands in 1492. When during the sixteenth century European colonizers developed a plantation system in the Caribbean, producing especially sugar for the world market, they began to import labor power to replace the Indians, first indentured laborers from Europe, then slaves from Africa, and finally, contract laborers from Asia, especially India. By the end of the nineteenth century, when large-scale migration to the Caribbean had ceased, several hundred thousand Europeans, approximately 3 million Africans, and more than half a million Asians had arrived in the Caribbean (Lowenthal 1972; Mintz 1974). The abolition of slavery in the British colonies in 1834 (effectuated in 1838) set in motion massive population movements within the Caribbean, as many of those who had been freed left the plantations to settle as small farmers in "free" villages in the rural areas or to look for work in urban areas. Others moved farther afield for better economic opportunities, first within the Caribbean basin, then to South America and North America. This migration continued throughout the twentieth century and was finally extended to include Europe (Richardson 1983; Thomas-Hope 1978, 1992). During the last half of the twentieth century alone, more than 2 million people left the Caribbean for Europe and North American (Cohen 1998: 22–27).

The long post-emancipation history of population movements for better social and economic opportunities has led some scholars to describe the Caribbean as characterized by a migration tradition or a migration culture (Richardson 1983; Thomas-Hope 1978). Indeed, the Jamaican anthropologist Charles Carnegie (1987: 32) has wondered why migration should be "regarded as the 'marked' phenomenon, and staying put as 'unmarked,'" because for "particular peoples at particular times . . . to move is as ordinary and expected a thing to do as to remain sedentary." What are therefore needed in the Caribbean context, he states, are studies of the cultural system that makes migration meaningful to Caribbean people (Carnegie 1987: 42) and the "potentially limitless social field" of reciprocal relations that enable them to migrate (Carnegie 1987: 36).

With the long history of population movements into, within, and out of the Caribbean, one can ask, however, what it means to be from the Caribbean or to belong to that category of people called Caribbean. In a critique of the tendency of historical anthropology to study historical processes in relation to particular localities, Mary Des Chene has raised the question, "If one's work concerns the lives of people who have more commonly been in motion than stationary—refugees, migrant workers, colonial district officers, academics—what makes the place where one happens to catch up with them in itself revelatory of that mobility and its meanings?" (Des Chene 1997: 71). One might paraphrase this question slightly and ask, "If one's work concerns the lives of people who have a long history of movements, what makes the place that happened to be the last site of departure in itself revelatory of that mobility and its meanings?" To address this question, it is necessary to examine how this place has been invested with social and cultural meaning and how variously positioned people have done this.

Migration research has tended to focus on immigrants of lower-class background. This focus may be explained by the fact that the very notion of migration has a class bias, because it tends to be associated with people who, as Bryceson and Vuorela (2002: 7–8) suggest, are "considered economically and politically deprived and seek betterment of their circumstances."[9] The neglect of the class diversity of migrants has limited the understanding of the processes whereby migrants become incorporated as citizens into a receiving society and the different communities and identities that may emerge in this connection (cf. Alleyne 2005). The class bias of migration research has therefore supported the tendency to perceive Caribbean people in terms of a homogeneous African Caribbean ethnicity. The limitation of studying migrants in terms of an ethnic or cultural background has been brought out by Aihwa Ong in her study of Cambodian refugees in the United States. She argues that " 'culture' (or 'race,' 'ethnicity,' or 'gender') is not the automatic or even the most important analytical domain in which to understand how citizenship is constituted. Rather, what matters is to identify the various domains in which these preexisting racial, ethnic, gender, and cultural forms are problematized, and become absorbed and recast by social technologies of government that define the modern subject" (Ong 2003: 6). In an American context, she adds with reference to Max Weber, "notions of the ideal citizen . . . are linked to the concept of the bourgeois individual" and "embedded in a variety of official programs and unofficial practices that participate in governing subjects" (Ong 2003:7).

Technologies of government, tied to notions of "the ideal citizen" and "the concept of the bourgeois individual," are well established in a Caribbean context. Indeed, they became an important basis of the British Caribbean society that developed during the post-emancipation period. During the long era of slave-based plantation societies, the Caribbean was characterized by a regime of extreme direct physical control supported by racist ideologies that defined the large slave population as socially dead, physical labor power (Patterson 1982). With the abolition of slavery, a new system of social technology was introduced by British missionaries, educators, and colonial officials who saw the adoption by the freed of (British) middle-class moral values and forms of behavior as the only means whereby they would be able to emancipate themselves from the debased condition in which they were seen to be left as a result of slavery and thus become proper members of society. This involved, among other things, forming nuclear families based on holy matrimony, acquiring a substantial home, belonging to a Christian church, and mastering the ways of acting and manner of speaking of the white middle class in colonial society. An important key to this transformation was education.

This complex of values and modes of behavior, which the freed and their descendants were expected to internalize and master, came together in the notion of "respectability," an ideal of citizenship that became an important ideological basis of post-emancipation colonial society, and thus of individual social and economic mobility (Abrahams 1983; Olwig 1990, 1993b; Wilson 1969, 1973, 1992 [1974]). The notion of respectability, however, became articulated with a complicated hierarchy of social distinctions tied to racial origins, connected with the still powerful plantation society. This hierarchical system maintained the significance of inherited social position and thus presented a barrier to individual efforts at social and economic mobility (Alexander 1973, 1977; Austin-Broos 1994a). The notions of respectability therefore were adapted to the social and economic opportunities available in specific local contexts. They were also reinterpreted in the light of cultural ideas and practices, emphasizing the significance of more community-oriented modes of life that emerged among the African Caribbean population during and after slavery (Olwig 1985, 1993b). These communities consisted of complex webs of relations of mutual rights and obligations based on notions of kinship or friendship and tended to valorize the significance of general sociability and mutual help rather than individual achievement and socioeconomic mobility. The British missionaries and educators regarded these ways of life as representing uncivilized, debased forms of existence that needed to be combated, and they therefore came to be seen as counter to the development of proper citizenship in the colonial society (Wilson 1973).

The British West Indies were dominated by old social technologies of control tied to notions of inherited social position based on a system of racial inequality, as well as more recently introduced colonial social technologies of citizenship linked to the British middle-class culture of individual improvement and achievement. The difficulty of navigating in this complicated field of contradictory social norms and cultural values has made migration an attractive way out for many people (Olwig 1993b). This means that they left not to get away from, and abandon, their place of origin but, rather, to achieve the "improvement" in society that could not be accomplished within the local community. Indeed, it is important to remember that Great Britain, one of the major migration destinations, was not, strictly speaking, a foreign country when the family members migrated but the mother country of an empire in which they had full citizenship until the early 1960s. Thus, the educational and religious systems, important avenues of social mobility in the island societies, were British. Furthermore, the tradition of viewing cultural values and modes of behavior associated with British middle-class society as a sign of high social standing meant that the migrants who traveled to Western destinations had a strong expectation that these societies would provide the opportunity to earn a position as respectable citizens if only they were ambitious and hardworking. They were not prepared for the discriminatory racial and ethnic regimes in the migration destinations, and this had an important impact on the ways in which they, and their descendants, perceived themselves as possible citizens in the receiving society and their Caribbean society of origin. The notions of belonging and identification that they developed in relation to their place of origin must be seen in this light. Thus, most of the second- and third-generation family members, born and reared outside the Caribbean, did not have the opportunity to choose their own identity and sites of identification, because they were categorized as a racialized other in the immigrant societies. For them, a personal identity rooted in their families' Caribbean place of origin therefore became an important way of countering a categorical identity as "blacks" associated with the lower ranks of society (Bashi and McDaniel 1997; Pierre 2004).

The following chapters detail how migration has become an integral aspect of Caribbean life as people seek to negotiate the complex field of societal differentiation and control, community-based relations of mutual rights and obligations, and individual desires and ambitions that they encounter in their place of origin. I focus on families because they provide important contexts within which this negotiation occurs. As a social entity, the family thus represents a group of individuals in society, and it thereby gives them a social identity and position in their place of origin. Yet as a constellation of relations that is not confined to a specific place, the family can explore opportunities in different parts of the world and thus aspire to social and economic mobility. The ways in which individuals define and practice their family relations and the kinds of migratory movements in which they engage therefore become mutually constitutive. Furthermore, they reflect specific forms of positioning in relation to the societal technologies of control as well as the social relations and cultural values that characterize the area of the Caribbean from whence they derive. This is illustrated in the three family narratives presented in the chapters that follow.

The Family Networks   The three families studied in this book were selected because they derived from different islands and were of different social and economic background. They therefore exemplify migratory trajectories associated with varying historical circumstances, cultural notions, and social fields of relations and, thus, specific notions of relatedness and place that emerged in these contexts of Caribbean life. The Muir family—to which Shelly belonged—originated in the "colored," i.e., racially mixed, middle-class segment of a small British colonial town, built in the heart of the sugar district in Jamaica, and was associated with commerce and trade. The Gaston family—of which Matthew was part—has its roots in the French Creole communities of small plantation owners and farmers that developed in Dominica during the early colonization of the island and had become affiliated

with the middle layers of educators in the colonial society. The Smith family—which included Susanna—came from an African Caribbean village of
small farmers and fishermen on Nevis founded by plantation laborers during
the first half of twentieth century. By looking at families that share an African
Caribbean past but differ in terms of their social and economic background
in Caribbean societies, I want to give an impression of the diversity of Caribbean migrants and notions of Caribbeanness and the ways in which this
diversity influences migratory moves and attachment to place of origin.
While the three families are of different class background and cultural orientation, I do not mean to imply that they are representative of the Caribbean as
such. Nor do I wish to suggest that they are typical of their particular island
background. Thus, one should *not* see Jamaican families as primarily upper
middle class; Dominican families as middle class; and Nevisian families as of
lower-class background. Nevertheless, the three families exemplify social and
economic developments that are particularly strong on their respective islands, as I will clarify further in the introductions to the individual family case
studies.

THE STRUCTURE OF THE BOOK

In the next six chapters, I present three different family narratives as related by
various members of the families from their particular social, economic, geographic, and historical vantage point. Through their life stories the members
of three dispersed families, defined by their common origins in a family
home in, respectively, Jamaica, Dominica, and Nevis, describe their background in the Caribbean, their migratory moves to different parts of the
world, the lives that they have lived in these various destinations, and their
relations with other family members and their shared place of origin in the
Caribbean. I begin each narrative by describing the ways in which the older
generations of relatives, born and reared in the Caribbean, situate their families through their life stories in a specific Caribbean context that confers on
them a particular place in their Caribbean society of origin. I also explore the
historical background of each family in the Caribbean, drawing on the life
stories as well as printed secondary sources. These narratives of origin provide the basis for an analysis of the notions of relatedness that underline and
define the three family networks. These notions provide an important inter-

pretive and expressive framework in which individual family members depict their life trajectories that, for many, entailed movements to different parts of the world. The particular circumstances of their movements—the socio-economic condition of the family and the opportunities for migration available at the time—are also accounted for.

After the presentation of the three family narratives (in chapters 1–6), I discuss the meaning of the notion of family relatedness, and associated Caribbean place of origin and identification, for individuals in the three families from their particular vantage point in the family network. Chapter 7 compares the migratory journeys in the three families, the lives lived by members of the three families in different migration destinations, and the ties that they have maintained with their place of origin. It shows that individuals in the three families account for their lives in terms of the family's foundational story and how this influences the ways in which they have experienced their migration experiences. It becomes apparent that the family networks define rather different places of origin in the Caribbean and that this has important implications for individuals' sense of identification as Caribbean people. In chapter 8, I explore how the foundational stories have been reinterpreted and practiced in the second and third generations, where most have been born and reared abroad. I focus especially on the complex ways in which individuals seek to construct a place of origin for themselves that allows them to develop a sense of belonging within the society where they live, while asserting their particular sense of identity rooted in a family of particular Caribbean background.

Finally, in the conclusion I discuss two dominant narrative frameworks in migration research, both of which represent the perspective of the receiving societies. The dominance of these frameworks, and their inadequacies, is challenged by approaches, such as the one taken here, that focus on migrants' narratives. By making family networks the ethnographic site of investigation, this study attempts to take seriously the anthropological dictum to take one's point of departure in people's lives, not the formal structures that frame these lives. The result is a questioning of established categories and concepts within migration research that may provoke some, but that is intended to present a richer ethnography that is closer to the lives of the people studied.

PART ONE...

.... **A JAMAICAN FAMILY**

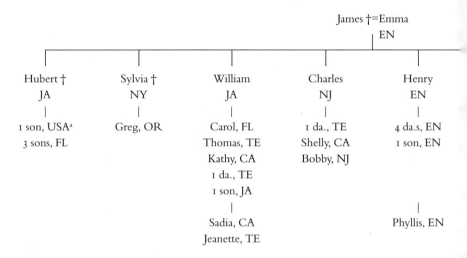

KEY: CA, California; EN, England; FL, Florida; JA, Jamaica; NJ, New Jersey; NS, Nova Scotia; NY, New York; ON, Ontario; OR, Oregon; SK, Saskatchewan; TE, Texas; USA, United States; WWI, Windward Islands; da., daughter; da.s, daughters.

[a] *The family did not know where in the United States this son was living.*

FIGURE I   The Muir Family, 1996. The figure lists and locates individuals identified in the body of the text. It is not a complete genealogy.

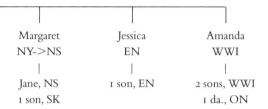

Margaret   Jessica   Amanda
NY->NS   EN   WWI

Jane, NS   1 son, EN   2 sons, WWI
1 son, SK   1 da., ON

Individuals in the elder generations of the Muir family described the family as part of the respectable middle class of Jamaican society. This social position was attributed to the family's ability to maintain a well-kept two-story home; the family members' mastery of good manners and proper English, which gave them the confidence and ability to move in the higher social circles of the colonial society; and the family's livelihood, which allowed it to employ people rather than be employed. A clear subplot of the narratives was that the family had gained its social skills over several generations of proper rearing and British education. This social mobility had involved, among other things, the move of Emma Muir, the "founder" and matriarch of this family, from the small African Caribbean village of Refuge to the British colonial town of Falmouth.

The family members' desire for upward social mobility within British colonial society, and their strong identification with British colonial culture, could be described as a form of identification with a hierarchical imperial system. This sort of analysis, however, would ignore the strong feelings of relatedness and belonging, rooted in a loving and caring family home, that the individuals emphasized in their narratives. The intent of this chapter therefore is to understand how the elder members of the Muir family, who grew up in Jamaica, viewed their particular family background in the colonial town of Falmouth—the ways in which it has given meaning and a sense of common purpose to their life trajectories and thus provided them with a source of belonging and identification of importance to them, wherever they have settled. The opening quote is from Emma Muir's narration of her life story:

> I was born in 1900, on the first of January, in a little village called Refuge. My mother was Elizabeth; my father, Sam Fernandes. I went to school there in the village. When I was fifteen I went to Falmouth to learn dressmaking, and in the afternoon I studied with a teacher in order to pass the student-teacher examinations so that I could become a teacher. These were my intentions, but they never matured! I sat for the first- and second-year exams, but when I was seventeen years old, I met a fellow. He was working on the Panama Canal, but because his mother was sick, he had come home for a visit, and he never returned. We were married in 1917. Then we started having children—first one girl, then four boys, and then three girls. We had eight children all together.

When I met Emma Muir in 1996, she was living in her daughter Jessica's home in a typical London suburb, with terraced houses, a high street with various shops, a green park, and easy access to the city via the "tube," the London subway system. In the 1960s, when Jessica and her family had moved into the neighborhood, it was almost entirely white English, but it had since become ethnically mixed, having had a large influx of immigrants from the former British colonies, mostly in Asia. Indeed, the home where I interviewed Emma might be described as Asian, Jessica's husband being Sri Lankan. Emma was one of the most recent arrivals, because she had moved in with Jessica just a month or so before I came, having lived most of her long life in Jamaica and the United States. It was not clear whether she was there for a prolonged visit or whether she was actually going to stay. This did not seem to matter to Emma because, as she explained, the family—wherever it was—was her home. When I asked Emma to tell me her life story, however, she dwelled on the life she had lived in Jamaica, particularly in Falmouth, where she spent most of her adult life. This was where she had married and raised her eight children, who, along with their children and grandchildren, provided the most important framework of her life. But it was also the place where the family had developed the sense of moral values and proper manners that Emma regarded as so essential and therefore had imparted to her children.

Today Falmouth is the small, sleepy capital of Trelawny parish, located a little more than twenty miles east of the fast tourist area of Montego Bay in northwestern Jamaica. When Emma was born, however, it was still a busy harbor city serving as a transshipment point for sugar cane grown on the large plantations in the surrounding countryside. Jamaica has been described as the "Caribbean core" because of its long history of plantation production, which meant that more than 800,000 Africans were transported to the island (Besson 2005: 17). Trelawny itself has been one of the main areas of sugar production in Jamaica, and in 1800, when the slave-based plantation economy was at its height, this parish had the greatest number of plantations in Jamaica (Besson 2005: 18). The plantation society was still strong when Emma grew up in the early twentieth century, and it has left an important legacy in the form of a hierarchical societal order based on race and class that still suffuses Jamaican society.

In her analysis of modern Jamaican society, Diane Austin-Broos (1994a: 218) notes that Jamaica has "at its core a sense of persisting hierarchical order. This is a sense of hierarchy that acknowledges ranked, inherited forms of difference." In this hierarchy, "social class and color groupings jointly present the major issues of status that constitute a Jamaican sense of hierarchy" (Austin-Broos 1994a: 214). Categorizing others on the basis of such distinctions, however, is no longer socially acceptable. Rather, a cultural value system has emerged where people are appraised according to their morals and behavior. As noted by Jack Alexander, "middle-class life and background is distinguished from lower-class life and background by virtue of being responsible in contrast to careless, civilized and socialized in contrast to unsocialized. So it is the presence of socialized and civilized characteristics in one party and their absence in the other party that results in the two parties having nothing in common" (Alexander 1973: 307). Jamaican society is thus hierarchical, not just because individuals have unequal access to vital resources such as land, education, and employment, but also in the sense that it is characterized by an intricate cultural system of differentiation based on perceptions of similarity and difference related to people's position in society.

While a "sense of hierarchy" permeates Jamaican society, Jamaicans have different ideas about the nature of this hierarchy and their place in it (Austin-Broos 1994a: 219), and notions of similarity and difference therefore are subject to a great deal of negotiation as people position themselves and others within the hierarchical social order. As Lisa Douglass (1992) has shown in her study of elite families in Jamaica, the family plays an important role in this negotiation and practice of hierarchy, especially among those who aspire to identify with the upper classes. It is within the family that a specific outlook on life and a certain mode of behavior, identified with a particular class position, can be acquired as a natural "habitus" (Douglass 1992: 247). Those who identify with the upper classes and the middle classes, and thus seek to demarcate themselves from individuals located lower in the social hierarchy, will tend to emphasize the importance of the family rather than kin. This is because the family can be defined as a more exclusive group of people with whom one shares "cultural principles of likeness, including ideas about the meaning and relative value of color, class, and gender." The family therefore can distinguish itself even by "minute types of differences gleaned in social practices," whereas kin is seen to comprise all blood relatives, regardless of their social position (Douglass 1992: 22). This does not mean that the family is an instrumental unit constructed for the purposes of mobility in the social hierarchy. Rather, the "cultural meaning, social values, and moral principles" associated with family life become the "content of family sentiment" (Douglass 1992: 265), or—from a slightly different theoretical point of view—that which leads to the sense of relatedness (Carsten 2000) that defines and gives meaning to a specific family unit and its position in society.

When Emma Muir began her life story in Refuge and moved on to Falmouth, she not only described her Jamaican origins in relation to named geographic localities. She also located herself—and her family—in a particular place in Jamaican society reflective of the kind of Jamaica with which she wished to identify. Emma's Jamaican identity, in other words, was rooted both in an island society that had since become an independent nation-state and in a very specific socially defined place in Jamaica. This was that of the middle class that emerged between the African Jamaican lower classes, struggling to realize their freedom after the abolition of slavery in 1834, and the upper class of British plantation owners and representatives of the British colonial regime, seeking to maintain their privileges in the plantation society. While Emma and her children described their Jamaican background in such a way that the family could be seen to belong to the respectable middle class, their narratives should not be viewed as merely serving the purpose of claiming a specific class position for the family in Jamaican society. As emphasized earlier, the particular mode of life that a particular family sees as its own becomes constitutive of family relations and sentiments and thus of the notion of relatedness that makes a family. As foundational family narratives, the life stories related by the family members therefore are selective, as any family's stories of the past will be (Douglass 1992: 92), because they seek to convey an understanding of that mode of life that family members cherish and have come to associate with their particular family and its Jamaican origins.

VILLAGE ORIGINS

Emma, as noted, began her life story by noting that she was born in Refuge and by mentioning the names of her parents and the fact that she had gone to school in the village where she was born. However, she quickly went on to relate that she had moved at a young age to Falmouth, where she met and married her husband and established a home. In the narrative that followed, she said no more about her roots in the village. When, in my second interview with Emma, I asked her to tell me more about Refuge, she did not paint a particularly favorable picture of the village:

> You wouldn't know it unless you go there. It is just a little backward village that I left when I was fifteen. Imagine, when I was in Jamaica recently, a relative of mine wasn't well, and a fellow I knew asked me whether I would like to go see him. And I said, "Sure!" So he took me there, and I went there in my ninety-seventh year. And it hasn't improved. There has been no improvement, just from driving through. It had an elementary school. And it had a Roman Catholic church and a Baptist church. It had no banks, no nothing. Just a small village.
>
> [But who lived in the village?]
>
> Oh, lots of people! Poor people, and people of little means, you know—not wealthy people, either. But there were lots of estates in those days, where the people worked. To make a livelihood.
>
> [Sugar estates?]
>
> Sugar farms, cane. English people lived there. They had plantations there. When I grew up, there were English people living there, all over on the estates. They

owned the estates. There was Oxford, there was Cambridge. You know all the names from here.

[So there were English estate owners and poor people who worked on the estates?]

Right, and afterwards there were factories, and, you know . . .

[Did the workers live in Refuge or on the estates?]

The workers had their little homes in Refuge, and they lived there and they worked on the estates.

When I asked Emma whether it had been difficult for her to move from the village to the big town, she replied, "No, I mingled well. I thought well of myself." She attributed the ease with which she had gained acceptance in the town to her mother's good upbringing, her mother having shown her "the right way." Thus, the mother had made sure that Emma attended school every day and took music lessons, sent her to Sunday School every week, and checked that she knew her "memory gem," a "verse, or a golden text" that she had to learn for Sunday School. And perhaps most important, the mother had insisted that Emma speak "proper" English, not the "broken" Jamaican that was widely spoken in the village. Indeed, her mother had spoken standard English very well herself. This was highly unusual, because black people—like Emma's mother—rarely mastered this form of English:

> My mother was dark in complexion. There were two Portuguese ladies living in our district, who looked after the Roman Catholic church. And one of them said, "When Elizabeth is inside speaking, and if you don't know, you would think that it is an English woman in there, speaking, because her speech is so lovely." And we couldn't speak the patois; we couldn't do this in those days. She would pull us up over the rope and correct us.

For Emma, her mother's insistence that she speak "proper English" meant choosing a better life for her:

> Some people haven't got the intellectual or common sense to grasp it [proper English], or don't even want to. They don't want to either, Karen, you know. They just want that language [the patois]. So we all choose our own way in life. Some

choose the patois; it is a choice that you have to make, what you want to make out of life.

This better life meant distancing oneself from other villagers who might be a bad influence—for example, because they spoke the patois: "I wasn't allowed to have too many friends. I wasn't allowed to roam about with everybody, mix with everybody. Not really, no."

Emma professed to have little knowledge about her mother's family, who had lived in the village for several generations and represented her black Jamaican background. She remembered her grandmother, who lived nearby in Refuge, and described her as "black" and "loving and caring," and added that "color didn't matter to you." When I asked her about her mother's father, she said she did not know anything about him or who he was. She knew her father's parents and was aware that they had come from Portugal, but did not know how they had ended up in Jamaica. They had "an estate, a cultivation" in the area, but she had never been there, she explained, because it was far away and she had no way of getting there. They did not own a big estate, she explained when I asked her about this, because such estates were all owned by the English people. However, she remembered fruit and sugar-cane juice being brought from her grandparents' estate to her home. Her father was in business and owned a number of stores that were run by "native" people.

By presenting herself as the issue of a local black woman and a second-generation immigrant from Portugal, Emma created a foundational story that fit into the upper- and middle-class pattern of tracing one's origins to the arrival in Jamaica of the first white male (Douglass 1992: 92). She did not say much about life in Refuge, the African Caribbean village where she grew up, or about the people who lived there. Her lack of interest in her African Caribbean past in Refuge may be regarded as remarkable in the light of the importance of Refuge in Jamaica's history. In an in-depth study of the history of the free villages in the Jamaican parish of Trelawny, the Jamaican anthropologist Jean Besson (2002) describes the history of Refuge, along with several other Jamaican villages. She documents how they were established during the free-village movement that emerged in the late 1830s, after the abolition of slavery. This movement was spearheaded by Baptist missionaries, who helped the freed slaves acquire their own land on which to settle in independent communities outside the sugar plantations.[1] Refuge was founded by the Baptist minister William Knibb, one of the leaders of the free-village movement, on ninety acres of land that had been purchased for village development. Knibb originally named the village Wilberforce, after the British abolitionist, but within a few years it had assumed the name Refuge (Besson 2002: 111–12). When Bessen did ethnographic fieldwork in Refuge, she found that it basically consisted of a few, large, interrelated cognatic descent groups who could trace their origins to slaves who were brought from Africa to work on the large sugar estates in the central area of sugar production in Jamaica.[2] She was able to locate villagers who could relate oral history about how their ancestors were brought from Africa to Jamaica, where they worked as slaves, and what sort of role they played in the establishment of the free village of Refuge (Besson 2002: 113–15). Besson depicts how the villagers turned the land they acquired in Refuge into family land held in common by large, inclusive kin groups, and shows that they still have family burial grounds on this land. According to Besson, this family land containing the graves of ancestors forms an important source of family identity for those who have migrated abroad as well as to other areas of Jamaica (Besson 2002: 140–41).

It is likely that Emma's maternal family was part of this village history. Given that Emma was born in 1900, her maternal grandmother, who also lived in Refuge, must have been born sometime in the middle of the nineteenth century, during the early period of village settlement. Furthermore, it is not unlikely that Emma, through her mother's family, was related to the large kin groups that made up the village and owned family land there. Emma's trip to Refuge to visit a sick relative a few months before I spoke with her shows that she still had family in the village. Her maternal relatives may therefore have lived in the area for more than 150 years. This aspect of the family past, however, did not figure in Emma's account to me of her life. The family's past in the village of Refuge was also absent in the stories related by Emma's children and grandchildren. When I asked Margaret, one of Emma's daughters, whether she had been there, she replied: "Refuge? I have passed by, but I never went there to look." A couple of the sons did recall having spent their summer holidays with their mother's father, but they emphasized that he lived on a large cattle estate, where he was a manager. They described being picked up in a horse and buggy and staying on the estate, where they went bird hunting, rode the horses, and helped with the cattle. They said nothing about having visited any villages nearby or the people living there. Family members, in other words, identified not with Emma's village origins, but with the British colonial society of Falmouth and the plantations in the surrounding countryside.

The fact that Emma had little positive to say about the village of Refuge does not mean that she had no regard for the childhood she spent there. On the contrary, as has been seen, she emphasized that her mother had had a tremendous positive influence on her later life. She also acknowledged that she received her religious grounding at the Refuge Baptist church she had attended with her mother and grandmother. Thus, even though she joined her husband's Anglican church when she married, she felt that she had "got the substance" in the Baptist church. When I asked her to compare the Baptist and Anglican churches, she declined to so do, saying that they are all about the same, but she did note, "I always had fond memories of the Baptists—the way they conducted to bring the young ones up, the streamline that they gave for the young ones."

Emma did not elaborate on what she meant by "streamline," but Diane Austin-Broos's study of the Baptist church in Jamaica gives some ideas about what it may have entailed. According to Austin-Broos (1997), the missionaries who founded the free villages, such as Refuge, were motivated by a strong belief that the freed African slaves needed to be saved from the "historical corruption" that they had experienced as heathens subjected to slavery. This corruption, the missionaries believed, had resulted in the development of local beliefs and ways of life associated with slave life on the plantations that they viewed as immoral and therefore needed to be replaced with another, moral mode of living. The missionaries attempted to accomplish this through the founding of free villages envisioned as communities of Christian farmers, owning their own property and living in respectable homes based on holy matrimony (Austin-Broos 1997: 38). In the churches and through the schools that they ran, the missionaries therefore preached against the local culture of the freed and sought to create a "New World Christian . . . through private property, education, and conversion" (Austin-Broos 1997: 41; see also Gordon 1963: 5; Mintz 1974: 157–79).[3]

Baptist missionizing was reflected in Emma's enthusiasm for self-improvement through the adoption of "the right way" and her rejection of local ways. It is easy today to criticize the Baptists' attempt to transform the

freed Jamaican population to "New World Christians" and the condemnation of African Caribbean culture that this involved. It is important to remember, however, that the Baptists did help the freed people establish villages
outside the plantations and made education available to the villagers, education being a primary means of upward mobility for the lower classes (Austin
1983: 235). While Emma Muir's fond memories of the Baptists and their
streamlining of the young people can be construed as a rejection of her
African Caribbean roots, it can be seen equally well as a realistic appraisal of
the importance of knowing the "proper" ways that had to be mastered to
make any headway in the wider colonial society of Jamaica and thus improve
one's social and economic situation.

To Emma, Refuge was important because it was where her mother and
the Baptist church gave her a good "foundation in life" and taught her the
skills to move upward in society. This meant moving away from Refuge and
the rural African Caribbean life that the village also represented. It is note-
worthy, however, that Emma did not display any moral condemnation of
those who did not follow "the right way." She merely stated that they had
chosen another way that she did not agree with. Furthermore, as shall be
seen, she described her move from Refuge to Falmouth not with smugness
about her personal achievements but, rather, with great humor, pointing to
her at times faltering attempts to manage modern life in the city. Emma lost
contact with her mother at a young age, because her mother emigrated to
Cuba, where she died after a few years. But Emma still recalled her mother
with gratitude: "To this day, I reverence her bones. I reverence her ashes to
this day, because I think that I was properly brought up."

A BEAUTIFUL AND ORDERLY TOWN

For Emma, moving the few miles from Refuge to Falmouth represented a big
step forward. "It was like going to New York City for the first time," she said
and added, laughing, "coming out of the bush!" This, however, was not how
she had thought of it at the time: "I didn't think of it as bush then. It was
home. But it is to further yourself, to improve yourself. For the improvement
of self." The significance of Falmouth as a civilized, modern place was quite
apparent when I asked Emma to describe the town she moved to as a young
girl in 1915:

It was a town. Beautiful buildings, beautiful laid-out streets. Different from Refuge, the country place with all the bush around. [Laughs]. It had wharves; it had different churches. Wharves, places where you stored rum. Store places. There was Trelawny Wharf, Scots Wharf. It was bustling business. It was a business town. And cars had come in. Cars were around. It was different from the bush. You never saw a car come up there.

With her marriage to James, Emma had very much become part of the busy commercial life of the town. James's father was a stevedore contractor who hired crews of workers to load and unload the large sailboats that brought goods from abroad and shipped sugar to foreign markets. He also owned fishing boats and hired people to pull nets. James went into his father's business and took it over when the father died. Falmouth was, at this time, still an important town in the leading sugar-producing district of Jamaica, although sugar cultivation had undergone a period of decline during the latter part of the nineteenth century.[4] The Muir business provided a comfortable basis for the new family, and within a few years James and Emma were able to purchase a house of their own, where they reared their eight children: Sylvia, Hubert, William, Charles, Henry, Margaret, Jessica, and Amanda.

Emma described Falmouth as both a modern commercial town and an important administrative and cultural center in the British colony of Jamaica. With its large Anglican church, its many substantial Georgian townhouses owned by affluent English planters, and its British courthouse and barracks, Falmouth was a very British town in the early twentieth century. Emma remembered how impressive it was when the inspectors and policemen marched together, wearing their uniforms:

We were under the British rule. When you saw the inspectors, dressed in their uniforms, they were all English people. And their wives and children. . . . And when they marched to go up to the courthouse, we all just loved to go to the windows and watch them, when they came up marching for the big court.

[They would march for big court?]

Oh, yes. They would march from down the barracks, where the policemen are. And the inspector would march with the policemen up to the courthouse. Grandeur. And you saw their uniforms: white tops, decorated, and black pants with red seams coming up. Very orderly, very orderly.

The British order suffused the colonial town, doing so from the legal and administrative system of the empire to the domestic life of the respectable citizens of the town. Emma was keen to adopt the way of life that was expected of her as a married woman in a good home. This was very much about knowledge of proper manners:

> Not all the local people were of the same caliber. Some locals you would not want your children to marry. We all have our prejudices. It depended on how you were brought up. If you were brought up the same way, you were on equal grounds. If you had manners. Proper manners are important.
>
> I did my part. I read books about what other people do, imitated the best, knew the good from the bad. But some people do what they do regardless of society.

One gets an impression of the way in which Emma and James presented themselves socially from a photograph taken of them when they were a young couple. It shows James sitting on a chair, wearing a suit and tie, and Emma standing behind him, wearing a long-sleeved dress extending from her neck to well below her knees, where her boots took over. When I asked Emma when the picture was taken, she explained, "I was twenty-one years old. We had just bought our home, and so we went to have the picture taken."

When Emma talked about the importance of good manners, she emphasized the moral dimension: Proper manners showed that you were a person of good caliber and "on equal grounds," and therefore worthy of respect. Emma's children, who grew up in Falmouth, were more conscious of the fact that, in Jamaican society, "good manners" signaled a person's position in the social order of the colonial town and defined, to a great extent, the kinds of people with whom they associated. Their accounts of their childhood in Falmouth therefore were much more explicit about the class system and the family's position in this system. When I asked Henry to describe his parents, he stated:

> My parents were reasonably middle class. They were able to employ three maids. My father was a stevedore contractor and employed quite a few laborers when

ships were in. He also had a fishing concern. He was a very able fisherman and had eight to ten boats. He employed people working for him.

Class defined, to a great extent, with whom one associated socially in the town. When asked how the family fit into the class system, William replied, "Upper middle class" and explained that this was

because of the people that we visited with, the youngsters we played with, the parties that we attended.

[What kind of people were they?]

I remember as a youngster I used to play tennis with the wife of a judge. She taught me tennis—or, rather, to improve my tennis. She had nieces who were good fun. We saw doctors, the pharmacist, those were the kind of families we associated with. . . .

[Why did your family fit into that layer of society?]

It was primarily education. We belonged to a certain social strat[um]. It did not have anything to do with color but education and upbringing, stability financially.

The class system, and the social distances associated with it, operated right in the home.

We had two maids, but we were not encouraged to be close to them or their offspring. It was not proper. The maids called us not by our first name. I was called Mas' Bill, my brother was called Mas' Hubert. You socialized with families of like social background. That holds true until today. It has not been broken down.

The maids clearly did not belong to the "circle" but were seen to be part of the lower classes. An important sign of this class difference was the kind of English that the maids spoke, language being a "clear marker of class" because it indicates "education and reflects who an individual's associates are" (Douglass 1992: 81). Thus, the siblings emphasized that the maids spoke only "patois," whereas they, the Muir family, spoke "proper English." William even claimed that he did not fully understand "patois": "I understand it for the most part, but if they speak very fast, some of it escapes me. The maids spoke only patois; they could not speak proper English." While the children emphasized the social distance maintained toward the maids, Emma described the family's relationship with the domestics as one of mutual respect. She explained that she taught her children "to respect our helpers in the house" so that the helpers would respect the family members and not do "anything out of the way" in the home. She therefore did not allow her children to correct the maids, she noted, but was the only one to do so.

The maintaining of class lines was most vehement in private social life and less important in other social contexts. Henry explained:

> We moved with those who had careers. That doesn't mean that we didn't have friends outside that circle. At school we played and were friends with anyone. I played cricket and football, the team was comprised of everyone who was good enough. There was no class distinction there. But when it came to inviting people to your home for tea or dinner, you only invited people of your own circle.

The family's home was also a significant indicator of the family's middle-class status. Margaret described it as an "upstairs and downstairs house" with a yard where the children could play. The daughters learned from an early age how to maintain a proper home. Margaret recalled, "We all had to make our beds before we went to school, and we had to put fresh flowers in the vases before school. We had a flower garden. And we had to wash our stockings and hair ribbons. And we learned cooking. We had to watch the maid so that we would learn."

Thus, the girls had to learn how to keep a nice home, but they did not do heavy physical housework. Indeed, some of the duties they were given, like picking fresh flowers for the vases, are associated with being "the lady of the house" in upper-class families (Douglass 1992: 207).

One does not receive the impression that the home was the center of an elaborate social life. On the contrary, Emma emphasized that, with so many children, she had little time for this. Nevertheless, Amanda noted that certain social activities took place in the home: "The home was comfortable, and the family was well known. It was a place where tea parties were held on the lawn to raise funds." She is probably referring to the women's groups that Emma participated in, such as one that sewed items for the Red Cross to send to Europe during World War II. Emma was also active in the Women's Federation, a movement that the wife of the British governor organized throughout Jamaica. Emma had gone to the meetings, when the organizers came from Kingston, but was not quite sure what it was all about, except that its purpose was "to help women." When a new governor came to the island, the movement petered out. Emma seems to have been drawn into these activities through women's groups at the Anglican church that she had joined when she married James, who was an Anglican. This social engagement—and the high moral standard that it indicated—also helped consolidate the family's position in the respectable middle class of the local community.

While the stevedoring and fishing business provided a handsome income for James and Emma when they married, it became less lucrative as the harbor in Falmouth declined in importance.[5] Emma did her best to maintain a respectable home by economizing—for example, by making the children's clothes: "I sewed for all my children. The first suit I tried to make for my boy, I had to laugh the way it turned out. So I sent for a suit from a mail-order company in the States. . . . I made a pattern from this suit, and I was then able to sew the children's clothes." James, who had grown up in a fairly well-to-do home, was not used to skimping and saving, and he had a reputation for being generous with money. Amanda recalled a steady stream of local people who came to the home to ask the father for favors or money. Emma, who had to make ends meet, conceded that it was nice to be so generous, sharing everything with people in need, but added:

> They preyed on him, really! [Laughs] A nice life, if you can live it, Karen. . . . I couldn't share as generously as he did. If a woman came to me and said, "I don't have anything, could you help me with something? Can you lend me a pound?" I lend her 5 shillings because I don't expect it back. [Laughs] He would give her the pound, but he wouldn't get it back, either. That's what I mean.

Emma explained that her husband had inherited this behavior from his father and noted that it was "in the blood." Her husband's parents had been independent financially, but not wealthy. People, however, "looked upon them as being wealthy," she added, laughing. Generous behavior toward the poor thus was associated with a middle- or upper-class position in society (cf. Thomas 2004: 108), whereas the more economizing behavior displayed by Emma was indicative of the modest financial situation of the family.

When James became ill, Emma began to worry about how she might be able to manage on her own:

> My husband took sick with a heart attack when I was forty-two. He was seven years my senior, and I wondered what to do. I had no profession. My father was a merchant, so I entered that field and opened a dry-goods store. It was very small. I had no money for a big place, so I started small. My husband said, "Don't worry about it. The folks will laugh about you having such a small place." But I said, "Well, suppose that instead I think that they are laughing with me, then it looks completely different." The attitude is very important, the way you look at it yourself. I had a section of the store with cakes, where I had a boy make ice cream—it was made by spinning it—and sell it for me. The store was right before the courthouse, and a gentleman from Montego Bay said to me, "Just watch us grow," and that was a big, big pat on my back. I had that store for a while and then moved to bigger quarters, because I did well.

It had not been easy to get James to accept that his wife was working because, as Emma explained, "A man in those days did not like a woman to go into business on her own. He wanted to be the full support of everything." It was not just a matter of men at that time not wanting their women to work, but of men who had James's social standing not wanting their wives to work. In a Caribbean society like Jamaica, where women in the poor segment of the population had always worked, the ability to support a wife was an important sign of high social standing. The Jamaican elite families that Douglass studied thus were characterized by a strict division of labor. Women, she writes, devote themselves to "the work of the family," which involves "managing the household, bearing and caring for children, and being responsible for the home and the social life of the family" (Douglass 1992: 213). Men, by contrast, concentrate on what she calls the "work of kinship"—the wider affairs of the kin group, which entails tending to "obligations outside the household: to business and career, to family financial matters, to community and politics." She adds that, even though women are responsible for the home, a wife "carefully ensures that her husband feels in charge of the household and family" (Douglass 1992: 214). Nevertheless, it is apparent that women, not men, are key figures in family life, and she refers to the "centralizing woman" as one who is "central to the daily life of family" (Douglass 1992: 217).

While the Muir family did not belong to the few elite families in the highest level of society, it clearly regarded these gender roles as ideal. Emma therefore emphasized that she went into business only because her husband had become ill. She also noted that a "gentleman" had given her encouragement, thus showing that the better segment of society approved of her economic activities. The significance of social approval was expressed more directly by Amanda, who described her mother's business as a modern store where the most respectable members of the local society came:

> We had a store with fabrics and everything for fabrics. There was a men's, a women's, and a children's section, and on the other side there was a restaurant where we sold milkshakes, ice-cream sodas, popsicles, patties, plantain tarts, soft drinks. It was lovely. Lawyers and doctors went there with their families. Mom was the main brain behind this business.

By depicting her mother's economic activities as the running of a store—even a restaurant—frequented by the upper levels of society, Amanda underscored that her mother's economic activities were a modern and respectable business. In this way, the mother was described as quite different from the economically active women in the lower classes, such as the higglers, the market women who have been involved in a range of economic activities since the early days of slavery. While the higgler, according to Douglass, is a "beloved folk figure" in the middle class and admired in the upper class for her "entrepreneurial spirit," she is a "woman of lower-class origins whose stereotypical image emphasizes her large size, her loud clothes, and her black skin," and she is often criticized for being "brusque and aggressive" (Douglass 1992: 244). She is the image of the poor, black, uneducated women, in sharp contrast to the image of the respectable and refined lady cultivated in the upper levels of society with which the Muir family identified.[6]

Even though Emma was careful to describe her business as a supplementary source of income that might become necessary in case her husband should succumb to his heart condition, it was apparent that she had in fact become the economic mainstay of the family. When her husband died some years later, she was a financially independent woman who both supported the family for a number of years and underwrote the cost of secondary education at some of the best private schools for several of the children, an important aspect in the further "improvement" of the family.

EDUCATING FOR SOCIAL IMPROVEMENT

While Emma Muir's children realized that the Jamaican society where they grew up was strongly class oriented, they did not necessarily see this as a problem, because class, as William noted, had nothing to do with color but was about "education and upbringing" as well as "stability financially." Class thus was a manner of achievement. In his study of Jamaican society, Adam Kuper argues that education has become "a functional alternative to 'race' in the ideological justification of Jamaican social inequality, but it is much better adapted to contemporary conditions. It presents itself as open to achievement, and as a channel for social mobility" (Kuper 1976: 75). Education, however, is "normally the consequence, not the cause, of high social position; but this is not generally recognized" (Kuper 1976: 74). The Muir children were well aware of the fact that it was a privilege to attend the secondary school, because some of the siblings did not have the opportunity to attend a well-known private secondary school. This was true for Henry and Charles, who explained that they would have liked more education but that their parents at the time could not afford to send them to a private school outside the local area for further education.[7] Margaret noted that she did attend private girls' schools in Kingston but married before taking the exams. Four of the Muir siblings, however, graduated from reputable secondary schools: Wolmer High School, a boys' school in Kingston that Hubert and William attended, and St. Hilda's Diocesan High School, a girls' school in Brown's Town, where Jessica and Amanda were enrolled. When I interviewed William, Jessica, and Amanda, they dwelled on the importance of this secondary education, whereas the other siblings who had not received an education at a private secondary school spoke much less about their schooling and were well aware of their more limited educational background.

William's, Jessica's, and Amanda's accounts of their school experiences underlined that secondary education constituted the ticket to full acceptance within the upper levels of Jamaican society. The schools did not emphasize practical or natural science subjects but focused, instead, on the classics, the arts, and languages while impressing the importance of a certain cultural refinement on the students. According to Shirley Gordon, secondary education developed in Jamaica "divorced from the interests and needs of responsible working members of this community" (Gordon 1963: 3)—following the model of British upper-class education.[8] The strong emphasis on academic humanistic subjects is apparent in William's enthusiastic description of his "first-class" education at Wolmer, where he was particularly fond of his Latin and English teachers. The influence of the British public-school system is also apparent in the emphasis on sports and in the prefect system, where certain students were appointed to keep order among their fellow students. In general, William described his schooling at Wolmer as an "exhilarating" and "memorable" experience that he recalled with great pleasure, and he still had the trophies and cups that he had won as a sportsman at the school, where he was captain of the boxing team.

Jessica and Amanda, who attended a boarding school for girls, described a much more controlling environment, where there was emphasis on "finishing" as well as educating the girls in the subjects necessary to take the Cambridge exams. Jessica explained,

> We were allowed to have three white dresses, and they could not have any patterns on them. In the evening we were to change from our uniform to the white dresses. We were also allowed three colored dresses for Saturday evening. And we wore brown shoes during the day, and black shoes with white socks in the evening. You had to report to the nurse every night, and she checked whether you had been to the bathroom, and if you hadn't been for two days, she would administer medication for you. . . .
>
> We were kept in check, and we received order marks if we did anything wrong. We were placed in three houses; they were not houses that we lived in but houses that we belonged to. And the houses competed as to who received the most points. If one person in the house received order marks, this would pull the others own. The houses were named after famous British persons: (1) Kitchener; (2) Nuthall; (3) Disraeli. We should have known who these persons were, but most of us didn't.

Amanda described St. Hilda as "one of the most prestigious schools on the island" and noted that her parents must have "had to sacrifice" to send her and her sister to that school:

> They must have wanted us to live our lives dotting our *i*s, crossing our *t*s, towing the line. It must have been what my parents wanted. But if you were applying for a job, you would be preferred if you were from St. Hilda. You learned to speak well, to eat with the queen, and be comfortable everywhere. It was very British. But I decided that if I had children, I would not send them to a place like St. Hilda.

She characterized the teachers as "frustrated spinsters who had come from England to teach." They did not allow the students to move beyond the school's gates, but on Sundays they had "letter-writing time" when the students could communicate with the world outside the school. This communication, however, was severely restricted, because they were only allowed to write three letters, one of which was expected to be addressed to their parents. Letters to men whose surname was different from that of the letter writer were censored. Students were not allowed to speak with maids at the school, because—they were told—the maids might be used as an intermediary in relations with boys. Jessica recalled that it was possible to receive permission to visit a day student if the school had approved of the student's family.

When I interviewed Amanda and Jessica, they were critical of the strict regime and the highly British curriculum, which was divorced from the Jamaican context. At the time, however, they did not question the school. As Jessica noted: "Jamaica had always been a British colony, and my parents were brought up like that. We learned no West Indian history and geography at the school, but ask me about England! In retrospect, you may wonder what on earth they thought that they were doing." There was no question in Emma's mind that she had done the best by sending her daughters to St. Hilda:

> St. Hilda was good, because it was very strict, it taught proper manners, and the teachers were good. I knew some of them. Some were English.
>
> [Were they better than local teachers?]
>
> I don't know about that, but they spoke proper English. We were an English colony, under British rule.

The exclusive nature of secondary education in Jamaica, and elsewhere in the British Caribbean, has led Shirley Gordon to suggest that the Cambridge local examinations became viewed primarily as "passports for most 'respectable' employment" (Gordon 1963:240). Along similar lines, Raymond Smith has suggested that education served a clear purpose, because it created an " 'intelligentsia' literate in English and in command of English manners, sharply distinguished from the mass of uncultured ex-slaves and indentured immigrants" (Smith 1996: 155). This Caribbean intelligentsia served an important purpose, he argues, because it provided "a new basis for the integration of society once slavery had been abolished." It thus filled the positions within the administrative, military, and legal system of the post-emancipation society and appropriated and maintained the ideologies, and associated colonial values, that underlined this system (Smith 1996: 155)

The experiences of the Muir family support, to a great extent, Smith's interpretation of the integrative role of the educational system. The family had a history of continued efforts to become integrated within the respectable layers of society through education, beginning with Emma's studies for a teacher's license and continuing with the Muir children's private secondary schooling. Both Emma and her mother appear to have accepted the sociocultural order of the colonial rule and sought to earn the best place possible for their children within this society. Emma's children also seem to have accepted this order in the sense that they recalled with great fondness their childhood in Falmouth and were proud of their family, which was well known and respected in the town. However, as shall be seen, all of them opted to leave Jamaica when they finished school, and all but one of the émigré siblings chose to stay abroad. An important reason they left was their realization that their foothold within the Jamaican middle class was tenuous and that further social and economic mobility within Jamaica was virtually impossible. Rather than accept this, they opted to migrate. The emergence of a large group of people who identified with middle-class cultural values and social norms therefore did not necessarily further the internal integration of Jamaican colonial society, as Smith suggested. Such integration occurred only insofar as this society was able to offer this segment of the population a position that was commensurate with their social aspirations and cultural orientation. When such a position was not forthcoming, emigration for better opportunities abroad was the only way ahead.

CONCLUSION

In this chapter I have shown how the elder Muir generations located their family background in the upper middle class of Jamaica, the notions of relatedness associated with this background, and the structures of differentiation vis-à-vis the lower levels of society that they implicated. The position of the Muir family in Jamaican society was informed by complex concepts of hierarchy related to notions of "race" and "class" that have a long history in Jamaica. According to Austin-Broos (1994a: 230), "Jamaican notions of 'race' and 'class' can be rendered as a discourse of heritable identity," which entails both "ideas of biological inheritance and ideas of environmental inheritance." The first notion of inheritance views social position as defined at birth and is associated with a static social order, where individuals have no social mobility. The second notion emphasizes the sociocultural environment—and individual achievement—as the most important factor determining the position of individuals in the social order. In this view, a certain social mobility is therefore possible, not through one individual's achievement, but through several generations of improvement in upbringing and education (Austin-Broos 1994a: 220). Whereas ideas of "biological inheritance" prevailed during slavery, ideas of "environmental inheritance" have become predominant today, although the two have always coexisted to a certain extent. Thus, Austin-Broos notes that notions of heritable identity that were quite different from notions of individual achievement were incorporated within Jamaican ideas of education (Austin-Broos 1994a: 218).

I suggest that the merging of the two concepts of inheritance has occurred, to a great extent, in the notions of relatedness that characterize the family in the middle and upper classes in Jamaica, especially in relation to the family. Thus, biological inheritance is associated with kinship, believed to be based on blood ties. Out of the wider network of kin relations, however, a smaller family group may emerge that seeks to improve its social position through education and proper rearing of the children, in the process "improving" itself and thus becoming of a "better" kind. It was apparent that the Muir family members regarded their family as having risen from the lower to the higher levels of society by virtue of "proper" manners, "correct" English, and "good" education that over several generations had become an integral part of family life. Emma described her mother as a key person who, because of her intelligence, had learned proper English and good manners and therefore was like a white person. As the issue of a white–black union who had benefited from her mother's strict upbringing, Emma had removed herself further, both biologically and culturally, from the lower classes, and she consolidated her upward mobility when she physically moved away from Refuge and married a member of the racially mixed, respectable middle class in the colonial parish capital of Falmouth.

Emma figured as an important foundational figure in the family narratives related by the siblings and their children and grandchildren. She was described as the central person in the well-known family home in Falmouth, where the children grew up. She had essentially supported the family and paid for her children's education at some of the best schools in Jamaica, and as the siblings left Jamaica and settled abroad, she became a central figure in the family network and an increasingly important source of identity rooted in the "certain ways" she embodied. When the children left Jamaica, their notion of relatedness, and the tradition of self-improvement that this entailed, shaped their migratory moves, their ambitions, and the kind of life and place in society that they desired wherever they settled.

The life stories related by the elder members of the Muir family served as foundational stories that situated the family in the respectable layers of Jamaican society. This social position served as a point of departure for the siblings' narratives of migration and settlement abroad. Their move out of Jamaica to metropolitan centers in North America and Europe can be regarded as a continuation of their mother's journey from the little "backward" village of Refuge to the bustling colonial town of Falmouth. As the siblings moved away from Jamaica, they left the colonial class system and the sort of social differentiation that it involved. This system, with its strong emphasis on education and good manners, had allowed family members to secure a position in the respectable middle class. The Jamaican racial hierarchy, however, limited their access to further opportunities in the local society. An important motivating factor for emigrating therefore was that of obtaining a higher education abroad that would allow the family to circumvent the racial barriers and thus increase its status in Jamaican society.

As the family members moved to various migration destinations, they encountered a global migratory regime associated with other systems of differentiation that had a great impact on their pursuit of social and economic improvement. One aspect of this regime was the nation-states' regulation of migratory flows. Great Britain, the imperial mother country, was an open migration destination for British West Indians until the early 1960s. Two of the siblings opted to go to Britain, one enlisting in the Royal Air Force (RAF) during World War II, the other training as a nurse at a London hospital. The United States was much more difficult to enter at the time because of a quota system that placed severe restrictions on immigration (Kasinitz 1992: 26; Waters 1999a: 34–35). Instituted in 1924, when non-European migration to the United States was increasing rapidly, the quota system was maintained during the economic recession of the 1930s, the war years of the 1940s, and the first two decades of the postwar period. When in 1965 the quota for Caribbean nationals was increased, it set off large-scale Caribbean migration to the United States. During the forty-year period, the highly restrictive quota system favored professionals as well as relatives of Caribbean migrants who had entered the country before 1924 (Kasinitz 1992: 26; Waters 1999a: 35). Most of this migration therefore involved people of middle-class background, resulting in the development of strong middle-class Caribbean immigrant communities in New York. American immigration quotas giving preferred status to relatives of immigrants enabled the Muir siblings to enter the country, because their paternal uncles had migrated to New York early in the twentieth century.

Another important aspect of the global migratory regime concerned the racialized systems of stratification in the migration destinations that differed from that experienced by the family in Jamaica. In the United States, non-white Caribbean immigrants were perceived as blacks and therefore identified with the black, lower-class segment of society, regardless of their middle-class background and their light skin color (Foner 2000: 150–51; Waters 1999a: 45). During the 1940s and '50s, this racial categorization entailed, among other things, segregation in black neighborhoods. As a result, the family members seem to have withdrawn into their own Jamaican communities of middle-class migrants. In Britain, where there was no sizable local black population except for the old, established black community in Liverpool (Brown 2005), Caribbean immigrants were regarded primarily as colonial British subjects. Until the early 1950s, many of these people had moved to Britain to pursue further education. While they were racialized, they seem to have been able to mingle in British society by using their British middle-class cultural skills. This was the case for the two family members. They therefore did not develop their own Caribbean middle-class communities but mixed with the local population, as well as with other immigrants from the British Commonwealth.

The siblings' accounts of leaving Jamaica and settling abroad, and their and their children's descriptions of the family life they developed in various migration destinations, revolve to a great extent around the varying ways in which they sought to maintain the ambitions and goals associated with the Jamaican social order, while negotiating the new structure of opportunities and limitations associated with the social orders in the receiving societies.

LEAVING JAMAICA

During the 1940s, the Muir siblings began to move away from Jamaica, and over the next ten years all but two of the siblings had emigrated. By the early 1960s, the whole family, including Emma, had left, with the exception of Hubert, who remained in the family home in Falmouth.[1] When I did fieldwork in the late 1990s, Charles and Margaret lived in the United States, while Henry and Jessica made their home in Great Britain, and Amanda resided in the Windward Islands. William, having returned from the United States during the early 1970s, was living in Jamaica. Hubert died in Jamaica in the early 1980s, and Sylvia passed away in the United States the year before I began my research.

The family constituted an important framework for facilitating the moves out of Jamaica. Most of the moves were planned and made possible with the help of various relatives and friends of the family, and the family network therefore offered essential practical help. The family also provided an important sociocultural framework of life that gave meaning and purpose to the siblings' moves. When the siblings related their departure from Jamaica at a young age, they described it as a natural consequence of the strong desire for further education that could not be had in Jamaica or of marriage to men who were pursuing an education or a professional career abroad. Migration therefore needed little explanation. It was regarded as an integral aspect of belonging to a family of this social standing and the personal ambitions that this entailed. When the siblings described the lives they had lived in various migration destinations, they related how they had sought to establish what they deemed to be a satisfactory way of life, considering their particular family background in Jamaica. Thus, their narratives of leaving Jamaica and settling in different destinations were not stories of the breakdown of a family being scattered on different continents. They were tales of the strong loyalty to family values and the aspirations to progress in society that this involved.

While the siblings generally emphasized the positive values that motivated them to migrate to progress further, William and Charles also recounted experiences that made them realize that they would be able to go only so far if they stayed within Jamaican society. William explained that he considered going into business on his own in Jamaica because his family did not have the funds to support his further education abroad when he finished his secondary education: "I visited a bank and outlined my proposition. I wanted to get involved in import and export business, but I needed start-up capital. I was told: 'Sorry.' They couldn't accommodate me. I felt as though I was rejected by my own country. I felt that to progress I had to go beyond Jamaica." Charles, who had not been able to attend a private secondary school, experienced how lower-rung employees were treated in the business sector:

> I worked at an ironmongery store, where they sold nails and so on. I worked there until I was eighteen to nineteen years of age. The head of the parish had made an order for a pane of glass of a particular size, and I did it. But the person brought it back and said that the size was wrong. I had a boss who was English-like, and he bawled me out, even though I knew that I had done it right. So I just walked out of the store and left it. My father agreed with me that I had not been treated right. Then I joined the Home Guards and spent four years with them.

William's and Charles's problems were caused by the hierarchical nature of Jamaican society, although they experienced this in somewhat different ways. Charles's expression of "feeling rejected by his country" indicates that he experienced the bank's refusal to grant capital for his business venture as being put in place: He had attempted to reach above his station in Jamaican society. Charles, in his account, leveled a more direct criticism at Jamaican society, depicting it as one where those at the lower levels had to accept blame for mistakes made by those high in society. Furthermore, Charles identified representatives of the unfair social order as the head of the parish and an "English-like" boss, both of whom would have been associated with the colonial system. Both William and Charles indicate that when they entered the Jamaican labor market it became apparent to them that their family's social status was not quite as elevated as they might have thought during their early childhood. Charles's reference to his father's approval of his walk-out indicates that the family may also have been disappointed at the treatment he was accorded. Only William and Charles made note of such experiences of being put in place. Furthermore, they do not elaborate on what must have been a central aspect of the lack of respect they received in the wider society—their background in a colored family of limited economic means and social status in society. Indeed, none of the siblings mentioned the difficulties presented by their family's place in the racial hierarchy of Jamaican society. On the contrary, the life stories generally were celebratory of the family's position of respect in Jamaican society and the personal ambitions, social expectations, and cultural values to which this naturally led. By downplaying their encounter with the racial hierarchy in Jamaica and emphasizing their sociocultural achievements in Jamaican society, family members presented themselves as part of the respectable layers of society who were entitled to be accepted in the established middle class of the migration destinations.

DESTINATIONS

The first migration destination chosen by the family was "America," where it would be possible to seek further education and where James Muir had three brothers. Both William and Henry applied to go to the United States, but Henry ended up in Great Britain:

> We had three uncles in America, and my brother and I had decided to further our studies in America. These uncles would send for us, help us get the papers so that we could study there. I waited for more than one month, and a couple of friends said, "Why not join the RAF?" I did, and two weeks after, the papers came through, and my brother went to America.

Charles joined William—and the uncles—in New York after his four years with the Jamaican Home Guard were over. Around the same time, Sylvia, who had trained as a nurse in Jamaica, moved to New York with her Jamaican husband who sought higher education abroad.[2]

Margaret also left Jamaica during the 1940s, but she went with her British husband, an Anglican priest, to Great Britain, where he was stationed in a new parish. She joined her siblings in New York several years later, when she left her husband. When Jessica was ready to leave Jamaica for further education in the early 1950s, the family found that London was the better place for her:

> For nursing, England was just the best at the time. So my mother asked whether I would like to go there. The local doctor, whom we knew well, was also very influential. He had studied in England. America was regarded as too wild. England was the mother country; it was better, especially for girls. Boys could go to the States. And I had a sister and brother there [in England], so that gave added protection.

Amanda, like her elder sister Sylvia, earned her nursing degree in Jamaica. In the early 1960s, she married a man from the Lesser Antilles who had received medical training at the University of the West Indies in Jamaica and moved with him to his island of origin.

The siblings' accounts of their emigration show that they moved within the British empire as part of the RAF, the Anglican church, or an educational program, within the family network, or within a combination of both. While family members could travel freely to Great Britain until 1962, they could not enter the United States without the help of the sponsoring relatives in the country. In his study of immigration to New York, Philip Kasinitz (1992) divides Caribbean migration to New York into three phases: (1) an early phase in the first decades of the twentieth century until immigration regulations in 1924, when a large group of Caribbean people entered the United States; (2) a middle phase from the mid-1920s until the mid-1960s, when Caribbean immigration was severely restricted and mostly involved migrants of middle-class background joining family who had migrated during the first phase or entered on student visas; and (3) the latest phase, since 1965, when liberalized U.S. immigration regulations made large-scale Caribbean immigration to the United States possible again (Kasinitz 1992: 23–26). William's, Charles's, and Sylvia's immigration, as noted, clearly fits the second stage of middle-class migration and depended on the uncles' having entered the country early in the century and being in a position to help their relatives immigrate.[3]

With the practical help that the family offered came certain expectations as to the migrating family members' achievements abroad. This was especially apparent in the case of Jessica and William, who migrated with the explicit purpose of obtaining an education abroad. Jessica's plan to become a nurse was much in keeping with the kind of work that a woman of her background would be expected to undertake. Indeed, two of her sisters also were trained as nurses. Jessica planned to return to Jamaica and therefore trained at the Fever Hospital, considered the best for tropical medicine. When she decided to marry another Commonwealth immigrant, from Sri Lanka, and settle in London, the family accepted this, since her sister Margaret had "approved" of her husband, the woman's primary position being in the home. The expectations as far as William was concerned were more ambitious, because the family was hoping that he would succeed in becoming educated as a medical doctor. Indeed, William's second wife claimed that William "was designated to become a doctor":

> When he left Falmouth as a boy, they all knew he was going off to the U.S. to become a doctor. So they called him doctor. Mom's earnings went to him becoming a doctor. It was difficult for her to support him. I didn't know him then. I was a child in Jamaica.

> [Why was it so important that he became a doctor?]

> Doctor, lawyer, Indian chief. It is a high point in any family. Jamaicans aren't business oriented; being wealthy is not seen as so great as being a doctor or a lawyer. Most families aspired to have a doctor. . . . Girl children had aspirations to marry well, marry one of those professionals. They didn't strive to become a doctor.

According to Gordon (1963: 240), the primary way in which the colored middle class might aspire to higher status in colonial society was by acquiring higher education in the professions—law or medicine—that allowed them to go into private practice upon their return to the Caribbean. Before the founding of the University of the West Indies in the mid-twentieth century, education in the professions was only available abroad. Several attempts to institute such education were rejected by the upper classes of planters, who feared losing their abundant, inexpensive local labor force and the development of an influential black middle class of professionals (Miller 1990: 54, see also Heuman 1981). The government scholarships introduced in the British

West Indies during the late nineteenth century and awarded annually to the most outstanding graduates of the secondary schools provided the only direct access to further education for those of lesser means, and there was intense competition to obtain the prestigious scholarship (Gordon 1963:240). For the vast majority of the students who did not have the family funds to pay for higher education abroad, and who were not among the select few to obtain an island scholarship, migration abroad to find work with which to finance further education was the only solution. With the high social prestige attached to entering the professions, William's education as a medical doctor therefore would constitute a personal achievement, as well as a major family accomplishment that would improve its status in Jamaica.

While only William's migration was surrounded by such high expectations, all of the siblings were keenly aware of the notion of progress and self-improvement that guided family relations. As explicated by Emma, this notion revolved around maintaining the "right ways," emulating the best, and mixing with the better elements of society. The migration destinations presented very different possibilities of living up to this family idea.

New York   For many years, New York was a major stronghold for the Muir family and the center of family life. James Muir's three brothers had migrated to the city early in the century, and during the 1940s three of the Muir siblings arrived. They established their own families there and were joined by Emma and Margaret, as well as by several nephews and nieces born in Jamaica. From the 1950s to the 1990s, more than half of the Muir family lived in New York for extended periods, and more have visited for shorter and longer periods.

When I talked to Muir family members about the departure from Jamaica, they never gave the impression that they intended for so much of the family to relocate in New York. It just happened due to a number of different life circumstances. William realized fairly quickly that he could not return to Jamaica as a medical doctor, when he married and had a child with a Jamaican woman he had met in New York while still in the premedical program. This led him instead to find a job at a large American corporation so that he might support his family. Charles described his move to New York as a temporary holiday that became extended when his uncle suggested that he stay; it became permanent when he married another Jamaican immigrant and, with William's help, obtained a job at William's workplace. Sylvia found a good job as a nurse, and by the time her husband had obtained his master of arts degree, they were settled in their own home and both doing well in their careers. When James Muir died, it was natural for the children to sponsor Emma's migration to the United States, and when Margaret separated from her husband, they helped her immigrate and found her a job in New York.

All of the family members settled in the Crown Heights area of Brooklyn, where Sylvia and her husband were living in a house they had purchased. This may suggest that these members of the Muir family were making their home in New York and becoming Americans. This is true to a great extent. The four siblings lived a large part of their lives in New York and reared their children there. Furthermore, they became citizens of the United States. However, they did not accept the place in society that they were accorded on the basis of their supposed ethnic and racial background as Jamaicans. The life stories related by the siblings and their children therefore reflected the conflictual relationship between the family members' shared identity rooted in a middle-class home in Jamaica associated with specific social relations and cultural values and the identities bestowed on them in American society by virtue of their being categorized as part of a racial and ethnic minority.

An important sign of the family's middle-class Jamaican identity, as noted, was its ambition that William become a medical doctor. William recalled how his mother had done everything possible to support his education:

> I remember in New York I was in the apartment building, back from college, and I was checking the mailbox. . . . I found a local paper from Jamaica there, and when I opened it, I found . . . U.S. dollar bills folded into the paper. My mother had sent them. She also baked plum pudding with money in it.

It was difficult for William to come to terms with his failure to obtain a degree in medicine, and in his life story he dwelled on his inability to live up to his family's expectations. He explained his later working life as shaped by his desire to make up for his educational failure by proving his worth in other ways:

> I had two full time jobs and worked ten to twelve hours a day.
>
> [Why did you work so hard?]

I wanted to make a success of my life. I had acquired six—seven parcels, properties, and was financially independent. . . .

[Was this success satisfying to you?]

Not really. I always had that restlessness. Not just a desire to acquire, but I never felt at peace with myself because I never accomplished what I had set out to achieve. That frustrated my desire so that I was not satisfied.

On the basis of this success in business William was able to purchase a house in a "good" neighborhood in Brooklyn that he described as "pristine and beautiful. It was a brownstone building by my wife's mother. The area was immaculately maintained. When I walked home I met the policeman who patrolled the area. The block was inhabited by mostly professionals, doctors, lawyers, dentists." William might not have become a doctor himself, but he had done well enough to live among professionals.

Another important mark of the Muir family's particular Jamaican identity was marriage to a person from the proper social circles. Both William and Charles dated primarily Jamaican women or women of Jamaican background who belonged to the Jamaican middle-class social circle in which they moved. Charles described a date with a woman of Jamaican parentage where they spent the whole time drinking tea in the living room of the girl's home under close supervision of her parents. While the spouses did not know each other before leaving Jamaica, they were part of the same network of colored families of a certain social standing, and this network had gradually become extended to New York, because there was a fairly substantial population of Jamaican middle-class background in that city when the Muir family arrived. There was therefore a great deal of socializing within this Jamaican network. As Emma noted, "Those who went to the States all married Jamaicans. In the States people are more clannish, so you tend to go with the crowd, and you get close to them."

The family members also demarcated their social status by purchasing a brownstone and keeping a "nice" home. The acquisition of a brownstone in "the stately streets of Crown Heights" has been described by the West Indian writer Paule Marshall as "the West Indian American dream, circa 1950" (Marshall, as quoted in Kasinitz 1992: 59). Several of the family members, including William, mentioned that they were living in a brownstone in

Crown Heights, and they described very nice homes, indeed. Kathy, one of William's daughters, remembered that her mother, Eliza, kept fresh flowers in the entryway and acquired a baby grand piano so the children could learn to play. Kathy's older sister, Carol, made reference to Eliza holding "tea parties and coffee hour" in the home for the various women's societies and women's groups in the Catholic church to which Eliza belonged. Many of the women who came for such events, Carol recalled, were white Americans. Being accepted in white society seems to have been of great importance to Eliza. Thus, when Kathy was told by one of her white schoolmates that her mother would not let her attend Kathy's birthday in the home, because "all niggers live in garages," Eliza marched with Kathy to the friend's house and insisted that the mother come and have a look at her house. When the mother saw the home, Kathy added, she exclaimed: "My God, you live in a nicer home than we do!"

It was important for members of the Muir family not to be lumped with black Americans, who generally were associated with a low position in society. When I asked William and Charles where in New York they had lived with their uncle, they replied, "Manhattan." When I inquired further about where on Manhattan they had lived, they described the place as the outskirts of Harlem, an area that was mixed white and black, the blacks being primarily from the Caribbean. This mixture, they said, made them feel more comfortable about living there. They had attended cultural events in Harlem that were patronized by whites as well as blacks, they noted, and William also described going to concerts in the parks during the summer, primarily classical concerts. For his further studies, William chose a Catholic university that was overwhelmingly white. Later he became one of the first non-white employees at a large American corporation, where he ended his career in a high-level position. When the Muir families moved to Brooklyn, they chose to settle in an area that at the time was largely white. Later, William and Sylvia's husband, Victor, built weekend houses in the Hamptons, described by Charles as "one of the richiest places on Long Island." A friend of the family noted that it had been necessary to purchase the property in this area through a white intermediary.

The family's attempt to become part of white, mainstream society was only partially successful. The white population began to move out of the neighborhood as an increasing number of people of color moved in. Thomas, William's eldest son, remembered this exit of the white population well:

My best friend was German from third to sixth grade. But overnight, most of the white families moved out. It all happened within a year.

[Why?]

Blockbusting. People panicked; they feared that their property value would deteriorate, and this caused a white flight to the suburbs. The neighborhood went downhill. As kids, we were innocent of race, but as we became older it changed. The family moved, and we had all intentions of staying in contact, but didn't anyway. Then my family moved when I was twelve or thirteen years old to another Italian–Irish neighborhood. Within two years, the same happened. We did not move. It was a very nice house, and we were in high school. About 80 percent left, and there were about one or two white families left on the block. Before the neighborhood had been 95 percent white.

With the white flight and the concomitant influx of a black population, the area of Brooklyn where the family lived changed character entirely. It was no longer an established, middle-class neighborhood of professionals, but turned into an immigrant community consisting largely of blacks of Caribbean origin.

By the 1980s, Crown Heights, Bedford Stuyvesant, and East New York were identified as a "Commonwealth Caribbean 'core district'" (Conway and Bigby 1987:77). In particular, Crown Heights has become known as an important Caribbean cultural center in the United States, largely because of the Carnival that is held on Eastern Parkway every Labor Day (Kasinitz 1992: 143). None of the members of this Jamaican family, however, described this West Indian transformation of the neighborhood in positive terms or mentioned having taken part in West Indian cultural activities in Brooklyn. Sylvia's son described the neighborhood as a rather rough and increasingly violent one, and he remembered having experienced a conflict between the black population that was moving into the area and his family:

The neighborhood had African Americans who were poor and had a very different outlook and way of doing things. My parents were Jamaican and professionals. My father was a chemist; my mother a head nurse in obstetric gynecology. I was having an education while the other kids were screwing around, playing in the street. There were some conflicts: "Who do you think you are?" "You think you are any better than us?"

Those who arrived from the West Indies beginning in the second half of the 1960s did not have the same class background as the Muir family. Even though they were West Indians, they represented a rather different sort of West Indianness with which the family members did not identify. While to Americans the Muir family and the West Indian newcomers might be perceived as black—or, at least, colored—immigrants from the Caribbean, the Muir family did not see it this way. Margaret explained, "In America, they prejudice by color. In the islands, the prejudice is by class. If you are not on the same level, you don't mix socially with those who are on a lower level." To the Muir family, the newly arrived Caribbean people were uneducated, lower-class people who did not share their cultural values and social norms.

The family protected their children against the changing neighborhood by raising them in a sheltered environment of family relations and friends who had the same Jamaican background as the Muir family. Kathy described growing up within a large extended family of aunts, uncles, and cousins:

> A close family member, Fay Miller Jones lived two doors down with her husband, Oswin Jones. Across the street lived a couple of West Indians, and at St. John's Place, Sylvia and Victor lived with their son. Sylvia passed away last year. Down the block lived Margaret Driver, one of my dad's sisters, and her two children (Jane and Ernest), and half a mile away were Alice and Charles Muir and their three children, Barb, Shelly, and Bobby. It was very much a family atmosphere.

This network, her brother Thomas recalled, was boosted by a steady stream of visitors from Jamaica or family and family friends who stayed for an extended period while they were settling in New York: "We always had family from Jamaica with us."

Just as important, the family sent the children to private schools. They did this both to protect the children from the rough public schools and to ensure that they received the best possible educational foundation for pursuing a degree in the professions. The parents, in other words, projected their own educational ambitions on their children, and they followed the children's educational progress keenly and supervised their homework closely. When Kathy expressed a desire to become a ballet dancer and was accepted at a high school for the performing arts, her mother made it quite clear that this was not acceptable:

My mother was against it. She asked me how many black dancers I had seen on stage in ballet productions. None at that time; they were all white dance companies. So what did I expect to get out of going to the high school—becoming a ballerina? She reminded me that I wanted to be a pediatrician, so I had to go to the San Andrews Hall Academy. They were hoping to have a doctor in the family. Eventually I married a pediatrician!

New York had offered a range of social and economic opportunities but also imposed a number of limitations because of the racial background of the family members, and the family essentially got stuck in an increasingly disadvantaged inner-city area of black immigrants. During the late 1960s and 1970s, the younger generation began to leave the city, as they went off to college and followed career trajectories in other parts of the United States. Later, the older generation moved away. During the early 1970s, Bill returned to Jamaica. After Sylvia died in the mid-1990s, Charles moved to live with his son in New Jersey, and when I did my fieldwork with the Muirs during the late 1990s, Margaret was in the process of moving to live with her daughter in Nova Scotia. New York had been an important destination in the family's initial migratory move out of Jamaica, not a place for family members and succeeding generations to settle permanently.

England   While the members of the Muir family who began moving to New York during the 1940s ended up creating an enclave of middle-class Jamaican culture in New York that celebrated the family's particular background in Jamaican colonial society and represented the kind of social relations and cultural values with which the Muir family would like to identify, the Muir siblings who migrated to England mixed with people in British society. They did this partly because there were few people of their Caribbean background with whom they could associate, and partly because they were able to mingle with the "right" sort of people from their point of view as members of the respectable Muir family.

On a sunny afternoon, Henry Muir picked me up outside the Sheldonian Theater in Oxford and drove me to his home in a small rural village nearby. As he drove me through the English countryside, pointing out the village church that he attends, the pub nearby where a famous novel was written, and the Thames River winding through the wooded area where he liked to walk his boxer dog, it was difficult to believe that I was entering the ethnographic field where I was doing research on Caribbean migration. Everything looked so English, and this impression was further confirmed when we entered Henry's home, located in a small development of semi-detached houses, and his English wife welcomed us with tea and homemade cake. Henry seemed to blend entirely with the English landscape. My impression of Henry as the image of a real Englishman received further support when he began to tell me about his life. He had joined the RAF at eighteen during World War II and played on the RAF cricket team, where he had served as captain of the cricket club at his RAF station for a while. When his club reached the final in the inter-station games, he even played at the Kennington Oval, the famous venue for international cricket games, and won. After leaving the RAF, he had played for the local cricket club for ten years and served as the chair of the team. He was active in the parish church and had been a member of the parish council for a number of years. Henry appeared to have become a quintessential Englishman.

The sort of Englishness that Henry had made his own—the British military, cricket, and the Anglican church—were very much part of his background in colonial Falmouth. Thus, when he joined the RAF and went to England, he was going not to a foreign country, but to the old center of the imperial culture that had suffused his early life. He saw no reason to seek out the company of West Indians but, instead, chose to mix with others: "When I joined the RAF at Abingdon, the captain said, 'We have quite a bit of West Indians; would you like to live with them?' I said, 'No, I will go where the trade takes me.' You should not try to be different; you should move along." While he did experience some racial prejudice, he brushed it off as merely incidences of the kind of stereotyping that many others experience:

> I have had racial abuses, but I took it in context. Somebody might yell, "Bloody West Indian," but then he would also yell, "Bloody Irishman" or "Bloody Welshman." People do have a chip on their shoulder. When you are a minority, there is a great feeling that you are being picked on. Of course it happens, and I would not deny that it happened. I am sure that even my children had problems because of me being their father, but they never brought it home to me. I always instilled in them to believe in their own self. They must stand on their own feet regardless. When

you show yourself capable, eventually people will respect you. You must gain their respect; it goes a long way wherever you live, work, whatever you do.

Henry showed that he was capable, he explained, and therefore he succeeded. This success, however, was not within the realm of material welfare or occupational prestige. When he had spent a year at a civil-service job in England after the end of the war, he realized that it offered little possibility of promotion and supporting his wife and their children. He therefore took a job in welding and went to work on the production line in the motor industry. This work gave little "job satisfaction," he explained, but he earned three to four times more money. With the income, he and his wife were able to settle in his wife's childhood village in a small housing project built after World War II. There, he and his wife reared their five children and became accepted in the local community. Henry emphasized that he had never sought out people because they were West Indian, only because they were nice people, and when I asked him whether his life in England had been different in any way because of his West Indian background, he replied, "Not at all!"

As he settled in England, Henry benefited from having grown up in the old colonial town of Falmouth, where he had socialized with English people. With his light complexion he did not particularly stand out in a crowd of white Englishmen, and with his training in "good" English and respectable British manners he had the cultural skills to mix in British society. And he made a point of doing exactly this, choosing to ignore the racial slights that he encountered. Henry's five children noted that even though they grew up in a small, white English village, their racially mixed family was generally accepted. This was, they explained, partly because their father was so involved with cricket, partly because he had served in the RAF during the war. It was also important that their father made a great effort to maintain a proper appearance in the village. Even though he worked as a welder, they remembered, he left for work and returned home in a suit and tie and only wore his work clothes at the factory. Because of his impeccably correct appearance and proper manners, he was called "Gentleman Henry" in the village. They were well aware that their father had hoped that they would receive a higher education, but none of them did. As one of them noted: "He was determined that we get an education, but he didn't earn enough for us to go to private school."

When I interviewed Henry, he had just had a weeklong visit from his brother Charles, who had retired on a comfortable pension from his job at a major corporation in New York. The meeting of the family the previous year in connection with Sylvia's funeral in New York was also fresh in his mind. This led him to relate his life story in contrastive terms vis-à-vis the sort of life that he might have had, had he left for the United States, as had several of his brothers and sisters: "I might have been materially better off, but not morally. I have been satisfied with the life I have lived. I would not have had the lovely wife and children and grandchildren. It was destiny, and I have no regrets."

The high moral quality that he attributed to his life rested to a great extent on the superiority that he attached to life in Great Britain compared with that which he had experienced during his visits in the United States. He emphasized that he could move freely in England without worrying about crime; that he had never had any problems becoming accepted in white English society; and that he preferred the British way of life to the American: "I am very pro-British. On the whole I find the American way of life very cosmetic, overreacting to most things, everything is bigger than big, and when it comes to the crunch to show your metal, they are not there." In this account, Henry also pointed to his family as one of the great achievements in his life. Indeed, he was the only Muir sibling who was able to enjoy close contact with his five children and many grandchildren on a regular basis. Three of the children had settled in the local area, and the others were living within easy distance. This physical closeness, however, also reflected the fact that most of his children had opted not for mobile professional careers but, instead, had married and settled in the local area.

Jessica did not express quite the same enthusiasm for everything British as had Henry. Nevertheless, like Henry, she emphasized in her life story the ease with which she had become part of English society when she moved to London in 1951, and she also related this to her training in English culture in Jamaica. Indeed, her long journey across the Atlantic Ocean had not entailed a noticeable change in sociocultural environment, she noted, because the private secondary school she had attended in Jamaica had already immersed her in a very English environment. Besides, as Jessica joked, the system of strict control maintained by the hospital where the nursing students lived was all too familiar from the Jamaican boarding school: "We had to be in at 10 P.M. We had to report to the porter at the gate, and we could get a late pass from the matron a couple of times a week to stay out maybe up to midnight." From a social and cultural point of view, Jessica in essence had migrated to England when she moved to St. Hilda's. Transporting herself physically to English territory in Great Britain just completed the migration process.

Jessica described her life in England as fairly uneventful. She studied to become a nurse, married a man from Sri Lanka, worked as a nurse, had a son, worked again as a nurse, and began helping in her husband's Sri Lankan restaurant after her retirement. Jessica did not make an issue out of having married a person from Sri Lanka; she merely mentioned it in passing. When I asked her how she had met her husband, she explained that at that time there were not many colored people in Great Britain and that she therefore began to go out with her husband. When I inquired further concerning what her mother thought about this marriage, she replied: "I don't know what my mother was thinking, but she voiced the opinion that she had brought us up a certain way. We must find ourselves a partner, and we must know whom to choose." By marrying a Sri Lankan, Jessica in some respects was mixing with somebody from a completely foreign cultural background. Not only was he from an entirely different part of the world; he was not even a Christian but a Buddhist, as she explained. At the same time, it is apparent that Jessica and her husband, despite their different origins, belonged to the same sociocultural group in England. They were both people of color born and raised within the British empire, and they had traveled to the center of the empire to take advantage of its social and economic opportunities.

The desire to become part of British society was also an important theme in Jessica's home. Jessica's son emphasized that his parents had chosen to move to an English suburb when they purchased their own house: "My parents were the only non-white people. It was quite something in 1962. They did not move into a black area like Shepherd's Bush, Brixton, where the immigrants tended to congregate." His parents worked hard to put him into a private school and provide a university education for him, and he did obtain the medical degree that was so desired in the Muir family.

While Henry and Jessica mixed in society, they both had close West Indian friends who were of importance to them. Henry had maintained a close friendship with a Jamaican friend from the RAF, and Jessica had become friends with a Barbadian woman who studied nursing with her. These West Indian friends participated in their weddings and served, respectively, as best man and maid of honor. Furthermore, Henry and Jessica visited each other fairly regularly and celebrated Christmas and other special occasions together. However, the Jamaican population in England was small and scattered before the middle of the 1950s, when mass migration from the West Indies set in.[4] In their everyday life, Henry and Jessica therefore did not emphasize their Jamaican background but used their competence in English culture to become integrated into British society. This English competence was closely related to the cultural values and social norms that they had been brought up to admire and emulate in their family home. When they acted English, they therefore also acted as good members of the Muir family. The members of the Muir family that I interviewed during the 1990s were in many ways fully incorporated into British middle-class society.

The Windward Islands   Like Jessica and Henry, Amanda moved within the British empire when she joined her husband on one of the Windward Islands in the Eastern Caribbean, but unlike her siblings who went to the imperial center in England, she traveled to the periphery—one of the smaller and lesser economically developed islands. She alluded to this when she explained that she had known very little about the island when she moved there: "I hardly knew where it was—it is terrible, but Jamaicans don't know much about the small islands, which they just think are little dots somewhere on the map. But I knew from geography that they grew bananas and limes."

Being married to a local medical doctor, she became part of the professional middle class and was able to keep the lifestyle that she was used to from her home in Jamaica. Thus, whereas her siblings in North America and Europe started out in modest accommodations, did the housework on their own, and relied on Emma to look after the children during the long summer holidays, Amanda moved into a spacious doctor's house that she described as "a fine, old wooden house with a lot of character" and had domestic help. When her husband became established as a specialist, they built their own modern home in a neighborhood in the capital inhabited mainly by professionals. Amanda explained that she had devoted her life to supporting her husband's career and being there for the children, which included supervising their education, sending them abroad for further education while they were still in their teens, and, later, spending extended periods of time abroad with her daughter helping to care for her children while she finished her exams at the university. She emphasized that she was also involved in the community on the island where she lived, being active at church and on various committees and helping to found a school for the "mentally challenged." She thus combined the "work of the family" described by Douglass (1992:203) for upper-class Jamaican women with more philanthropic work common in the middle classes.

Amanda saw her Jamaican background as an important part of her identity, and her children described her as keeping quite a Jamaican home:

> We always knew lots about Jamaica. She talked about Jamaica, read Jamaican books, like the Anancy stories that are big in Jamaica, she would sing Jamaican songs.[5] I sing them now. Jamaican culture was a big part of the home. And we ate Jamaican food. Mom has an *akee* tree—she is the only one who has it [on the island]—and she supplies *akee* to all Jamaicans [there].

A number of the Jamaicans on the island would have been women married to local men educated at the University of the West Indies and professional Jamaicans who worked within the West Indian administrative system. Jamaican culture therefore represented a "big island" culture on a small island and a Caribbean culture associated with the upper, educated layers of society. Furthermore, Jamaica became an independent nation-state in 1962, whereas the smaller Caribbean islands achieved political independence considerably later. As nationals of a newly independent country, Jamaicans regarded folk tales and folk songs, even when performed in the local dialect, as important elements in the new national culture to be celebrated and preserved in books and on records. Singing Jamaican folk songs and reading Anancy stories for the children therefore did not represent a return to the family's roots in rural Jamaica such as Refuge but the teaching of a culture that had gained social acceptance as national heritage in postcolonial Jamaican society. The local "folk" culture had not yet achieved this level of recognition, and the speaking of the local dialect was not allowed in the home.

THE NETWORK OF FAMILY RELATIONS

To a great extent, the life stories related by family members can be characterized as narratives of dispersal. The elder generation of siblings talked about how they had moved away from the family home in Falmouth, Jamaica, and settled in different areas of North America and Great Britain, as well as the Caribbean. Many of their children described further moves to even more scattered places. But if family members were scattered geographically, they insisted that they were emotionally and socially close. This closeness revolved around a sense of relatedness grounded in acts and statements that confirmed the cultural values and social norms believed to form the substance of their family. It also resulted in a network of relations involving visits, letters, telephone calls, and the extending of various kinds of help.

Emma was described as playing a key role in keeping the family together. In doing so, she was essentially maintaining her role as the "centralizing woman" in the family in the sense that she remained "central to the daily life of family" (Douglass 1992: 217). With the dispersal of the family, she carried out this role on a global scale. This centralizing role had economic, social, and emotional aspects. William noted, as mentioned, that his mother sent economic support to him when he studied in New York, and Henry recalled that she "put something in the letter" for his children when they were small and he had little money to spend on them. Emma herself emphasized that she had traveled to be with her daughters when they had their babies and had stayed with them for quite a while afterward to help care for the children. For several years, Emma also cared for her grandchildren when they visited her from New York in her home in Falmouth for long holidays. And when she turned over the family home to her eldest son, she began to travel within the family network, visiting children and grandchildren and offering her help wherever it might be needed. She sent birthday cards to all of her children, grandchildren, great-grandchildren, and great-great-grandchildren, as well as to many of their spouses. After she had left the family home in Falmouth, she stayed for a number of years in New York, where most of the family was living. When the family scattered, the relatives themselves—wherever they lived—became her home, as they sent her tickets and asked her to visit. In her old age, she was being cared for by her children and grandchildren, and she was immensely proud of her family, saying, "I am enjoying life, the best of everything. It is like red carpet treatment!"

While everybody described Emma as the central person in the network of family relations, her children and grandchildren also emphasized that they maintained close relations with one other, among other things by extending help where it was needed in various ways. William and Sylvia, who were well off in material terms, were described as having been instrumental in sponsoring the migration of a number of Caribbean relatives to the United States. Furthermore, they had opened their homes to newly arrived relatives when they needed a place to stay in New York. Henry and his children in England related that William and Sylvia had sent boxes of children's clothing. Margaret noted that when Sylvia became seriously ill, she took over all domestic work in the household, and Jessica explained that she traveled from London to nurse her sister in her home for a couple of months. William's youngest daughter described how Amanda had taken her into her home in the Caribbean for several years when her mother died. Amanda's daughter related that her mother traveled first to Jamaica and later to Canada to stay with her when she had her babies. When I interviewed family members they seemed to be up to date on the most recent events in the family, and there appeared to be a network of communication with a few key people who were particularly well informed about family matters. Margaret was described as one of the key people in this network of communication. When I asked her whether she had talked to anybody in the family during the week before I saw her in early December, she replied that she had called her two children in Canada, her mother and sister in London, a grandson in Canada, and her brother in New Jersey, and that she had been called by her sister in the Caribbean and her son in Canada. Belonging to the family was defined to a great extent by being part of the information network, and this meant talking about and knowing the whereabouts of various relatives as well as being the subject of talk by other relatives.

The importance of knowing about the family was brought home to me when I interviewed Charles's son, Bobby. Even though he had grown up in New York within the circle of relatives living there, he said that he had felt isolated and never fully part of the family, because he was deaf and did not share a language with his relatives. Speaking to me in sign language—so fluently and masterfully that the friend who interpreted for us had a hard time keeping up with him—he explained: "There certainly was love. I love them all. But I was isolated because there was no communication. I could not lip read. Because I was not strong at lip reading, I did not develop that closeness and connection with them." Having never communicated much with the family, Bobby had very limited knowledge about what was going on in it.

More important, perhaps, he did not know the subtleties of what went into being a Muir relative—the hopes and aspirations that had led his parents' generation to leave Jamaica for different places of opportunity abroad and the memories of Jamaica that they maintained through stories about their shared family past. The family members did not seem to be aware of Bobby's feeling of isolation but regarded him as part of the family, partly because he had grown up in New York with many other relatives and partly because they maintained contact with him through his father Charles, who lived nearby.

While many of the Muir relatives emphasized the closeness of the family, it was apparent that the family was not defined just by the frequent visits, the extending of help, and the sharing of stories about the family's past and gossip about individuals' lives in the present. The family was also defined to a great extent by that which it did not talk about, by the silences. These silences provide important keys to understanding both how members of a family wished to present themselves in society and the types of conduct that they did not want to identify with and sought to disassociate from the family. This became particularly apparent as I began to interview the siblings' children, who spoke more freely about certain relations and events that had been silenced for many years within the Muir family and even displayed a certain ironic distance toward the elder generation's insistence on keeping good appearances.

RELATED AND UNRELATED LIVES

Narrative theory has shown that life stories are credible when they are related in such a fashion that they follow socially accepted conventions that bestow on them a certain order and coherence (Linde 1993; Rosenwald and Ochberg 1992). Within the context of a family, Jerome Bruner states, life stories "are made to mesh with each other" according to the "miniature culture" that the family comprises (Bruner 1987:22). From a slightly different angle, one can argue that by telling their life stories in such a way that they "meshed with each other," relatives affirm the substance of their relations, and hence their belonging in a particular family group. As I listened to the life stories related by various relatives in the Muir family, it became apparent that in some cases meshing was only possible by simplifying—that is, standardizing certain family relations or deleting them altogether from the life story. This was the case as far as the issue of illegitimacy was concerned. Emma and her children often described all relatives as the offspring of married couples, even though some were, in fact, the result of extramarital sexual relations. In other cases, they simply forgot to mention the offspring of extramarital relations. This "simplification" of family narratives reflects the ambivalent attitude in the middle class toward such relations, which primarily involve middle-class men and lower-class women.

According to Jack Alexander, "Illegitimacy is an improper yet expected feature of middle-class Jamaican life. It provokes shame and silence, yet there are no structurally generated sanctions against it; indeed it is a structured feature of middle-class family life" (Alexander 1984: 160). In the Muir family, some of the outside relations were quite well known, whereas others seemed to be less so. Some members of the Muir family claimed, for example, that it was not general knowledge that certain relatives were born of illegitimate unions. I therefore was not the only one who was subjected to highly edited accounts of family history. Indeed, some of Emma's grandchildren remembered incidents in which they realized that there were certain things that were hidden from them. When I asked one of the cousins about his paternal grandparents (his father had married into the Muir family), he replied:

> Something happened there. My parents were really secretive about that. I never heard. Something was said in my presence, I think I was seven, and Aunt Eliza said, "Hush, he doesn't know." There were things that happened, something that my parents felt they would protect me against. . . .

> [Why did they hide these things?]

> They had their reasons—they were things that they were not proud of, and they were trying to present an image to the younger generation about where they were coming from. The family culture, they were on top.

By keeping silent about certain matters, family members therefore were able to turn their model *for* family life into a model *of* the family (cf. Geertz 1973).

Most members of the Muir family were aware of the fact that three of Emma's sons had children out of wedlock in Jamaica before they married. One of the children, a son, had been recognized by his father and even lived with him for a while, but when this son emigrated to the United States, the family lost touch with him. It seems that he emigrated illegally, indicating that the family did not help by applying for a visa for him. The two others had become fully incorporated into the Muir family, but only some time after they were born. This delay was not so much caused by the family's actively refusing to acknowledge the children as by its silence about the existence of the children. When the mother of one of the grandchildren born out of wedlock asked the Muirs for help with the child, Emma took it immediately into the family home, rearing it as her own. Later on, this grandchild moved to New York and stayed with Muir relatives there. Most of the Muir family did not know about the existence of the third child born out of marriage for many years. Apparently, the mother informed the family in Falmouth when the child was born, but since she was from a middle-class family in Kingston, no help was requested from the Muir family. The existence of this granddaughter therefore was ignored, and she did not meet her father until she and her mother had a chance encounter with him in Kingston. She remembered it well:

> My mother took me to the [American] embassy for the visa, because my uncle wanted me to spend the summer holiday there. A gentleman came up, and my mother said, "Bill, fancy seeing you here!" Then he hugged and kissed my mother, and she said, "This is your daughter, Carol," and he reached over and hugged me and cried. It was very dramatic. He took all the information and came over to see me before he left. . . . Then arrangements were made for me to meet the family, and I met them in Brooklyn. They were so exited to meet me, and we hit it off. The only thing was that they couldn't get over that I didn't eat chicken. My stepmother gave me a beautiful pearl necklace and earrings as a gift. The kids came to Jamaica on vacation to spend time with me, and I kept going up. Then the rest of the family came.

As long as children born out of wedlock were not generally known to exist, they seem to have been conveniently forgotten. They therefore did not, in effect, figure as relatives who were born outside the proper marital unions. Once their presence became known, however, they were accepted, and when I asked Emma about her sons' involvement in outside sexual relations, she shrugged it off:

It happens today, it happens tomorrow, it happens all the time. [*Laughs*] That is the way life is. Whatever happens in life depends on how you look at it, how you accept it. Whether you are going to be miserable and make a big fuss over nothing. No, no, that is just not my approach to things.

Emma's children generally shared her pragmatic attitude. Those who had children born out of wedlock presented all of their children as if they had been born within marriage. Yet when I asked them about their having had children before marriage, they readily acknowledged this.

This understanding of family relations is somewhat similar to that described by Lisa Douglass for Jamaican upper-class families. Family are those with whom one maintains close relations and who are part of "the intimate daily interactions of a household." Kin denote "individuals who would appear on an objective genealogy based on the criteria of consanguineal or affinal relations. . . . [They] sometimes represent a kind of netherworld that the upper class would rather not see or acknowledge" (Douglass 1992: 22). Whether or not kin are included in the family, Douglass states, depends on whether they are able to conform to "cultural principles of likeness, including ideas about the meaning and relative value of color, class, and gender as well as in the minute types of differences gleaned in social practices" (Douglass 1992: 22). Thus, the phenotypically white granddaughter who was born to a poor Jamaican woman of European background and adopted by the Muir family at a young age conformed easily to the "cultural principles of likeness" that defined the family, as did the granddaughter who was born into a middle-class family. The grandson, who was the issue of a black woman of the lower classes and reared mainly by his mother, was less easily accepted into the family.

Race was another issue that the family apparently preferred not to speak about openly but that was very much present in family relations. Emma and her children described their Jamaican background as one where race was not an important concern. Emma acknowledged that her mother and grandmother were of dark complexion but emphasized that this did not matter because of their love and good manners. By stating that a dark complexion was outweighed by love and good manners, she, of course, indirectly stated that race, in fact, did matter. With her good upbringing and move to Falmouth, Emma had left her black past in Refuge behind, and she seems never to have taken her children back to the village. While Falmouth clearly was a highly racialized place, the family did not make any reference to this. Rather, they emphasized that the family mingled with the respectable layers of society. Thus, William and Charles chose not to mention race as a factor when they described the poor treatment they received that led them to leave Jamaica. It was clearly not good form to refer to the color of individuals within the family if they were of dark complexion. One of Emma's grandchildren in New York remembered asking her father how her brother could possibly be her sibling since he was so much darker than she was and being admonished by him that God had created all equal and that color did not matter. While she admired her father for his refusal to acknowledge the significance of color, she realized that her brother felt that he stood out in the family because of his dark complexion.

It was apparent that the family, despite its claims to color blindness, was in fact quite conscious of color differences. Several noted that certain in-laws had been unpopular in the family because they were black and therefore considered unsuitable marriage partners. Nobody, however, claimed to hold such views. Rather, all attributed the feelings to others in the family. While the family sought to maintain color blindness within the family, it was keenly aware of racial categories in American society and their social and economic implications. Family members therefore attempted to avoid being lumped with black Americans, realizing that they were connected with the lower segments of society. Furthermore, the family distanced itself from more recent black Caribbean immigrants, who it considered belonged to the less-cultured lower classes in the Caribbean. In Britain, family members made a point of settling in white English areas and did not associate with more recent black migrants from the Caribbean. Thus, by demarcating themselves from these racialized groups and by insisting on being themselves part of a well-educated, well-mannered Jamaican middle class where race did not matter, they sought to create a place of respectability for themselves in society.

The family's refusal to openly recognize race as an issue of any importance caused problems for some of the children, because they were subject to racial discrimination when they were placed in all-white environments. This was especially the case in New York. Kathy, who was sent to a white Catholic school, recalled a number of instances of ill treatment, ranging from being forced to stay outside the classroom when she started primary school because the teacher "didn't want to have a nigger in the room" to being told by a student counselor that she was fit only for agricultural work. She wondered why her parents had kept her in the Catholic school, where she clearly was not welcome: "They may not have realized how bad it was, and they were intent on paying for my good education. They took the stiff-upper-lip approach that good schooling is most important. It was the ticket to life."

The color differences in the family became an increasingly important issue when Brooklyn became "black," because some of the "white" relatives began to feel uncomfortable in the area. Margaret's daughter, who married a white Canadian man, explained that when they visited her mother in New York, he was shocked about the area's appearance and told her that he would never go there again. She herself was upset when, later, her son and his stepbrother insisted on visiting her mother there, explaining: "It simply is not a place for whites!" The transformation of the neighborhood into an all-black area therefore made the existence of color differences within the family painfully apparent. The neighborhood had changed from being a place that brought the family together to a place that divided the family along racial lines. The family's refusal to openly acknowledge the significance of differences based on color and legitimacy can be related to the notions of "heritable identity" that Diane Austin-Broos (1994a) sees as central in Jamaican society. Austin argues that such notions, while usually "marked by a reference to color," are often stated "in social class terms alone" (Diane Austin-Broos 1994a: 217). Furthermore, they are historically specific:

> Due to Jamaica's historical specificity, Jamaicans have also construed the experience of "class" in particular ways; ways that make the representations of difference presumed to be embodied in diverse productive roles something specifiably Jamaican, related to but not identical with color classifications. Such a meaningful content of class I found in the language of "inside" and "outside" which proposed ideas of manners and education, associated with certain productive roles, to be inherited characteristics. These antimonies pertained to three areas of life: work life, domestic life, and procreation. Each of these domains, paradigmatically, was organized in an educated "inside," or an "outside" way that connoted lack of education. (Austin-Broos 1994a:217)

Within the Jamaican historical experience, dark complexion, birth out of wedlock, and lack of education would be associated with "outside" relations that did not belong within a respectable middle-class family as defined in Jamaica. When relating their life stories, individuals in the elder generations therefore preferred to "forget" about these matters to maintain their understanding of the family as a respectable one entitled to a high status in society. The younger generation of cousins, as shall be seen, was not concerned about respectability in terms of an inheritable identity associated with a certain class position, and some of the cousins were critical of their parents' social ambitions. But they were proud of being part of a family that had a position of respect in Jamaican society; migrated for better social and economic opportunities; created warm, close-knit, and supportive families in various migration destinations; and succeeded at maintaining ties to relatives living in different parts of the world. This legacy, as shall be discussed in chapter 8, became an important source of identity, especially when family members were confronted with their ethnic and racial background in the migration destinations.

CONCLUSION

In this chapter I have examined the Muir family's migratory moves to different destinations. I have argued that the foundational narrative of the family as part of respectable middle-class Jamaican society provided an important framework within which the siblings presented their own life trajectories and their hopes and aspirations for themselves and their children. When the racially mixed Muir family members migrated to the United States and Britain, they insisted on what they regarded as their rightful place in society. They settled in white, middle-class neighborhoods; sent their children to the best possible educational institutions; and refused to identify with the black lower classes. When the family members in the United States were excluded from the American white middle class, they formed their own circle of friends from the racially mixed Jamaican middle class, where they might cultivate the way of life that they knew and cherished.

All the siblings maintained and further developed a strong Jamaican identity, rooted in the family's position of respect in Jamaican society, within the close-knit network of family members living in different parts of the world. This network helped individuals maintain their middle-class status by extending considerable help in the form of, for example, sponsorships for visas, air fares, money for further education, and clothing for the children. It only reluctantly accepted those who did not "naturally" belong in the family, such as children born out of wedlock and spouses of the wrong color and class. The family also kept a tight lid on "problematic" behavior within the family that did not fit into the respectable norms but pragmatically accepted, and quickly adapted to, a state of affairs that could not be changed. Far from merely emulating British middle-class culture, the family, and its network of close friends, therefore developed its own understanding and social practices in relation to its Jamaican social and cultural background.

While the global network of relations was close-knit, individual family members seem to have experienced their migratory moves in quite different ways and to have drawn on their family background in varying ways. William emphasized that racial discrimination had prevented him from becoming fully recognized as a (middle-class) American and that this was a major reason he had decided to return to Jamaica. Henry, by contrast, downplayed the difficulties that he encountered and underscored that he had become accepted in British society because of his good family background and had led a culturally and socially fulfilling life. Their differing stories reflect not their individual achievements by any objective social and economic measurement but, rather, the extent to which they succeeded in inscribing their family narrative within the family legacy and the "heritable identity" that this gave them. By marrying an English woman and settling in an English village, Henry was able to become part of the English culture and society that was associated with the middle- and upper-class status in colonial Jamaica. He therefore achieved the family's social goals, even though his occupation and economic situation did not match this social position. William had a fine career from an economic point of view, but he remained a man of color, and therefore socially marginalized, in American society. He was only able to convert his economic capital into the symbolic capital of social status in Jamaica, where he, with his business venture and his prestige as a returned migrant from the United States, was able to become part of the upper class.

The other siblings were less clear-cut in their accounts of their migration experiences. In hindsight, several expressed some criticism of the highly class-conscious Jamaican society in which they had grown up. However, they were not critical of the social ambitions of their own family, and they emphasized that their home had taught them important moral values and social skills that had given them a feeling of social worth and a sense of direction in life. Furthermore, they were keen to pass on those family values and ambitions to their children and grandchildren. In the last chapters of this book, I will discuss how the siblings' children and grandchildren, living under widely different social and economic conditions in disparate parts of the world, perceived and experienced this family legacy, which gave them a social identity as members of the respectable middle class in society yet was tied to Jamaica's colonial heritage.

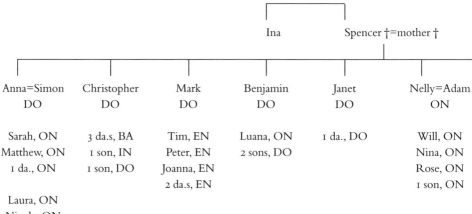

THE GASTON FAMILY, 1996

					Ina	Spencer †=mother †

Anna=Simon	Christopher	Mark	Benjamin	Janet	Nelly=Adam
DO	DO	DO	DO	DO	ON
Sarah, ON	3 da.s, BA	Tim, EN	Luana, ON	1 da., DO	Will, ON
Matthew, ON	1 son, IN	Peter, EN	2 sons, DO		Nina, ON
1 da., ON	1 son, DO	Joanna, EN			Rose, ON
Laura, ON		2 da.s, EN			1 son, ON
Nicole, ON					

KEY: BA, Barbados; DO, Dominica; EN, England; FL, Florida; IN, India; NY, New York; ON, Ontario; USA, United States; da., daughter; da.s, daughters.

[a] *I do not know where in the United States these children are living.*

FIGURE 2   The Gaston Family, 1996. The figure lists and locates individuals identified in the body of the text. It is not a complete genealogy.

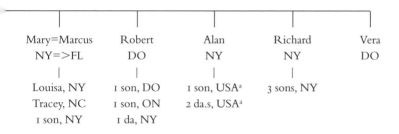

Mary=Marcus Robert   Alan   Richard   Vera
NY=>FL   DO   NY   NY   DO

Louisa, NY 1 son, DO 1 son, USA[a] 3 sons, NY
Tracey, NC 1 son, ON 2 da.s, USA[a]
1 son, NY   1 da, NY

THREE ....

.... **THE VILLAGE ORIGINS**

The Gaston family was proud of its origins in a French creole village in Dominica, where the family had lived for several decades and the children were born and reared. This meant that the family identified with a small community of peasant proprietors who had lived fairly independently of the British colonial society. Within this community, land ownership and government employment, rather than race, would have been the strongest demarcators of social status. Most of the villagers were of French creole origins and therefore of light complexion. Indeed, this was one of several French creole villages in Dominica considered to be more "light skinned than others" (Honychurch 1982: 9). This attention to the "color" of villages in the wider society indicates, however, that race was of social import in Dominican society, and it therefore also became a factor in the local community.

While family members saw themselves as part of the local community and described having participated fully in village life, it was apparent that they were also somewhat apart from it. Their father was the local schoolmaster, an outsider who had moved to the village to educate the local people and introduce them to the modern ways of the world and the British colonial regime. Even though the father died during the early 1960s, he remained a towering figure in the life stories that his children related during the 1990s. The siblings described their father's impact as an educator who demanded only the best from his children; the difficulties he experienced as both a member of the local, relatively egalitarian community and a proponent of change and socioeconomic upward mobility; and the ways these difficulties had affected their childhood. They portrayed their mother, a local woman who devoted herself to religion, as a warm and spiritual person who brought a more human dimension into their lives.

This chapter discusses the Gaston family's complex origins in an isolated community that members of the family celebrated and cherished yet had sought to reform and eventually left for better social and economic opportunities elsewhere. The values that emerge from the siblings' narratives of their village origins revolve around love for the simple rural life, excellence in education, and dedication to serve others. The siblings fully acknowledged that this involved a great deal of self-discipline. They saw this discipline not as a negative form of subjugation involving self-denial, however, but as a constructive force that built a family with a mission that could not be realized within the confines of the village community. Thus, although family members traced their strong values back to their village origins, they all nevertheless left the village. The opening quote is from Benjamin Gaston's narration of his life story, and his personal life in many ways came to exemplify the cultural values that became the defining mark of this family:

I was born Benjamin Gaston on January 18, 1934, in Sainte-Anne [a pseudonym]. I was the third of my mother's children, the fourth in line of my father's—you know, Anna.[1] We were three boys, three girls, three boys, and one girl—ten of us. We grew up as boys would. It was not an urban but a rural area. My father was headmaster of a primary school. We did all the things boys in the village did. Apart from helping our parents, we went to school and did games. We made scooters, but they had no engines, so we had to push uphill! Things were so primitive that we used soft breadfruit, which had dropped from the tree, as grease for the wheels' axle. We had made them ourselves [with] hammer, nails, and saws.

From early on, dad had got us into gardening. There was a school garden, and we had a vegetable garden in the yard. There was also a tract of land that mom's family had. We went there on Saturday. We looked forward to that— fishing crayfish, bathing in the river, picking coconuts. We had to be home early so that our clothes would be ready and our shoes would be shining for Sunday.

The three most important forms of influence we were exposed to were:

(1) The school. Daddy was strict. He wanted us to achieve and get interested in the outside environment.

(2) The environment and feeding ourselves. He sent us to clean people's yard, and the leaves would be used in his compost heap. And we collected ashes from the ovens in the village and brought them home. When the ashes were cold and mixed with water, they would make good compost together with the leaves.

(3) Religion. We had a religious upbringing. Mom was very devoted and never missed mass in the church; she went there every day. We boys became acolytes, not just at the local church, but also in town.

Benjamin Gaston was describing his childhood in a village in Dominica. He did so with great fondness and clarity from the point of view of a person who had lived a long and productive life and had considered carefully how this early, formative period influenced him and his ten siblings who grew up in the family home in the village. He depicts a wonderful childhood where games, cultivating the land, enjoying the natural environment, and going to school and church all blended into an extremely active and industrious life under his parents' careful guidance. His father was the educator with the rational approach to agriculture and an ambition for his children to do well scholastically, his mother the religious devotee who got them involved in the church. The programmatic way in which Benjamin presented the "three most important forms of influence" he and his siblings received during child-hood suggests that they had come to be seen as important pillars of the family. Indeed, as I interviewed Benjamin's siblings Anna, Christopher, Mark, Janet, Nelly, Rose Mary, Robert, Alan and Richard,[2] it became apparent that the pillars also figured prominently in their life stories, although they were pre-sented and interpreted in somewhat different ways in accordance with the particular lives that they had lived as members of the Gaston family.

When the siblings represented themselves in relation to their origins in the village of Sainte-Anne, they claimed a central locus of belonging in Domini-can society. Originally colonized by the French, Dominica did not become a British possession until the Treaty of Paris in 1763. When the island came under British rule, it had become "a new frontier for poorer whites and freed slaves" who had been squeezed out of the surrounding French islands of Martinique and Guadeloupe where a large-scale, slave-based plantation system had been instituted (Honychurch 1995: 50). In scattered areas with arable land in mountainous Dominica they established small settlements of modest coffee estates operated with a few slaves, and by the time the British arrived, they encountered what Cecilia Green has called "enclaves . . . saturated in a culturally and linguistically Afro-French creole and paternalistic Catholic tradition" (Green 1999: 44). Although the British set out to develop a plantation economy on the island, their "attempt to impose a classic sugar plantation economy upon this base was doomed from the start" (Green 1999: 44). By the late 1700s, thirty sugar plantations had been given up, and only fifty were left (Honychurch 1995: 100).

While most of the Caribbean islands saw the emergence of a strongly hierarchical, color-graduated society dominated by European plantation owners and representatives of the colonial administration, Dominica presented a more complex picture. The British had a strong presence in the capital, Roseau; the second town, Portsmouth; and the limited lowland areas where the sugar plantations survived. While the rural communities were incorporated within a wider British political and economic system, they consisted of largely self-sufficient, French creole-speaking settlements of peasant farmers whose most immediate contact with the outside world often was the local Catholic priest (Baker 1994; Green 1999; Honychurch 1995). It was only in the course of the twentieth century, when attendance at the British schools in the villages became common, that the British influence asserted itself throughout the island (Christie 1982: 43).

The strong tradition of self-contained local communities in Dominica does not mean that this was an entirely egalitarian society. Rather, other forms of differentiation relevant to the village hierarchy were of significance. During the 1930s, '40s, and '50s, when the siblings were growing up in the village, land ownership gave status and admittance to the local community of peasant proprietors. Additional income through other economic activities, such as shopkeeping, gave higher status in the village hierarchy. Above—and to a certain extent outside—this local hierarchy were the Catholic priest as well as the schoolteacher and the policeman, who usually came from the outside. Their status derived partly from their ties, respectively, with the Catholic church and the British colonial system and partly from their salaried income, which gave them economic stability (Baker 1994: 117; Eguchi 1984: 171; Green 1999: 69). This village hierarchy was a rather contradictory one, referring partly to a local community of peasant proprietors who emphasized autonomy rooted in a traditional rural way of life, partly to the Francophile Catholic church, and partly to the British colonial system.

The Gaston family was very much a product of this history. Family members had a family tree prepared by a Catholic priest showing that the first Gaston arrived on Dominica during the eighteenth century, settled, and founded a family that somewhere along the line mixed with the local population of African and native Carib Indian origin.[3] By tracing their descent from a French ancestor, the Gastons did not wish to claim their origins in a high-status family of European origins. On the contrary: Family members rather liked to emphasize their modest background in a rural Dominican community. They explained that the first Gaston had come as part of the French militia, and that the family never was involved in large-scale plantation cultivation. They noted that their father was born into a family of peasant proprietors but had chosen to give up farming for a career as a schoolteacher. He had therefore left his home as a young man to receive further training in the Dominican educational system and eventually ended up in Sainte-Anne, where he became a head teacher. It was apparent that the Gastons were keen to point to the family's deep roots in the old villages on the island and its rise to middle-class status through education.

Through their descriptions of their childhood in the old French creole village of Sainte-Anne, where their father was a head teacher, they claimed a source of identification that gave them a place of belonging in modern Dominican society. After political independence in 1978, the villages came to be seen as foundational to the nation-state of Dominica because of their long history of relative cultural, economic, and social autonomy (Honychurch 1982: 8). However, none of the family members who claimed this village-based Dominican identity were living in Sainte-Anne, and as they related their life stories, it was apparent that the family's position in the village had been a rather contradictory one. As an educator and representative of the colonial system living in the village, their father had played a key role in mediating between the local and outside worlds. This gave the family high status in the community. However, the family had also been heavily involved, both economically and socially, in village affairs. This intermediary position, where the family sought to be *of* the village while looking *beyond* its limited horizons, was fraught with problems that could only be resolved by leaving the village. When the Gaston siblings described their particular background in a French creole village they therefore not only rooted themselves in Dominica but also explained their moves away from this village, the kinds of lives they and their children have lived in widely different parts of the world, as well as the prominent role many family member have come to play in modern Dominican society.

THE HEAD TEACHER'S VILLAGE

> What was different about us was dad's belief in education. He said the land will stay. If you are educated, let people fight for the land.

In these brief sentences, Richard, the last son, summarized what made Spencer Gaston and his family unique in the village. They regarded land, the solid and necessary foundation of any community of farmers, as less important than education, a much less tangible resource that might seem somewhat remote from village ways. Other siblings concurred. Their father's greatest gift to his children, as well as the community where he served as head teacher, was his dedication to education. Spencer Gaston was one of very few people in the village who had books in the home. The Gaston children were also encouraged to visit the Catholic priest who lived in the presbytery next door and who had a library. Alan remembered going there with his brother Robert to read *National Geographic*. To broaden the horizon of his family and other villagers, Spencer acquired a radio, and Christopher recalled one of the first major news items from the wider world that he heard on the radio:

> My father got the first radio in the village in 1939. I remember hearing about the outbreak of World War II and being asked by my father to go to the French priest to tell him about it. We listened to BBC, and it meant a lot in terms of bringing the village in contact with the rest of the world. Everybody in the village would come and listen to the radio.

The father sought to widen the horizons of his children even further, taking his children for walks on moonlit nights to tell them about the stars, his eldest daughter, Anna, remembered.

The Gaston family asserted its status as the educated segment of the village population by speaking English rather than French-lexicon patois. With the British colonization of Dominica, English became the formal language, and it was the language of instruction in the schools established in the nineteenth century, after the emancipation of the slaves. This caused considerable problems for a large majority of the children, who did not know English, and school attendance was quite low well into the twentieth century. As late as 1937, when the oldest Gaston children were attending primary school, only 62 percent of school-age children in Dominica were enrolled in school (Green 1999: 65).[4] While education may just have been deemed a luxury by peasants, who could make good use of the children's labor in the family's farming activities, by the middle of the twentieth century many Dominicans had become aware of the importance of education and government employment as avenues of social mobility. English therefore began to be "considered the language of the relatively sophisticated and educated urban dwellers" (Green 1999: 45).[5] Nevertheless, in more remote villages, such as Sainte-Anne, patois remained the spoken language much longer, even though, as Christopher noted, it had low status.[6] "It was only the illiterate who spoke it, and it was regarded as nothing but the language of the illiterate people." While the Gaston children spoke English in the home—at least, when their father was present—they were only able to communicate with the domestic helpers, and virtually all of the villagers, in French patois. They thus learned to speak the language, even if their father frowned on it.

The children said little about what was taught in school as such but emphasized that their father was a disciplinarian. Anna explained: "He was hard, a good disciplinarian. 'Spare the rod and spoil the child' was his motto." Anna's positive description of her father as a "good disciplinarian" reflects the fact that physical punishment of children by parents as well as teachers has been widespread and generally accepted within the Caribbean.[7] Liberal use of the rod therefore would have been regarded not as a sign of child abuse but, rather, as an indication that the teacher cared about the children and wanted them to learn at school. By this logic, the stricter the disciplining of the pupils, the more concern and interest in them the teacher was demonstrating. According to this mode of understanding, Spencer Gaston was an excellent teacher, because he kept good order and discipline in the school. He disciplined his own children the most, as Mark well remembered: "I remember being out picking berries during the lunch break, and we would be five minutes late. I would get the strap, but he would let the others go, because I should set the example, and I should have known better."

An important aim of this disciplining seems to have been to instill a work ethic in the children. Janet emphasized that they learned the value of hard work:

> Learning, education, and the work ethic he gave us. People would say, "Look at the teacher's children, how they work!" We were examples for others. He worked the land and was not interested in "things of the world," possessions. He made us work to where we are. He taught us that you must work for yours.

At the same time as Spencer Gaston taught his children about the significance of a strong work ethic in relation to learning and education, he involved them in a range of economic pursuits, some of them entailing a great deal of hard, physical labor. The siblings emphasized that these activities showed that the family was part of the local community,[8] but they clearly also offered a welcome supplement to the headmaster's meager salary, which could hardly support such a large family. According to Mark, the children performed a variety of tasks:

> We, the children, had to help in the shop. We were taught how to cut the cod fish so that they [the customers] got some of the good and some of the not-so-good parts of the fish when they bought. But if somebody asked for a quarter pound of fish, I would just cut a piece of the best part, right in the middle of the fish. And I would give too much. This was because I knew the people. And for this reason I was banned from the shop. I never was so happy! I was glad not to be in the shop.

> [Did you have other tasks?]

> We had to cut wood with cutlass. And we had to climb four ridges and valleys to get to the garden where we had our provisions. In Sainte-Anne there was just the school garden. My father had permission to plant on an estate. And when we went there to work, I was the chief cook and prepared food for everybody. And then the provisions had to be carted down. We would make a cradle on the back to put them in. But I enjoyed those days. We had to do it, but we also looked forward to it, even though the journey was tough. All the boys went. The girls didn't go so much.

And we had to go get the goods for my father's little shop. The goods were brought in . . . wooden boats to [the bay] below Sainte-Anne, and then we had to carry the goods up a steep road to the village. And often the goods were wet (and partly ruined) with the salty seawater because of the rough seas—rice, sugar, and so. But we had to carry them.

The girls might not have participated so much in the father's agricultural venture on more distant estate land, but they participated in most of the other work. Indeed, Janet saw her mother as the driving force in the family's farming activities in the mountain areas, and she remembered the entire family going there to spend the day together. These trips seem to have been somewhat less "disciplined," with more room for playful activity:

My mother loved to work her garden. Her type of agriculture was in the mountains, where she grew root crops. I have fond memories of going to the mountains with her and other relatives to plant there. We would roam in the hills, cook meals there, because it was an all-day affair, cut trees, plant root crops, go to the rivers to catch crabs.

Several of the siblings, especially the girls, had pleasant memories of visiting the mother's family. Nelly, for example, recalled that her grandfather had "an accordion, a mouth organ, and we would dance and sing, and he told stories."

The shop integrated the family into the community because, as Mary related, it was located in the middle of the village and was a place where villagers met and socialized:

We lived centrally. Four roads met in front of our store. Men met there and talked. There was a church in Sainte-Anne, and all came there to go to mass. Many would come up Friday, if there was a feast, and some had tiny homes in Sainte-Anne, where they would stay until Sunday. There was the police station, the store, the school, and the church. We were in the middle, and we did well with the dry goods, groceries, and the liquor store. They came for their drinks. My father was well known, he was the head teacher, and all loved mom.

Robert described the shop as a place where the local villagers and people from the surrounding countryside met and socialized: "Sainte-Anne was the parish center, and people would come in from the other villages in the area. So it was a social gathering place. We sold alcohol, and they played dominos. As children we helped at the shop."

The family's close integration into the rural community was underlined by the parents' active involvement in community affairs. According to Robert, his father had helped organize one of the first village councils on Dominica in Sainte-Anne, and he was a leading member of the council for a number of years. The council in Sainte-Anne provided various services to villagers, Janet explained, including "bathrooms and toilets, with running water, before it was common in Dominica." According to the Dominican anthropologist Lennox Honychurch (1995), the instituting of village councils in Dominica in the early 1940s initially met with stiff opposition in many villages. In some, he notes, people threw stones, making it impossible to hold elections for the council (Honychurch 1995: 196). In Sainte-Anne, opposition to the council apparently continued for quite some time because the village council had visions for community development that were too grand for many of the villagers. When the council began construction of a swimming pool where villagers could learn to swim, the nearby Atlantic Ocean being too rough for swimming lessons, villagers refused to pay, and the project had to be stopped. It survived, however, in a Carnival song. Janet remembered:

> My father was a very strong and influential man. Everybody looked up to him. Daddy and a group were even trying to build a swimming pool, and they instituted taxes in the village for the village council. . . .
>
> [My] brother-in-law collected and he had a folk song about father and his taxes, which was made at Carnival. It is in patois and says, "Why did he make them dig that hole?" But it didn't say anything about the public baths and toilets.

If the father was the great organizer and leader of community affairs, the mother seems to have led a much more quiet life. Janet described her as a "very devote Christian Catholic woman" who "went to church meetings." Through the mother's active participation in the church, Janet said, the family became involved in church life together with the villagers. The mother also "reached out in the community" and helped villagers by sending soup to the sick, and Janet remembered that as children they "always had to go to somebody with soup." Unlike the father, the mother was a local person, and her parents and other relatives lived in the area. They belonged to the group of landed peasant proprietors in the parish and were active in the church. Apparently, this respectable family background played an important role when Spencer married his wife, as Janet explained: "When daddy wanted to marry, he went to the priest and said that he wanted to marry a good wife and asked whether he could recommend one. So grandfather and grandmother were close to the priest, and he recommended my mother, their daughter."

While the mother led a much less public life than the father, she was quite active in various economic activities.[9] Apart from cultivating crops on her family's land in the mountains, she was a seamstress, and she made straw hats and artificial flowers for Christmas that were sold in the store. To the children, the mother was the mild-mannered, religious, industrious person who represented the moral values of the family. Benjamin said:

> Mother was like a saint. She worked very hard, and she never saw her grandkids. That was hard. She had a hard life, but she bore it with faith. She sewed and made clothes. She must have died from many debts that the villagers owed her because of her sewing for them. She taught many girls to sew and was a godmother to many.

Because of their active involvement in the community, the siblings regarded themselves as part of the local village. This does not mean, however, that they were just like the other villagers. Their engagement in village affairs gave them special status in the community. Robert explained:

> Few were in secondary school; many never went to primary school. They couldn't read or write. The teacher might be the only person, he had to read and write letters or legal document for people. . . . So this left the teacher as the key person in the community to provide services. That accounts for my father's stature in the community.

Robert emphasized, however, that as children they did not in any way feel that they were superior:

> I don't recall any division. There was no elitism. We were very much part of the village: did fishing and mixed with the villagers. And our shop was the meeting place for people. . . .

Father was involved in growing vanilla and other crops. He had helpers working the ground, but we worked with them. We had to fetch firewood. There was no separation because of the status we enjoyed. This is not something that is just vaguely familiar to me.

And he later added, "I don't remember status playing a role in Sainte-Anne at all. We just blended in." Janet similarly stated: "We were just one of the village people. Daddy brought us up to think that because you have privileges, you must serve. Being the headmaster's daughter did not mean that you were on a different level or that you had services available. Because you were educated, you must do something." If they had any advantage, they emphasized, it was their education, and this did not give them any privileges, only an obligation to help and serve. The parents made it a point to teach them to be polite to everybody in the village—to the extent that, to Benjamin, it seemed like almost ostentatious politeness: "We were extremely polite to people, almost condescending—tip your hat."

While the siblings did not feel superior when they grew up in the village, the family kept a certain distance from some of the villagers. Several of the siblings observed that they were admonished not to keep "bad company" who would "track you down the gutter." "Bad company" included, according to Benjamin, those children who would "play truant, curse, not say 'good morning' or 'good afternoon.'" Richard suggested that they might have been "people hanging around, who didn't have much education or purpose in life. They would be drinking, saying useless talk, getting into trouble, getting women pregnant. I never questioned it."

The notion of "bad company" seems to have been quite a bit wider, however, because Janet remembered being discouraged from "mixing too much with the village children" or "going to people's houses": "He was very protective of us and didn't like us to follow their way of life. He didn't want us exposed to bad influence. He wanted us to have certain values and not just to pick up any attitude." The speaking of French patois, Mark recalled, was regarded as an important sign of "bad influence": "I had friends, and I liked to mix with the population in Sainte-Anne. They all spoke the patois. But we could not speak it in the presence of my father, because he associated it with bad company."

The family's understanding of its status in the local community was a complex one. On the one hand, the siblings were quite aware that they had higher status in the village by virtue of their father's position as a headmaster and the family's ownership of a store. Furthermore, they realized that the family distinguished itself by its usage of English, a language that was not generally spoken in the village. On the other hand, the siblings insisted that they were part of the village and did not feel superior to their fellow villagers or set apart in any way. The contradiction between being part of the village while maintaining a different social identity seems to have been resolved by moral arguments. Thus, while members of the family were friendly and polite toward everybody and helped those in need, they did not mix socially with villagers who were defined as having a "bad influence"—at least, not on a personal basis. By explaining the refusal to have social intercourse with certain people by their failure to live up to proper social standards, what might have been a class issue was therefore turned into a question of the morals and respectability of the individuals involved. Such considerations undoubtedly would have been of utmost importance to a family whose social status was closely tied to the father's position as headmaster in the village. This position, however, was only one aspect of the family's status in the community. The complexity of social and economic relations that made the family part of the village was thus closely connected to a local village hierarchy where the family was placed right at the top.

A FAMILY OF ''SUBSTANCE''

In an analysis of Wesley, a primarily Methodist village in Dominica, Michel-Rolph Trouillot (1988) distinguishes between several different socioeconomic groups in the local community. The group with the highest status is composed of what he calls "the outsiders," those born outside the local community and who often live outside the community proper. They are owners of estates and various religious and public officials such as ministers and policemen brought in from the outside. This group of people, who tend to be lighter skinned than most local people, does not intermarry or socialize with native villagers but provides some domestic and agricultural employ-ment to locals (Trouillot 1988: 233). According to Trouillot, villagers do not consider "the outsiders" part of the "immediate social hierarchy" of the local community (Trouillot 1988: 234–35). When he asked villagers to rank people who belonged in the local community of Wesley, they ranked a few individuals considered "big farmers" first. These were people of peasant background who had succeeded at acquiring enough land to employ others to do most of the heavy agricultural work, usually as poorly paid task work. Members of their family, however, were actively engaged in most agricultural tasks. This group of highest local status was followed by "the entrepreneurs," a similarly small group of people whose families were engaged in various forms of business, such as transportation and shopkeeping, as well as various agricultural activities. Entrepreneurs were important economic mediators between the villagers and the outside world and were admired for their economic success, which was thought to be the result of their own hard work, not the exploitation of others, as was the case with "the outsiders." And finally, at the bottom of the social hierarchy, villagers placed "the peasants," the 80 percent of the local population who made a living on cultivating small plots of land and working for others (Trouillot 1988: 234–41).

A similar system of ranking based on education, landownership, and entrepreneurship has been documented in other studies carried out in Dominican villages, and it therefore seems to have general applicability throughout the island, although the particulars vary.[10] I suggest that the Gaston family can be viewed as an especially powerful blend of "the outsider" and the "entrepreneurial" categories. As a headmaster who had been appointed to the village school by the colonial authorities, Spencer Gaston belonged to the high-status group of "outsiders" who had close contacts with the colonial society, and he came from another part of the island. However, by marrying a local woman, purchasing his own home in the local community, and running a shop and engaging in a number of local agricultural activities, he joined the local "entrepreneurial" group that also had high prestige in the community. Spencer Gaston seems to have used to great advantage this combined identity that reinforced his position as an intermediary between the local community and the wider society. At an intellectual level, he brought "outside knowledge" to the local community—knowledge about the wider world and new knowledge of relevance to local ways of life. In the school garden he introduced crops that were unknown to the villagers, such as a type of manioc now locally called "*toloma*," and he taught the children new agricultural methods, such as composting. He also, as noted, acquired a radio where villagers could listen to the BBC—for a small fee, according to one of the elderly villagers who remembered going to the Gaston house to listen to the radio. This was therefore an instance where intellectual concerns merged with economic interests. At an economic level, Spencer Gaston imported goods by boat to sell them at his store, and he cultivated and purchased locally grown vanilla beans, dried and cured the beans in the attic of the school building, and sold them for export out of Dominica. This economic venture would have been quite profitable during the 1940s, when vanilla production was a major economic activity in Dominica.[11]

Jonathan Wylie, who did ethnographic fieldwork in a Dominican village during the late 1970s, has argued for the existence of a single group of high-status people, "men of substance," who combine the qualities associated with the categories of "big farmer" and "entrepreneur" described by Trouillot. Apart from mediating between an external and internal socioeconomic system, these men, according to Wylie, also attempt to combine and reconcile in their own persons the values of reputation and respectability (Wylie 1982: 443, 465; 1993: 369–73). Wylie is here referring to the dual value system of reputation and respectability that Peter Wilson has described for Caribbean societies. According to Wilson, reputation is associated with local ways and played out in egalitarian relations within the local community—for example, among people who socialize in the rum shop or among groups that help each other with tasks pertaining to fishing or farming. Respectability, however, is closely linked with the formal, more hierarchical European-based institutional framework of the church, the school, and the colonial system (Wilson 1969, 1973, 1992 [1974]). In several later studies, it has been argued that the notions of reputation and respectability should be seen not as two different value systems but, rather, as closely integrated aspects of a single cultural system that takes different forms and attains particular meaning in specific historical and social contexts (Miller 1994; Olwig 1993b; Scott 2002). Furthermore, as Roger Abrahams (1983) has shown, the ability to keep the two dimensions of the value system in check—to balance the notions of reputation against those of respectability—is an important aspect of social life in Caribbean local communities. A successful man of substance who desires to serve as a successful mediator between the villagers and the wider colonial society therefore needs to be able to combine aspects of reputation as well as respectability in his person. This means that he must be able to both socialize with local people in the rum shop, with the drinking and joking that this involves, and display his mastery of proper social conventions in the higher levels of society. The attempt to combine elements of reputation and respectability appears to have posed a great challenge to Spencer Gaston.

When Spencer Gaston moved to Sainte-Anne, he made a great effort to become a respectable member of the local village. He married a local woman, purchased land in the middle of the village, and settled there in his own house. He was, as described by Janet, careful in his choice of a wife, because he married a woman from a local family who was recommended by the Catholic priest. He might have had other motives for doing this as quickly as possible, however, because when he arrived in Sainte-Anne, he had had a child by an extramarital relationship with his domestic helper while he was a schoolteacher in another village. He took the daughter resulting from this relationship into the home and reared her together with the other children as part of the family.

During the first years in Sainte-Anne, Spencer Gaston seems to have led a "respectable" life as a schoolteacher, educating the pupils, participating in community affairs, engaging in a number of economic pursuits, and providing for the intellectual and material needs of his family. He also went to church and joined the Holy Name Society, a Catholic organization that had local chapters and drew its membership from the upper levels of local communities. At about the time the eldest children had moved to Roseau to go to secondary school, however, Spencer Gaston began to spend an increasing amount of time in the rum shop, drinking and socializing with the customers. He became a heavy drinker and smoker, and eventually he stopped going to church. As Spencer Gaston became an alcoholic, he underwent a drastic change. Whereas he had been the embodiment of respectability—so much so that Mark remembered the villagers joking about it—he subsequently began to neglect his outward appearance: "My father used to go to school with white, starched jacket and tie and white clean pants. He was nicknamed 'stone coat'; it was like a straightjacket. People would say, 'Stone coat must be mad!' And when he was drinking, he would forget the tie and the jacket."

The mother seems to have reacted to the father's drinking by becoming even more religious. She attended all Masses in the Catholic church, and when her husband came home, drunk, she would say to the children, "Let us drown his noise in prayers." When the mother died suddenly after a heart attack, the father's drinking escalated, and he became an example of the kind of bad company that he did not want his children to mix with. Richard, one of the youngest siblings and, therefore, one of the last to leave the home, noted, "My father was a teacher. One of the most painful things for me was having to pick up my father from the gutter. When my mother died, he deteriorated." For the youngest siblings, who did not recall their father before he became an alcoholic, their memories of growing up in Sainte-Anne were full of such incidents—to the extent that they tended to overshadow the positive memories that they might have had of their childhood.

When I asked the siblings whether they had any idea why their father began to drink, they offered various explanations. Some thought that the father might have felt stuck in the village where there was little intellectual company; others thought that he, perhaps, had a medical affliction, such as a brain tumor, that changed his personality; yet others pointed out that heavy drinking was quite common and generally socially accepted in the village— indeed, the father continued to be respected as a good schoolteacher even after he became an alcoholic. While the educated siblings attempted to ac- count for the father's behavior within a framework of rational, intellectual explanations, the villagers had a different theory as to what had happened to the father. According to Mark, many of them believed that "somebody put something in his drink to mess him up." According to Mary, her mother shared the villagers' beliefs because, to her, nothing but "*obeah*," or witch- craft, could explain how her husband could become an alcoholic:

> Witches were not believed to have the power to kill, but mom felt that what was happening to dad could have been caused by a *sukuyā* kind of witch]. When she met him, he was a strong advocate of no drinking and so on.

> [How would this *obeah* work?]

> Somebody in the village who was envious would put something in a drink. She could not understand how somebody could change so much, so she believed it. He was a good person, and then he became an uncontrollable drinker. So she believed it was something that people did to him.

Belief in witchcraft has been widespread in the Caribbean and is closely related to notions of socioeconomic relations and local status hierarchies. The explanations of misfortune that witchcraft provides point to the difficult position that the man of substance occupied in the local status hierarchy. A man of substance, in Wylie's analysis, is a person who has become wealthy within the local economic system of farming, fishing, and shopkeeping; one who is married, attends church, and belongs to the Holy Name Society. In the village where Wylie did his fieldwork, many villagers believed that the two wealthiest men were *lugawu*, "men who have contracted with the Devil in order to win riches at others' expense" (Wylie 1993: 372–73). Apparently, this is accepted as long as the wealthy men are generous—they share their wealth, for example, by giving free drinks in the rum shop and sharing fish. By sharing their wealth, these men of substance therefore were seen to be, in essence, "obeah-workers 'on God's side.' " Furthermore, because of their occult powers, they were thought to be able to avert counter-*obeah* performed by weaker people, *sukuyā*, who tended to be socially and economically marginal women, often widows who are believed to bring "sundry misfortunes on people without gaining anything for themselves" (Wylie 1993: 376).[12] If a sukuyā succeeds in hurting a man of substance, this must therefore be a sign of weakness in his position.

As somebody who had grown up in a Dominican village, Spencer Gaston must have known how social and economic relations are played out in a local community and what would have been expected of him as a man of substance in the village. The family clearly was well aware of the need to be generous, because several siblings, such as Spencer's oldest daughter, Anna, emphasized their parents' generosity:

> My father helped in the village. He had a boat, and he would let the villagers use it to fish and get a share of the catch. He could not go out to fish himself. He did this to encourage the villagers to work. He also had animals—sheep, goats, cattle—and he would give them out to people to let them rear them from young, and then he would get his share of the animals, perhaps half. He lived like that, sharing. That is how I knew him.

The family, as Janet noted, also gave soup to the sick, and as Benjamin mentioned, their mother was not strict about collecting the debts that people owed her when she sewed for them. Nelly emphasized the importance of sharing for a family that had a high position in the local community: "People looked up to our family. We didn't feel above them, though we had a little more. We shared, and this made us feel like the others."

While the family was generous, it did earn a living from shopkeeping, and it therefore had to make money from the sale of goods. Though the father might have let the men keep some of the proceeds from fishing and animal rearing, he also had a keen sense for business, where others might not think so far ahead. Alan recalled that his father purchased flying fish when in season, cleaned and smoked them, and sold them at a profit later when there were no fish. Similarly, the siblings also related that the father purchased vanilla beans from local farmers and sold the cured vanilla, probably at a handsome profit. The villagers may not have liked this entrepreneurial approach to local resources, and some lodged an official complaint about his appropriation of the school's unused attic for the treatment of the vanilla. As Christopher noted, "My father was very entrepreneurial, and that, combined with the fact that he was an outsider to the village, might have made him unpopular." His insistence that the children speak English in the home, and his refusal to let them associate with children who spoke patois, may have made him even more unpopular in the village. There is no doubt that he was impatient with the villagers' skepticism toward local development—and showed it. It was a struggle to establish the village council, and some of his grand plans for the village, such as the construction of the swimming pool, had to be given up and were ridiculed in a calypso.

The legacy of Spencer Gaston as the head teacher who taught the villagers a great deal, who had high expectations of them, and who had no time for their obstreperous behavior seems to have survived in Sainte-Anne. When I visited the village in December 1999, I met a young man born in the village who had just returned after finishing his education as a Catholic priest. He recalled that when he attended the local village school as a child, they still called it Teacher Gaston's school. Curious to learn more about this person he had never known himself, he took me to some of the elderly people in the village so that we might ask them about the former head teacher in the village. The owner of one of the rum shops remembered Spencer Gaston well. As the young priest translated from the French patois, he explained that Spencer Gaston was trying to help the village, but that they did not understand what his goals were. People thought that he was attempting too much. He told people how to live in the village: to send their children to school, work in the school garden, and be ambitious.

Teacher Gaston said: "When I die, Sainte-Anne will go down like the tail of the ass."

[Was he right?]

Yes, he was. Don't you see the people up there? [He pointed to the corner, where the Gaston house used to be and where a group of young fellows were hanging out]. Young people are into drugs. Drugs have become the problem. With any sign of the destruction of new life, of non-industry, or of non-progress, people go back to Gaston's saying and say that he was right.

Spencer Gaston's turn to alcoholism can probably be related to many different aspects of his life. However, from a more general point of view it can be seen as a response to, and reflection of, the many contradictory expectations and demands that he experienced in his complex position in the local community. None of his children sought to carry on his work in the village. They all left Sainte-Anne at a fairly young age, thus avoiding the perhaps impossible task of having to combine the "respectable" mode of life, associated with education, religion, and individual achievement, with the "reputation"-orientation way of life, associated with an—in principle—egalitarian rural community.

CONCLUSION

In their life stories, the siblings described themselves as having grown up within a small, isolated Dominican village as members of the local community. Yet at the same time, they prided themselves on being part of the educational mission that essentially regarded village ways as inferior and therefore sought to educate the villagers and bring them within the realm of the civilized world. The siblings' narratives of the kind of life they had lived in the village showed that the family's attempt to be both part of and apart from (if not above) the local community was fraught with conflicts and tension. In the end, the father seems to have succumbed to the pressure.

Before the father's problems with alcohol, however, the elder siblings had already begun to move away from the village. The safe distance of the Dominican capital, Roseau, or various migration destinations abroad made it much easier to combine the community-oriented ethos of the Dominican

village with individual achievement and upward social and economic mobility. Thus, from the vantage point of the professional office or the well-kept
suburban home, the siblings could turn the family village identity into a
relatively abstract ideal, involving the simple life in the rural surroundings,
discipline, personal ambition, and dedication to serve. This ideal served the
Gaston siblings well. As the next chapter will describe, it became the defining
mark of the Gaston family and gave it a special name and position of respect
in the national and transnational Dominican community that emerged after
the country's independence.

In their life stories, the Gaston siblings identified closely with Sainte-Anne and described in glowing terms the natural surroundings where they spent their early life. Yet they considered the village not a place to stay as members of the rural community but as a place of origin. It was thus both a specific locality that gave them a village-based identity in the independent nation-state and a formative social space where their parents had given them the personal qualities that allowed them to become the sort of people that they were. Narratives of Sainte-Anne therefore described the stuff out of which the Gaston family was made—it provided a good point of departure for their movements and accomplishments in life as well as a site of identification that allowed them to return to Dominica.

The geopolitical landscape that the Gaston siblings had to navigate, as they left Dominica, was shaped by Dominica's particular colonial history. As a formerly French island with a strong Catholic church, there were strong ties with Catholic institutions of higher learning abroad, among them a university for men in New York State. As a British possession, the island was also well connected with universities in Britain and the British West Indies. Furthermore, labor migration to Britain was possible until 1962, and from the early 1960s labor migration to Canada began to open up. Family members availed themselves of all these opportunities, and they therefore left under quite different social and economic circumstances.

The family members' encounters with the migratory regime were molded by both the circumstances under which they were able to emigrate and the social and economic conditions in the migration destinations, including the ways in which they were received as non-white immigrants. In Britain, where the Gaston family members arrived during the 1950s, race relations had hardened in response to the large influx of Caribbean immigrants into the country. In the United States, the racial barriers were being challenged by the Civil Rights Movement when family members came during the 1960s, and antidiscrimination legislation was being put in place. In Canada, an important migration destination for family members beginning with the early 1960s, the first family members to arrive were presented with a sea of white people who regarded black immigrants mostly as a curiosity. The family members dealt with these varying racial situations by drawing on the duality of their own family background. They were, on the one hand, well educated and ambitious and therefore willing to work hard for self-improvement, regardless of the racial problems that they might encounter. On the other hand, they were also morally committed to "serve," and several of them became actively engaged in helping those in need, primarily poor black people. While they identified with "black" people, they therefore did not necessarily live in a black community. Rather, they saw themselves as leaders within the black community. These two aspects of their family identity came together in their notion of livelihood.

The pursuit of a "proper" livelihood (Olwig and Sørensen 2002) was a central aspect of the Gaston family. This livelihood was one where the learning and mastering of a profession, as well as devotion to a morally upright life, were the key underpinnings. Economic gain and social status were not, in and of themselves, important aims. As they described their journeys out of Sainte-Anne and the various destinations that these journeys entailed, it was apparent that individuals sought to construct their lives in terms of the livelihood that the family had made an essential part of its identity and that had made the family well known among Dominicans. This was clearly easier for some than for others, and the narratives reflect a tension between a strong pride in being part of a well-known family and the difficulty some members of the family experienced living up to the high expectations that this family's fame entailed.

THE ESTABLISHMENT OF A FAMILY TRADITION

Measured on a map, the distance from Sainte-Anne to Roseau is not very far. Dominica is twenty-nine miles long and sixteen miles wide, so even the remotest villages are not many miles from the capital. The mountainous terrain of the island, however, makes travel on the island difficult, and when Christopher and his siblings moved to Roseau, travel to the capital was a major journey that the siblings had rarely undertaken.[1] Benjamin, for example, told that when he, at twelve, went to Roseau to attend secondary school, he had only been in the capital once before, when he was five years old. Janet remembered dreading the journey:

> We had to walk the nine miles to [the closest port], where we had to take a boat to Roseau. I got sick traveling by boat, which was stopping at different places. Just the diesel smell! Sometimes we had to carry our suitcase on our head, walking the nine miles. Sometimes we could take a truck part of the way, and I would get sick on the winding roads.[2]

It was quite apparent to the Gaston siblings that the townspeople in Roseau regarded them as backward country people. Janet recalled: "There [in Sainte-Anne] we had been the headmaster's children. In town, we were country people. They mocked my accent, because it was different. We were 'country boukeys come to town.'" The "mocking" that the children experienced in Roseau because of their rural background should be seen in the light of the historical divide between the French creole-speaking villagers of peasant farmers and the English colonial town of civil servants and merchants. When the Gaston children began to enter secondary school, during the 1940s, they were spearheading an influx of rural people into the capital, and into its British colonial society. This generated some animosity and name calling among townspeople.[3] The Gaston children took this in stride, however, because they knew that their father had prepared them well. Mary noted, "In Roseau it was different. I felt less than middle class. People dressed better; I couldn't afford it. But our education was superior; we were well educated."

The Gaston children might have come from humble village backgrounds, but when it came to education, they had no reason to humble themselves.

Indeed, if they had not excelled educationally, they would not have been able to attend secondary school, as Christopher explained:

> I was able to go there because I received a scholarship. There were three scholarships for the island: one for the town, one for the country, and one which was open. I got the country scholarship. Only people who could afford to pay went there. Very few country people went there. It was mostly people from the town. The fathers were merchants, doctors, lawyers, property owners, businesspeople.

Several of the siblings did so well on the entrance exam that they were awarded scholarships for secondary school. While the scholarship paid for tuition and, at least in some cases, for the books needed to attend the private secondary schools, it did not cover living expenses in Roseau.[4] Spencer Gaston solved this problem by renting a house in Roseau and establishing another family home. It was headed by his youngest sister, Ina. For the younger siblings, like Robert, going to Roseau therefore essentially meant rejoining the older siblings who had relocated:

> It was a tradition in the family to go there. My older brothers and sisters went there. And going to Roseau was like being with the family again. My mother died when I was in the second form, in 1954. We were all living together there except for the youngest brothers and sisters, and old friends visited. We didn't have the freedom we would have liked, because our aunt controlled our activity and made sure that we stayed on the straight and narrow.

The agricultural activities maintained by the family in Sainte-Anne essentially sustained the siblings in Roseau. Benjamin recalled: "We took boxes of ground provisions with us, because in town everything had to be bought, and mother also sent [things] for us by the boat that went about once a week. Of course, we had to buy fish and meat regularly, but we only bought meat on Saturday so that we had it for our Sunday lunch." Richard, the youngest son, remembered well the trips to Portsmouth carrying ground provisions for the elder siblings in Roseau: "I would be up at 1 A.M. to go there with the maid. We had a load on the head and walked with a lantern through the mountains and the hills to get to the boat and back before school. I did this quite often." The education of the siblings therefore was a family project. When Ina decided to leave for England in 1958, Janet, who at that time had completed secondary school, became head of the household in Roseau, backed up by Christopher, who was then married and living in his own home. According to Alan, this did not mean any relaxing of the discipline in the home: "The older ones took care of the younger ones. I got a spanking because I played cricket instead of polishing the floor, which was so polished that you could see yourself in it. Janet called Christopher, and he came and spanked me."

The siblings were not allowed to lose sight of the primary purpose of their stay in the town: going to school and obtaining a secondary education. Robert commented, "Father was stern when it came to school performance. He did not accept bad reports, so we were motivated to do well." When Mark showed up with a bad report card, he received a lesson from his father that he would never forget:

> When I first came to Roseau, I played too much—football, cricket—so I failed my first term in high school. When my father got the report card, he just pointed to the mountain where we had gone to cultivate the provisions and said, "For the rest of your life, you will climb that mountain!" The next term, I got a second grade.

The father's message was crystal clear: Secondary school was not for having a good time with friends but a way to escape the toil associated with peasant life.

Most of the siblings did well in school and completed their secondary education successfully. The most successful ones, by and large, said rather little about their schooling. Mary noted in passing that she had "studied a lot" and "liked the school." Janet made a brief reference to taking the A-levels, the British university entry-level exams. Christopher stated that he enjoyed Latin and was sorry there were no teachers to prepare him for the higher Cambridge certificate when he attended the grammar school. From a modern Western perspective, it may not seem to be particularly remarkable to attend secondary school and pass the final exams. In Dominica of the 1940s and '50s, however, extremely few children from the rural communities attended secondary school, and even fewer passed the exams. A study of secondary education in Dominica carried out in the early 1960s showed that a mere 10 percent went on to secondary school, and only "an extremely small percentage" of those passed the exams (Fleming 1964: 3). Christopher attributed the Gaston children's success to their father's good education and the intellectual environment in which they had grown up: "We were fortunate, we were coached by a head teacher, and we had access to books and everything there."

As the siblings relocated in the family home in Roseau to attend secondary school, the relations among the children centered even more on education, because admission to a secondary school was necessary to become part of the family home in Roseau. This meant that attending secondary school was an important aspect of belonging to the group of siblings. When the father did not want to send Nelly to secondary school because she did not do well enough on the exams to receive a scholarship, she felt both "put down" and excluded from the sibling group:

> After I had finished elementary school, I had to write an exam to go to high school. If you didn't do well, you had to pay for high school. Father was then an alcoholic, and . . . he put me down. I felt inferior. My sister after me was very bright, Mary. I felt that it was true what he said. He didn't want to pay for me at high school. . . . At that point, my godfather, Mr. Hutton, paid for me. He was a manager of Melvin Hall, a company there. Dad paid for the others, not me, so I had an inferiority complex. . . .
>
> [It was important to go to Roseau because] friends were going there, and my other siblings went. It got to the point when I thought that I wouldn't be able to go, when my godfather stepped in.

Anna, the eldest sister, never had the opportunity to attend secondary school, nor was she part of the family life associated with education in Roseau. There may be several reasons for this. One may be that she, as the eldest daughter, was thought to be needed in the family home, another that the tradition of going to secondary school, and the family home in Roseau, had not yet been established when she finished primary school. As she described her childhood and youth in Dominica, however, Anna made no mention of lost educational opportunities in Roseau or missing out on living with her siblings. Rather, she chose to emphasize that she was an integral part of the family in Sainte-Anne and developed a much closer tie to her father and stepmother than did her younger siblings:

> I helped in the store, and I taught in the school and in the home. I loved my
> stepmother. I didn't feel left out. My stepmother sewed. She was a seamstress, and
> she taught me to crochet. The little things I can do is through her. She was a very
> hardworking lady. The other kids went to school in town, but I lived in the home,
> and therefore I knew her better. Daddy wanted me to stay and teach in his school. I
> was paid by the government. I taught for ten to fifteen years before I left.

She made clear, however, that staying in her father's home and teaching at his
school was not her choice: "I wanted to be a nurse, but my father didn't like
it. At that time, people had bad sores, and I think that he didn't want me to
work with that. But that is what I wanted to do. I didn't do it because I didn't
want to displease him."

Even though she never received a higher education like most of her
younger siblings, Anna underlined that she had been a good student and had
received valuable teacher's training:

> They used to have a teacher's college [in a local town]—not like now, where they
> go to the university and take higher education there. Before, we never did that. I
> took seventh standard, and you had to do well on that to be allowed to teach. And
> after the seventh standard, you took teacher's training.

Nelly's and Anna's accounts of their early lives in Dominica thus show how
educational pursuits became an important social context within which family
relations developed.

MOVING UP IN SOCIETY

The Gaston family valued education in and of itself, but they also saw it as a
means of social and economic mobility. When the children finished secondary education, they therefore were not expected to return to Sainte-Anne.
When I asked Christopher why he did not return to his home village when
he had finished secondary school, he explained:

> Those with education had no opportunity there except in farming. . . .
>
> [You never considered farming?]

No, because of the educational system, which gives no opportunity of earning a living in farming. Education was based in the classics and the sciences. There was no living in farming. Only if you had lots of land, like the Shillingfords, who had an estate and could employ people. If you had to do it on your own, you could not make it. You wouldn't see a future for yourself. There was no export in farming, and most people did their own farming, so you could not sell anything in Sainte-Anne. It was no livelihood.

Anthropological studies show that while a livelihood may ultimately be about the procuring of a material basis of living, the choice of a particular livelihood is never solely determined by the natural resources available. As stated by Sandra Wallman (1979: 1), the "working relationship between man and nature is never unembroidered"; it is shaped by cultural notions. If Christopher did not see a livelihood for himself in Sainte-Anne, this was not just because of the limited material basis of life in a rural community. It was also because, given the symbolic order of things in the social world he entered when he began his secondary education in Roseau, peasant farming would not have been considered a proper livelihood. A secondary education, with its emphasis on the classics and sciences, gave students a certain level of intellectual refinement and "culture" associated with the upper classes of colonial society. A graduate of a secondary school therefore could aspire to a career in civil service or other kinds of white-collar employment in the capital of Roseau and, hence, to a position in the upper layers of colonial society. This step would have been an impressive one for a person of village background, because, according to Lennox Honychurch, until the 1960s "island affairs from shop clerks, bank cashiers, and office staff to key posts in the civil service" were entirely dominated by people from Roseau (Honychurch 1995: 236). By sending his eldest son to Roseau for secondary education, Spencer was therefore introducing him to a new set of livelihood opportunities available to educated persons in the colonial capital.

Spencer's main goal was to secure for his children jobs in teaching, banking, or the colonial administration. When Christopher passed the Cambridge exam, the headmaster of the grammar school helped him get a job as a trainee chemical engineer at a newly started, Greek-owned fruit-processing plant. His father did not like this:

I started work outside the government, but he was not happy about that. . . . He got me into government service. . . . My father spoke to the chief secretary for the government who was a local person (over him there was an administrator who was English) and asked him for a job for me.

[Why did your father prefer for you to work for the government?]

He didn't like me in a small firm. The government gave status in the community, and it was a secure job.

The father's preoccupation with social standing became even more apparent when he retired from his teaching post in Sainte-Anne and joined the remaining children in Roseau. He was then blind and in poor health. Nevertheless, when he realized that his daughters were seeing young men whom he judged to be below the family's social status, he rejected them. Marcus, who later married Mary, recalled: "I went on weekends to read the newspaper for the blind father. When he found out that I did not just come to read the newspaper, he didn't want me to come any longer. I was not suitable, because I was from a poor family." According to Mary, her father and an aunt in her mother's family had other plans for her: "[They wanted me] to marry a bank guy who worked at Barclay's. This was a product of colonial days. It was a white guy with influence and money."

The siblings emphasized that color had little significance in the rural community of Sainte-Anne and that they were not concerned about it. Along with several other French creole villages, Sainte-Anne was known to be one of the "more 'light-skinned' " rural communities in Dominica (Honychurch 1982: 8). Christopher did mention, however, that color was one of the factors taken into consideration when determining a family's status in the local community. Color was clearly of significance to Spencer Gaston, because he was very cognizant of color differences among his children. Richard explained that his father took notice of his darker complexion, which he did not think belonged in the light-skinned Gaston family. Similarly, Alan recalled that his father refused to vote for a local black candidate for political office, preferring instead a white English person.[5] In the colonial society of Roseau, color was an important element in the social hierarchy, and not all educated people had equal access to government jobs. The highest positions in the occupational hierarchy were only filled with whites or very light-

skinned people. As Alan stated, "With light skin, you got more opportunities. I never saw any blacks in those positions." The Gaston children's
light complexion therefore was an advantage in the wider society. Most of
them noted this with apparent embarrassment, however, emphasizing that
color to them had no intrinsic significance.

While most of the siblings lived and worked in Roseau for a while after
completing secondary school, Christopher was the only one who decided to
make his career in the colonial society of Dominica. This was partly because
he did not have the qualifying exam to attend a British university and partly
because he saw in government work a great opportunity to learn about
public administration. He describes his career as one characterized by a great
deal of hard work where he drew on his intellectual resources:

> I was in the best possible position, and I made the most use of it. I was lucky. I had
> access to everything. . . . I had a key position. Others also had good positions, but
> they didn't take the same advantage of it. They went home as soon as their
> workday was over. I just loved working and did extra work. So I came close to the
> top positions in colonial government as a young person and was given good
> challenges and more responsibility than I should have had at that age. I also read
> everything, and I had an excellent memory, so many people would come to me
> and ask me about something in the colonial government that they didn't know
> about.

As part of his career, he was offered further training in colonial administration
in Great Britain, and he went for extended courses on two occasions. When
he was in his late thirties, he had reached the top of the colonial system in
Dominica and decided that he had to move out in order to move further up.
Like his other siblings, he therefore also ended up spending a good part of his
life outside Dominica.

Christopher's siblings did not wait so long to leave. Much to the father's
disappointment, they did not see attractive career possibilities in government
jobs. Mark recalled: "I had my first job as a clerk in customs. I was the excise
officer in tobacco. There were a lot of rules and regulations, and that was not
my line. So I resigned at twenty-one. . . . My father didn't understand. It was
the best job to him." One after the other, the siblings left Dominica. In the
early 1950s, Benjamin went to Jamaica to pursue medical studies. A couple of

years later, Mark moved to England to study optometry. He was followed by Anna and their aunt Ina, who went to England together in search of work. Richard then left for the United States to enter a Catholic order that was in charge of the Catholic secondary boys' school in Roseau. Janet and later Mary traveled to Jamaica to study at the University of the West Indies, and at about the same time Nelly went to Canada on a domestic scheme, a program admitting Caribbean women into Canada to work as domestic servants. Finally, Alan and Robert left for the United States to attend a college run by the Catholic order in Dominica, and Vera went to an institution in Trinidad for the mentally handicapped. The fact that so many of the siblings, originating in the home of a village head teacher of limited means, succeeded in pursuing higher education and professional careers in Dominica and abroad became an important distinguishing mark of the family.

EXTENDING THE FAMILY TRADITION

An event of great significance in the establishment of the family tradition of higher education and professional achievement was the award of the prestigious island scholarship to Benjamin: "I was first on the exam, and this meant that I got the only scholarship, which was given out every two years. It was an important event, because my father could not have sent me to medical school."[6] Benjamin realized the great possibilities inherent in the scholarship, and he chose his area of study with care: "I won the island scholarship, and this allowed me to pursue any career. But those who won the scholarship usually studied law or medicine, because this was the most prestigious thing. Medicine was most often chosen; there were few lawyers." He added, however, that obtaining a medical degree was not primarily a way of winning social status. He had become attracted to the medical profession as a child in Sainte-Anne, where he experienced the great need for doctors:

> As a boy, the doctor [from the nearest town] used to hold clinic in Sainte-Anne, and he would take his meals with my family. . . . As boys we would go to the clinic to collect the little saws that were used to break the pills. The nurse used to throw the saws out of the window, and we would collect them there. The smell of the medicines was very attractive to me. I saw a lot of suffering at home. People would die for simple things. Like a person would bleed to death for a little cut. And I liked science.

By pointing out that the medical profession allowed him to contribute to Dominican society, he downplayed the status aspect of education and emphasized the new possibility of serving others that this education offered. In this way he described his educational choice in terms of a central Gaston family value, and in his recounting of his life story, he substantiated this further. As soon as he had finished his medical studies in Jamaica, he returned to Dominica to practice medicine. He only left Dominica again to acquire his specialization and returned as soon as he had passed his exam, even though this meant a great deal of work and limited opportunity to use his specialization:

> [When] I got through and had my qualification for my specialty, I was told that I must come home right away. The only surgeon at the time had to leave the island, and I had to relieve him. I found myself doing my specialization and everything else. . . . The work at the hospital was heavy, and it was difficult to get sleep.

Many who obtain an island scholarship only return temporarily to fulfill the work requirements stipulated in the government scholarship.[7] Benjamin, however, emphasized that he had always intended to return because he wished to serve the country that had helped him obtain his education: "I felt that my medical training was obtained as a result of the contribution of the Dominican taxes and that I must give service for that privilege." Furthermore, he preferred the life close to nature that he could live in Dominica: "I like the climate and to be in the garden every day. I like to be in the open every day, not just weather permitting. In the States, it is not a friendly climate. I could cope, but I would not like it. And I like the fishing here." Benjamin had a long career in Dominica, contributing to the island's public-health system and developing a much needed medical specialization that had hitherto not been available on the island.

Benjamin's life story is in many ways an ideal migration story, because he accomplished exactly what he had set out to do during his sojourn abroad, and then he returned to assume a highly respected position as medical doctor on Dominica.[8] Furthermore, he did not have a privileged background but came from modest origins in an isolated village. As a doctor, he made a major contribution to the development of health services in the budding nation-state of Dominica. Finally, he married and settled in Roseau with his wife and children in a good middle-class neighborhood. Benjamin's life trajectory is by no means a typical one. Very few obtain an island scholarship; indeed, for most people it can only be a remote dream. Furthermore, it is rare that everything goes according to plan. Migration stories often describe at considerable length why things developed differently than envisioned. This does not mean that those who do not return have had less successful lives. Some never intended to return; others found more attractive opportunities abroad. Nevertheless, Benjamin's life story—with its clear goals that were amply fulfilled—is extremely important because it is the kind of success story that many Caribbean people would like to tell. For the Gaston siblings, it became an important ideal to emulate, and Benjamin's life was often mentioned as exemplary. While the siblings did not directly measure their lives against Benjamin's, they related their life stories within the framework of a family that emphasized the importance of education, serving others, and maintaining high moral standards and social respectability—values that his life exemplified so well.

Seven of the Gaston siblings initially left Dominica to study abroad. These siblings said relatively little about why they had left. It went without saying that they would continue their studies, if possible. Janet mentioned in passing that she had applied for, and received, a government scholarship to study at the University of the West Indies. Alan noted that he did well enough at the Catholic secondary school to be awarded a tuition scholarship for the American university operated by the Catholic order. When I asked Robert, who received a partial scholarship to study at the same university, why he went to study in the United States, he merely replied: "The opportunity was provided." Studying abroad had simply become the done thing in the family. This means that those who were not able to obtain a scholarship for further studies at a university, or who did not travel for higher education at all, were quite aware that their life trajectory did not fit the family ideal. They therefore had more to account for in their life stories.

Mark described his move to England as an attempt to live up to the family's ideal of further education, despite the fact that his exams at secondary school did not quite qualify him for this:

> I wanted to do something with myself on my own. As a clerk at customs I got magazines from abroad. And in one of the magazines I saw something on a part-time course [in optometry] in England.

I wrote for the information about the course but received the reply that since I did not have math, I could not be accepted. But by then I had already paid my passage to go, and therefore I decided to train as a nurse. I applied [to] three nursing schools and got accepted at all. And the training in nursing helped, because I got exempted from some of the course work [for optometry] later on. While I did nursing I got my math exam, and then I went to Bradford College to become qualified as an optometrist.

What should have been a fairly short course in optometry ended up involving more than six years of hard work that included training as a nurse, which enabled Mark to go to Great Britain and take the needed math exam, and, later, factory work that supported him during his part-time course in optometry. For Mark, obtaining an education was an important means of proving himself to the parents, and he therefore regretted that he took so long: "I left for England. . . . I wanted to come back to surprise them [his parents], but they didn't live to see my achievements."

Nelly did not travel to attend a university when she left Dominica. Nevertheless, in her life story she also paid heed to the high value that the family placed on education:

They had a special scheme to Canada to go as helpers in a home. You had to work in a home for one year, and then you could become a citizen. I came with quite a few girls, and we settled with families. . . . There was not much to do in the island. I said that I wanted to be a dietician. It was a way to get in. The government paid part of the fare, and you became a citizen after one year. We did nicely. The family encouraged me to study, and I stayed with them for one-and-a-half years.

While Nelly explains the move to Canada in terms of her ambition to become a dietician, the phrase "I said that I wanted to be a dietician" indicates that she might not have been too concerned about this plan. Indeed, she never did become a dietician. In her migration story, she emphasized the Gaston value of helping others as a central quality in her life: "The lady's mother lived there then, and I helped care for her. The lady said that she would never forget what I did for her mother. She was very grateful for that. I lived with the family, took care of the two kids and took them out for walks. I didn't mind."

Anna, who did not have the opportunity to attend secondary school in Roseau but stayed on with her father in Sainte-Anne, described her departure from Dominica as caused by the increasing problems she experienced with her father:

> My father was diabetic, and he was blind. And he started to be alcoholic and upset the family. And he drank and smoked and didn't want me around. I had some change [money] from teaching, and I traveled to England with Ina. I stayed with her in London. I had thought that I would go to my brother in Bradford, but my auntie wanted me to stay with her in London. . . . The hardest part was that I left Vera, Richard, and Al still there. It hurt me the most. But I left a girl there who was helping them. It was my own decision to leave.

She went on to explain that while she initially had to take any available work to make a living, later she was able to draw on her teacher's qualifications and pursue her interest in nursing—the occupation of her choice that her father had denied her:

> First we took anything, because we needed work. We worked for Lions, a sweets factory. Later I went to live with a family. . . . This was a Jewish family, and I took care of the kids. I taught them math, and I helped them with their homework. The parents were jewelers. I also took a nursing course.

Like Nelly's life story, Anna's account is moral in tone, emphasizing her sorrow at leaving her siblings behind with an alcoholic father and her willingness to sacrifice her own interests (joining her brother) for the sake of other people (staying with her aunt). By pointing to the value of personal relations and moral values, Nelly and Anna created a story that represented somewhat of an alternative to the more career-oriented life trajectories presented by their siblings.

MOVING ON IN LIFE

In the course of their various movements, four major migration destinations for family members emerged: Jamaica, England, Toronto, and the New York area. The siblings accounted for their migratory moves to these different geographical locations in North America, Britain, and the Caribbean largely in terms of opportunities for further education. Thus, they seem to have moved to the locations where specific opportunities presented themselves at vital conjunctures in their lives (Johnson-Hanks 2002), whether in the form of further education (Jamaica, Great Britain, the United States) or the possibility of legal entrance into a foreign country (Great Britain and Canada). Apparently, Jamaica represented only a brief interlude that gave the three siblings who studied there the qualifications necessary to move on in life. Thus, they said little about their stays at the university there and nothing about Jamaica as such. England, Canada, and the United States, where some of the siblings spent a considerable period of time and some ended up settling permanently, figured quite prominently in the life stories.

England   When Mark, Anna, Christopher, Janet, and Benjamin traveled to England during the 1950s and early 1960s, they were part of a major migratory move from Dominica to Great Britain. According to Robert Myers, "Approximately 8,000, or 13 per cent of the population" had emigrated from Dominica to Great Britain by 1960 (Myers 1976: 118). Unlike most of the Dominican migrants, the siblings did not end up staying in Great Britain. Christopher, Janet, and Benjamin left after relatively short periods of study; Anna and Mark left after living for a number of years in the country. Whereas Janet and Benjamin said little about their stays in England, perhaps because they had already spent several years at the university in Jamaica and regarded their stay in England as a continuation of their studies, Christopher vividly remembered his trips to England as his first experience of life outside Dominica. Christopher's, Mark's, and Anna's accounts of their encounter with English society are remarkably different. This reflects their particular position in Dominica and the Gaston family and the different vantage points that this gave them to experience British society, as well as their interpretations of these experiences in the light of their later lives.

Christopher may very well have had the highest expectations of his British sojourn. Like his younger siblings, he had desired to go on for further education at a university, but with no senior Cambridge certificate he did not have the necessary entrance exam and therefore could not be accepted at a British university. He spoke with great enthusiasm about his studies at the grammar school in Dominica and remembered with fondness learning Latin because it taught him about "the roots of the English language." When I asked whether his secondary education had seemed very British to somebody living in the Caribbean, he replied that he never thought about this:

> It was part of the system to study Great Britain, and we didn't question it. At grammar school it wasn't questioned either. . . . I remember the island observing the Queen's Birthday on May 24 and Imperial Day. They were national holidays, and there was a national parade. We all marched past the Union Jack and had to sing "God Save the Queen," "Land of Hope and Glory," and "Rule Britannia." We never questioned it.

When he traveled to Great Britain to study colonial service in Oxford he therefore did not think that he was going to a foreign, unknown land, but to the imperial mother country. Yet he felt that he got a cool reception and that he, as a colonial subject, was being questioned by the British: "The English are naturally cool, and they didn't introduce you, they just watched you and wanted to see how you behaved. How you ate, what kind of manners you had at the table."

Christopher realized that he was regarded as coming from the outer periphery of the British empire, where the well educated spoke a form of English quite different from that of the British center. Furthermore, they knew little about even the most basic aspects of British life: "I had never eaten in a restaurant before. Just ordering the food and what you ask for when you order, I didn't know anything about. And then to talk to the English people: They were hard to understand, and they had a hard time understanding me. It was a little traumatic, but I adjusted." He emphasized that he got along well with the professor and his fellow students, most of whom were international, many of them West Indians. He returned later for another course in public administration, this time with his family. But again, he did not like life in Great Britain. When a few years later he looked for job possibilities abroad, he had excellent offers from Great Britain and Barbados. He and his family chose Barbados so they might stay close to Dominica and avoid going back to Great Britain. When they went to Barbados, they found that the hardest part about living there was that the Barbadians were so "English" in their ways.

Unlike Christopher, Mark had not particularly enjoyed the British curriculum at school, including learning about the Latin roots of the English language. Indeed, he decided that Latin was "rubbish" and dropped it as a subject on the final examination. When I asked him about his encounter with Britain, he related the classic story of the immigrant who is ill prepared for the harsh realities that await him:

> We arrived in Southampton, and I wanted to go back home. I was seasick from day one on the boat. The place looked so dull, all the soot, the chimneys. I had expected something nice. I had little money, and I just made it to the hospital [where he trained to become a nurse] before running out. There was housing in connection with the hospital, but there was no space for male students. There was one Dominican there. They called him Roy Blackman. Roy was a staff nurse. He was so black that he was almost blue. He went with me looking for lodging. My shoes split because we were walking through the snow, and it was terribly cold. The doors were slammed right in our faces. Finally, I had to ask Roy to stay at the corner while I went to the door, and the very first place accepted me because I was alone.

I have often heard similar stories recounted by West Indians who went to Great Britain during the great migratory moves of the 1950s and early 1960s. They were disappointed, having expected a more glamorous place, and they were not prepared for the racial discrimination that they experienced. Most of these immigrants were of lower-class background, relatively uneducated, and black. When they encountered racism, they could do nothing but continue to knock on doors until they found somebody who was willing to let them in. Mark, however, was more privileged than most, because he could ask his black Dominican friend to stay behind while he, the light-skinned person who might have looked white to British people unfamiliar with color nuances in the West Indies, could approach the inhospitable hosts on his own. Nevertheless, by incorporating Roy Blackman into his story, Mark was expressing his sympathy with the plight of his black countrymen who were treated badly in Great Britain. Mark's story was not only a narrative display of solidarity with the less-privileged black immigrants to Britain, however, because it served as an introduction to more than twenty years of personal experience with British life that had been difficult for him and his family.

For Mark, Britain was a place where he hoped to obtain an education quickly so that he could return to practice as an optician in Dominica. He

therefore took the initial difficulties in stride. When he had settled in Bradford, where he began his studies in optometry and worked for a firm making
glasses, his Dominican girlfriend joined him, and they married and had a
family. They stayed on for several years after he completed his education
while Mark worked full time, but then they moved back to settle permanently in Dominica. It did not work out. Mark became heavily involved in
Dominican politics and spent a great deal of his time and money on political
campaigns. Eventually, the family had to give up life in Dominica and return
to England. He explained:

> I was so deeply involved in politics in Dominica that my profession suffered. I was
> not with the [ruling party], and therefore people wouldn't patronize my business. I
> didn't see any way out economically. So I sold the house that we had and went
> back up to England and took up employment for the same company.

The children were not told why the family was moving, and only the eldest
had an idea of the trouble that the family experienced in Dominica. Peter, a
younger brother, remembered not understanding what was going on, but he
quickly realized that the move did not represent social and economic improvement for the family:

> We were just told that our parents had decided to go to England. That was it. . . .
> Dad went on a recognizance trip to England and brought pictures of property in
> Ipswich that we could afford. We were amazed. It was a picture of a semi-attached
> [house]. I thought it was a big house, but I couldn't understand why there were
> two front doors. He had to explain that it was only one half we were buying. We
> lived in a fabulous house [in Dominica]—parquet floors, several bathrooms and
> bedrooms, lots of land with fruit trees, mangoes. It looked like a come-down from
> the lifestyle we were coming from.

When the family arrived in England, the oldest children were placed in a
grammar school with virtually no black students. Tim, the older brother,
summed up the experience this way:

> It was a nightmare because I had mixed with everybody in Dominica, but England
> was a white, racist culture, so it was a big shock. It was not overtly racist, but they

didn't talk to you. The trendy people didn't talk to you, only the other outcasts. Those who didn't fit in talked to you, like the fat ones. It was hell because they didn't speak to me. I didn't make friends for two years. It was a shock coming to a culture which didn't want to know you.

While the children eventually found friends, and mixed, they described their parents as living rather isolated lives revolving primarily around work. Mark had employment within his profession, but his wife, who had trained as a schoolteacher in Dominica, had to do unskilled work in a factory until she found clerical work in a tax office. After another ten years in Great Britain, Mark and his wife finally returned for good to Dominica. His children opted to stay in England, where they had by then settled. When I interviewed Mark on Dominica, he said little about the bad times he had had in Great Britain, but he did call his retirement in Dominica "the happier years of my life."

Whereas both Mark's and Christopher's families were critical of British society, Anna, who had lived in England and Canada, described England in glowing terms when I asked her what she thought about her British experience: "I liked it. I loved it. People were more social. I had a neighbor, a lady down the street, who taught me to type. And we would go around the place. There are lots of places to see, historical places and so that we used to visit." After having lived in Sainte-Anne virtually all her life, Anna experienced her move to England as an exciting opportunity to meet new people and visit the many impressive sites. One of the people she met was her future husband, Simon, a Dominican who had studied to become a chiropodist (podiatrist) in Great Britain. When he established his own practice, the family seems to have done its utmost to blend into English society. The family resided in a mainly white neighborhood and tried to live as "British" as possible. According to the eldest daughter, Sarah, her father "never went anywhere without wearing a shirt and tie," and the "rose bushes out front had to be trimmed and neat and tidy." The family's trips to historical places, described by Anna, can also be seen in the light of its efforts to become British. Sarah had almost only fond memories of her early life in England:

I still refer to England as home. I have not been back, but I plan to take my daughter. It was comfortable, close. I had family there. My parents kept the home very open and often cooked for the others. There were moments when it was hard. I had to change school, because it was hard to be black in the school where I was, so there must have been racism. But I don't remember—perhaps I just chose to let the bad parts go. I just remember the nice and warm, the neighbors. There was one neighbor, whom I called Auntie Lill. She was nice, kind, and I wrote to her until she died. My memory of England is a child's rosy memory. It is difficult to look back and know how realistic those memories are, because I see England through the child's wonderful rose-colored glasses. There is an English store in town that sells candy that I remember from England as a child. So I took my daughter there a couple of times to buy that candy.

Apparently, Anna did not challenge Sarah's and her siblings' rosy child-hood recollections of England, nor had Sarah chosen to go back during her many years in Canada. Sarah's vague memories of having to change schools because of racial problems indicate, however, that there were other than rosy things to remember. Indeed, her siblings' blurred memories of England also suggest that the family had its share of problems there. Sarah's younger sister remembered a rock being thrown through the window to their father's office, and Matthew, their younger brother, recalled a tense evening: "One evening dad did not come home directly from work, and he was in the hospital. I remember my mother was very upset and angry. I can't confirm this, but I think to this day that there was some violent racism involved in this incident." The racial problems indicate that the family was not entirely successful in its attempts to be accepted in British society, and this seems to have been a contributing factor when the parents decided to try their luck in Canada.

It may seem striking that Mark's and Anna's descriptions of England are so dissimilar, given that they lived there around the same time. The reasons probably should be sought not in major differences in their experiences in England when they lived there but, rather, in their life trajectories after they had left England. Whereas in Mark's family England became the place to which the family was unhappily forced to return because life in Dominica did not work out, in Anna's family England became the country that family members remembered with great fondness when things did not quite go as planned in Canada.

Canada   Toronto was a main stronghold in the Gaston family for many years. Nelly was a central person in the development of this center of family life. This was partly because she was the first Gaston to move into Canadian society, gaining entrance through the domestic scheme.[9] She related that when she arrived, she enjoyed going out with the other West Indian girls who had come with her, and she remained close friends with some of them. Still, she missed her family, and within a few years she helped her future husband and three sisters move to Toronto. In this way she reestablished a sense of home in Canada:

> I felt better, more secure. I felt at home again. There was someone to talk to, to tell problems to. The phone bills were very expensive.
>
> [Why is family so important in relation to having friends?]
>
> We are close as a family. The family understands, I grew up with family, and we hold on to certain values. It is nice to have family around. You also have a good time with friends, but it is not the same.

Nelly presented herself as a true family person. She performed the main caregiving roles in the family for whom she worked, looking after the elderly mother as well as the young children, and she emphasized that this was gratefully appreciated.[10] Although the family was Jewish, this posed no problem, she explained, because the family "respected her religion"—they found the closest Catholic church she could attend and even purchased a Christmas tree for her. Nelly was also a central person in her own family. She helped her sisters when they needed assistance, offering Janet and Mary a place to stay when they wanted to explore opportunities in Canada and sponsoring Anna and her family so that they were able to immigrate. But she also wanted to have family around because it was understanding and maintained "certain values." By pointing to the importance of family closeness and religion, Nelly was emphasizing values associated especially with the mother. Indeed, Nelly identified with her mother, saying, "I am the one who looks the most like my mother."

The other relatives described Toronto as a real family place. This was largely because Anna, Janet, Mary, Vera, and their aunt Ina moved there as family members, helped by Nelly, rather than as part of a clear career trajectory. Except for Mary, who moved to New York within a couple of years, this cluster of close female relatives lived in the Toronto area for more than two decades. In the early years, Janet and Anna lived near Nelly, and the children remembered seeing each other on a daily basis and enjoying the large parties at which the whole family would get together. Nelly's eldest son recalled:

> When we lived in Downsview, we were close to auntie Janet and uncle Simon [Anna's husband], who were also living in the downtown area. I could easily go to Simon and hang out with Matthew. Every year there were big family get-togethers, the extended family with Jessica and . . . a friend of my father's who played cricket with him. Always at Christmas we had dinner with relatives.

The "extended family" here included family friends. For instance, Nelly's children often referred to Josephine, a friend from Dominica who had traveled with Nelly to Canada on the domestic scheme, as aunt Jessie.

Family members were closely involved with Dominican, and West Indian, migrants in Toronto during their early years of living in that city. Nelly sought out the company of the Dominican girls who had arrived with her on the scheme, one of the few possibilities for Caribbean people to migrate to Canada (Henry 1994: 121). Most girls, she explained, had graduated together from secondary school.[11] When Nelly's husband, Adam, came about two years later, he helped form the Dominican Association of Ontario. The other family members attended events in the Dominican Association, and Janet, who was then still unmarried and had long summer holidays as a school-teacher, became involved with the Caribana. This annual Caribbean festival was initiated in 1968, when the Toronto Caribbean population increased dramatically after 1962, following changes in Canadian immigration policies favoring immigration from the Caribbean.[12] Janet recalled,

> We were a group struggling to create this Caribana parade on a Saturday before August Monday, and we had difficulties coming up with the finances. . . . I was just part of it. I remember I did organize a band dressed in creole, the national dress. St. Lucia and Dominica wore the same national costume, so we joined up with the St. Lucia group, and we had the parade in Toronto.

By the early 1970s, Nelly and her husband had decided that the downtown neighborhood where they were living was becoming too rough for the family because of rising crime rates and increasingly tough behavior among children on the street. They moved out to the suburbs, and soon after, Anna and her family followed to another suburban area. They were leaving at a time when, as Nelly's daughter Rose noted, "There was an influx of West Indians." These West Indians would have been of lower-class background than the early West Indian migrants, who tended to be relatively well educated (Henry 1994: 121). As the families moved, they withdrew to a certain extent from their engagement in Caribbean activities and turned toward a more family-based form of social life. Sarah recalled:

> We always saw each other on weekends. We dropped in and out of each other's home. Somebody would come and stay for dinner. The door was open; you were free to drop in. At Easter and Christmas, one person would invite the entire family over for dinner. On Sundays we would go for picnics or have dinners at each other's houses. We did a lot together.

Moving to a better neighborhood was a way to demarcate the family's improved social and economic condition. Nelly's son Will recalled the move from the "rough and tumble" inner-city neighborhood to the affluent suburb, where he was "one of three black kids at the high school," as a rather drastic one. He was not so much impressed by the shift in the racial makeup of the area as by the social and economic change that the shift implicated. He knew that his parents had skimped and saved to "scrape enough money together to purchase the house," whereas the other residents were mainly professionals with handsome incomes. Within a few years after his parents had purchased their home, the neighborhood turned into one of the wealthiest residential areas in Canada. When Will worked for an electrician during a summer holiday, he got a close look at the large houses that had been constructed by the new residents: "One house had a hallway as long as a bowling alley. You could sleep in a different room every night. It was obscene." Living in this affluent part of the Toronto area was important to the father, Will believed, because it was a way of showing that he had done well: "He wanted to look successful. Moving to [that suburb] was part of that."

One of the reasons living in a good neighborhood might have been a measure of success for Anna and Nelly's families was that they did not experience the same educational achievements that many of the other branches enjoyed.

Adam went to Toronto with the fond hope of studying to become a dentist. Due to visa regulations, he and Nelly had to marry within twenty-eight days of his arrival. When they had their first child within a year, he reluctantly gave up his studies for a career in civil service. Simon, who had left his practice as a chiropodist in England when he moved to Canada, discovered that he needed an American license to practice in Canada. This, as his daughter Sarah expressed it, was "devastating for him." When he opted to go into social work rather than take two years of coursework in the United States in his professional field, Anna was sorry: "He did a lot of courses at college and university to get his BA in social work. It was not hard for him. But the other work would have been better, because he would have worked for himself. With social work, he was employed." Simon seems to have hoped that his children, especially his son Matthew, would make up for this loss of a profession, and he was disappointed when Matthew instead went into music. Matthew noted, "My father insisted that I study something. He wanted accounting, law, or medicine. I went into acoustics engineering. But I decided it was not for me."

When I did fieldwork in Toronto in the summer of 1997, only Nelly's family and Anna's children were still living there. Janet had returned to Dominica with her young daughter after the sudden death of her husband, a Dominican she had met in Toronto. She decided that in Dominica her four brothers, who had by then settled in Roseau, could help her and be father figures for her daughter. She settled in Roseau, continuing to work within her field of education. Anna's and Simon's return was more planned: They moved back after they built a retirement home in Dominica. Adam also would have liked to return, but Nelly refused. She had made a home in Canada: "When my husband retired, he said that he wanted to go home to settle. But I don't have the urge because of the children and grandchildren. I could go for the winters. The family is close; they come up here. I would only settle if I had something to offer to the country." While she liked to portray herself in terms of the Gaston family's emphasis on the values of caring for and helping others, she realized that this tradition also involved serving others in a wider context than the family. In Dominica, this meant serving the new nation-state. This was unproblematic for somebody like Janet, who had a degree in education and long experience working in special education. It was much more difficult for Nelly, who did not have any higher education. Nelly, however, seemed content with staying in Toronto, where she was surrounded by the children and grandchildren and still able to remain in close contact with the family in Dominica. Nelly's home was clearly still an important center of Gaston family life. Thus, when I visited Toronto, Janet, Ina, and Janet's daughter were staying with Nelly; Mary and her husband had visited recently; and Benjamin and his wife were soon to follow. Nelly noted:

> You get so used to changes [her sisters moving back to Dominica], and I got used to it. It is part of life. But I had to cut down on phone calls. And there is always somebody coming up or down with letters, parcels, etc. Always at Christmas. It is amazing how that sort of thing works. People move down and have a container, and I send a barrel in the container. Every month I send something for Janet—Janet more than the others—and auntie Ina.
>
> [So you feel part of the family?]
>
> Yes, there is always news, letters, passing of messages.

By staying in Toronto, Nelly therefore was able to maintain her central role in the family—both as a good sister who continued to help her siblings and as a mother and grandmother who was there for her children and grandchildren.

New York   Three of the brothers went to New York State, and Mary joined them later when she married her Dominican boyfriend who had settled in New York. The Gastons who went to New York were the model of the hard work and educational achievement so admired in the Gaston family. Alan and Richard acquired Ph.D.s, Robert completed a master of arts degree, Mary earned a second bachelor of arts, and her husband obtained a bachelor of arts while pursuing a full-time, comet-like career at a major bank. All had good jobs within their professions, and when I interviewed Alan, Richard, and Mary, who stayed on in the United States, they were living in comfortable houses in Westchester County, north of New York City. Mary and her husband, Marcus, were in the process of moving to Florida after Marcus's retirement from a top position at the bank. They all could look back on productive and successful lives with satisfaction.

If family members in the New York area had done extremely well, they all emphasized that it had been a struggle for them to reach so far in life. Alan described the round-the-clock toil he endured to make it through college:

I had only a tuition scholarship, so I had to work for my books, rent, and food. Occasionally, I received a basket of something or a box of food, toothpaste, and so on from my sister Nelly in Canada. I am very close to her, and it was very useful. I managed by working in the college library, in supermarkets, and for a while at McDonald's. I got a job at the National Bank of Westchester, where I put checks through machines to balance the incoming money. I worked there sometimes from 5 P.M. to 2 or 3 A.M., and then I had to go to school in the morning. I did this for three years. I also had a job cleaning a bar, where I had to mop the floor and chairs. I would be up at 5 A.M. to clean the bar.

Mary related that her husband had worked his way through college and promotions in the bank, spending most of his waking hours outside the home. At the same time, he helped his family in Dominica, inviting several of them to stay in their home for extended periods of time. Richard described his many years of service as a priest in the Catholic order and how he agonized when he realized that he wanted to leave the order:

> I didn't like converting people. I never felt I was better, just different, because I had more expertise and knowledge. I became disillusioned. And there was favoritism in terms of color, though people were not conscious of it. . . . I had made my final wows, and so I had to write to Rome for a dispensation.

When he finally did leave, he had only a small suitcase and five hundred dollars in his pocket. If the siblings had had fine careers, it was made clear, this had not come about easily.

The siblings also emphasized that they had used their education to help other people, much in line with family tradition, because they had all worked with people who were in various ways disadvantaged. Alan, who had a degree in psychology, was involved with community psychology skills and trained guidance counselors before focusing on the mentally retarded. When I talked to him, he was making good use of his French creole-language skills in his work with Haitian immigrant children. Richard was directing a program to help disadvantaged, primarily black and Hispanic students acquire further education. Mary, after rearing her children, took up work with the disabled.

Although their careers loomed large in their lives, the Gaston siblings also saw a great deal of one another. When Mary established a family in New

York with Marcus, their home became a gathering point for the family. Mary's children remembered growing up surrounded by family. Her oldest daughter Louisa related:

> I had few friends, and my parents had no friends that were not family. On weekends everybody came, and it was one happy playtime. Uncles would play basketball. It seemed that for a while every weekend someone had to be taken to the emergency room with something broken or sprained. The home life was fun. New Year's Eve they had a party where about a hundred people came. They danced, and there was music until five in the morning. Tracey and I watched them from the staircase.

The family in New York also had close ties with relatives in Toronto. As Alan noted, Nelly sent him care packages when he was struggling through college. When Nelly married, Alan went to Toronto for the wedding, and the families visited each other frequently on holidays. When Mary was studying to finish her American bachelor's degree, her daughters stayed with Nelly for an extended period. Alan regretted that he was not closely involved with the family for several years because of marital problems. He started dating his wife, a white American, as a young college student, and when her family found out that she was seeing a non-white person, they rejected her. He felt that the most honorable thing to do was to marry her, but the marriage did not work out, largely, he believed, because she did not appreciate the closeness in Caribbean families. When I asked him whether he felt that he had married out of his culture, he replied: "Yes, my wife's friends were white. My wife refused to go to parties in my family. I took my children to my family. But for a while I saw my family very little, when I was agonizing over the relationship. I didn't want to share the problems; they might have problems of their own." He remained married much longer than he would have liked to, because he felt that it was out of the question for a Gaston to get divorced: "I was the first in the history of the family to get a divorce. That kept me married longer. I stuck it out for thirteen years. I should have divorced the first year. I kept the marriage for religion and family history." When the marriage finally broke up, he asked to have it annulled: "I wanted my nephews and nieces to understand that divorce is not easy. One must take marriage seriously."

When I visited the Gaston family in New York, Robert had been back in Dominica for more than twenty-five years. In Dominica, he explained that he never intended to stay in the United States but had left somewhat earlier than anticipated because he became politically active:

> It was the height of the Civil Rights Movement, and this helped create an aware-
> ness of race and justice and social issues at the time. Martin Luther King was active.
> We knew in the Caribbean the Black Power movement, which was transplanted to
> the Caribbean. Many of the political activists were of Caribbean parentage—
> Stokely Carmichael, Marcus Garvey. . . . Many of us got involved in the march in
> Washington, and I was there when Martin Luther King gave his "I Have a Dream"
> speech. We went together in a group of students.

This social engagement led him to become concerned with politics in Dominica, which was in the process of changing its political status to an independent nation-state: "I was always interested in Dominica, in the local happenings. I was concerned about the country's direction, the totalitarianism, the nepotism. I got involved in it and wrote political articles." This political interest, he explained, made him decide to return to Dominica before completing his Ph.D. so that he might devote himself to working with educational and political issues in Dominican society.

Robert's three siblings had no plans to return to Dominica. Alan and Richard did not see a career for themselves in Dominica and wanted to ensure their young children's further education in the United States. But both emphasized that, at some point, they wanted to go back to contribute in some way to the country. Mary and her husband, who were retiring, had planned to build a house in Dominica where they could spend the cold winter months. A visit to Dominica made them change their minds and choose Florida instead:

> I have lived so much of my life here, and in Dominica there is a lot of [my
> husband's] family. I like to be away. I love my family, but they talk back and
> forth. . . . They would be in and out, my house is your house—they would be too
> much involved, the family would be over constantly. I felt that I needed more time
> with [my husband]. I was selfish. And the kids are more excited about Florida. It is
> easier to travel there.

INCLUSION AND EXCLUSION IN THE FAMILY

The intertwined ideals of educational achievement, serving others, close family relations, and high moral values linked to the Catholic church provided a basic frame of reference in the life stories related by the first generation of siblings in the family network. Sharing these ideals, and upholding them in practice, defined the siblings and their children as a family group and gave a particular identity to the family name. This identity was not just a private one, nourished by family members. It received public recognition in Dominica, where the Gastons have become a leading family in the independent nation-state because of their outstanding contribution within health, education, public administration, and politics. The elder generation was modest about its achievements and emphasized that it had enjoyed being part of, and contributing to, the island society and saw this contribution as a natural continuation of the family legacy of serving others left by the father. It was apparent, however, that the siblings were keen to protect the family name. When Mark's eldest son, Tim, grew up in Dominica, he was quite aware that the family was well known: "Their father had been a schoolteacher in Sainte-Anne. All knew him in the village, and the brothers were all in the professions. It was not necessarily because of money. It was more the perception of a family name and a profession." Like most of his cousins, Tim lived in a "good" middle-class neighborhood and attended private Catholic school, and he was told not to mix with the wrong crowd: "What they called vagabonds, or particular families, girls with a bad reputation. They were very protective of the family name." Christopher's children, who lived in a more mixed area of Roseau, remembered being conscious of the great social and economic differences in the town. These differences were never talked about, however, and when I asked one of them whether she had been discouraged from making friends with children from the lower-class families in the area, she replied, "No, it just didn't happen. I don't remember they ever said not to go to a person's house."

Whether they grew up in Dominica, Great Britain, the United States, or Canada, the siblings' children were aware of the importance of obtaining a good education, preferably in the professions, marrying, and leading a "good" family life. The life stories of the siblings' children are full of references to their parents' high expectations and the consequences of not living up to them. Particular moral values were also impressed on the children through their upbringing in the home and their religious instruction in church and, for many of them, the Catholic school. Those who failed to stay away from the "bad crowd" tended to disappear from the family, as Alan had done when he experienced marital problems. Louisa remembered that a couple of her cousins vanished for a while when they had children out of wedlock:

> Once [they] became pregnant and [weren't] married, we didn't see [them] much.
>
> [Was it shameful?]
>
> Very, horribly. [They were] not excluded, but [they] knew about the disapproval. And when Will let his hair grow, it was regarded as weird.
>
> [So some did not live up to family expectations.]
>
> Yes. It is a very judgmental family.

The ability to live up to the family name thus had become an important criterion of belonging in the family.

CONCLUSION

In this chapter I have examined the Gaston family's pursuit of a "proper" livelihood outside the village of origin. In their narratives, family members emphasized that this livelihood had its roots in Sainte-Anne, where the family was engaged in uplifting and enlightening the villagers through education, community programs of various sorts, and the Catholic church. When the siblings left Sainte-Anne, they further developed this family tradition by engaging in other areas of public service, such as secondary education, health services, public administration, and the political system, which in some ways were of higher status. Family members asserted a respectable position in society, but they in no way rejected their rural background. They pointed with pride to their origins in a French creole community and emphasized the joy they derived from visiting the countryside, cultivating the land, and fishing. This celebration of the family's rural heritage also fit the recent origins of the Dominican middle class in the self-contained villages that until recently had characterized Dominica. It positioned the family centrally in the modern independent nation-state.

By depicting the village origins with its combination of the simple life of the rural community and the educational mission to uplift the villagers, the family downplayed its close connection with the British colonial system and the status that this had given them. Theirs had been a position of leadership based on devotion to education, hard work, and "high" morals tied to a respectable family life—core values in the new professional middle class in the modern Caribbean societies—not one grounded in privilege. This was what had brought family members so far and given them a central role in the development of the independent nation-state of Dominica. This image of the family framed the life stories related by family members. To inscribe themselves within the family, individuals therefore had to account for their lives in such a way that they could be seen to exemplify family ideals. For most, this meant pointing to their educational achievements and dedicated service to Dominica; for others, it meant emphasizing their devotion to helping others, especially the family. For all, however, it meant the upholding of the moral values of respectability. Those who failed to live up to these values therefore were seen as detracting from the family name and often chose to withdraw from the family.

By pointing to the importance of moral worth, the family downplayed the significance of social status. Thus, if they did not want their children to socialize with certain people, this was not because these people were of the lower classes, but rather because they might be a "bad" influence. In their professional life, however, the siblings were actively involved with people of the lower classes, whether as health officials, educators, or political leaders. Thus, family members distinguished themselves by being able to help others. The family's identity as one of well-educated professionals who were compassionate and helpful toward others, yet "judgmental" in their opinion of those who failed to live up to their moral standards, meant that they were both closely involved with, and socially distanced from, their fellow Dominicans of the lower classes. The Gaston family members abroad had been involved in social causes, such as the Civil Rights Movement; they had organized Dominican social and cultural activities; and they were active in educational programs for the disadvantaged and psychological counseling for ethnic minorities. In Dominica, they had been central figures in the development of the health and educational sectors of the independent country. Yet at the same time, most of them settled in middle- or upper-class areas and socialized mainly within their own circle of family and friends. In this they are not different from many other middle-class professionals. However, for the family members living abroad, it meant that they lived far away from most other Dominicans in mainly white areas. This, as shall be seen, had an important impact on the identities developed by their children.

PART THREE...

....

....

..............................**A NEVISIAN FAMILY**

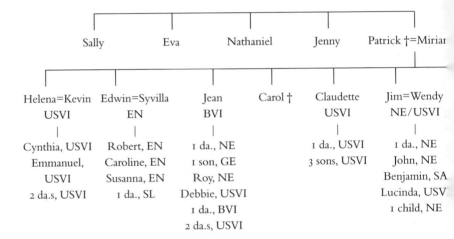

THE SMITH FAMILY, 1996

Sally	Eva	Nathaniel	Jenny	Patrick †=Miriar

Helena=Kevin	Edwin=Syvilla	Jean	Carol †	Claudette	Jim=Wendy
USVI	EN	BVI		USVI	NE/USVI
Cynthia, USVI	Robert, EN	1 da., NE		1 da., USVI	1 da., NE
Emmanuel,	Caroline, EN	1 son, GE		3 sons, USVI	John, NE
USVI	Susanna, EN	Roy, NE			Benjamin, SA
2 da.s, USVI	1 da., SL	Debbie, USVI			Lucinda, USV
		1 da., BVI			1 child, NE
		2 da.s, USVI			

KEY: BVI, British Virgin Islands; EN, England; GE, Georgia; SA, South Africa;
SK, St. Kitts; SL, Scotland; USVI, United States Virgin Islands; da., daughter;
da.s, daughters.

FIGURE 3   The Smith Family, 1996. The figure lists and locates individuals
identified in the body of the text. It is not a complete genealogy.

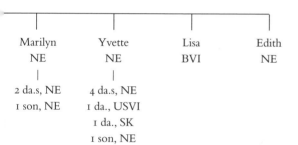

| Marilyn | Yvette | Lisa | Edith |
| NE | NE | BVI | NE |

2 da.s, NE	4 da.s, NE		
1 son, NE	1 da., USVI		
	1 da., SK		
	1 son, NE		

FIVE . . . .

. . . . A FAMILY HOME

The Smith family's life stories took their point of departure in Richmond Village (a pseudonym) on the Leeward Island of Nevis. The village emerged on abandoned sugar fields when the old English plantocracy finally gave up sugar production in the early twentieth century and sold parcels of land to their former, landless laborers, the black descendants of the slaves freed in the 1830s. Since there were no major urban areas on the island—and, hence, only a small middle class—the island tended to be polarized between a white upper class and a dark-skinned lower class. With the departure of the white upper class, the island society became largely black, and land owner-ship and occupation tended to be more important than race. Nevertheless, as in most of the old British West Indian plantation societies, a system of color differentiation developed, associating the light-colored population with high positions in the colonial society.

The development of Richmond Village by black, newly landed small farmers seeking to build a social existence amid the ruins of the old sugar regime meant that the establishment and sustaining of a respectable, well-kept, independent family home represented a great accomplishment. The life stories related by the Smith siblings revolve around how they experienced the struggle to maintain a family home during their childhood. This is the topic of this chapter.

The Smiths' narratives of childhood gave prominence to the family's difficulties, but theirs were not only tales of hardship. The siblings were proud of their parents' success in keeping a decent and well-functioning home that won respect in the village, and they were proud that they, as children, had played a part in this. Out of their collective efforts to maintain the home, they developed a strong notion of relatedness based on an unquestioned willingness to share whatever limited resources became available. A wider notion of relatedness also existed toward a larger group of relatives, and to the local community as such. In their impoverished community, however, this broader sense of solidarity often clashed with the more immediate concerns of the home of the smaller family group. In this situation of scarce resources, as shall be seen in the next chapter, migration for social and economic opportunities became an attractive solution.

This chapter opens with a quote from a life narrative related by Lisa, the second-youngest in the large group of children. By the time she grew up, her father, as well as many of the older siblings, had long since emigrated.

> I know that my mother and father had it tough. . . . My father used to work the land at home and at [a nearby estate]. He was up early in the morning to work. My mother would go down there, but she would get something for us to eat before she left. They didn't have much in those days. We ate things from the land and the animals. Sweet potato mashed into milk. Sometimes we got bread and some kind of relish, cheese, or eggs, because we had a lot of fowl. We lived on the ground provisions and the farming—milk from the cows and eggs from the fowl. Because my mother was away working the land from early morning, my older sisters and my brother got us ready for school. Jim would plait our hair. All helped, and all went to school.

Lisa was telling me about her childhood in Richmond Village, where she grew up during the 1950s and '60s. She had migrated to the British Virgin Islands about ten years before our conversation took place, and her account of a childhood in poverty and hard work might be considered a natural point of departure for a story of emigration and settlement in a new place of better social and economic opportunities. Indeed, Lisa did enjoy her job. The relatively good wages she was earning and her improved material standard of living, which included having her own car. She did not, however, see a future for herself in the Virgin Islands and looked forward to returning to Nevis as soon as possible. In fact, her tale of the hardship that her family endured when she was a child in Nevis was not intended to be a prelude to an account of moving away for a better life abroad. It was a story of the feeling of closeness, and sense of relatedness, that had been created among family members through their struggle.

This strong sense of relatedness, grounded in a common family home, was also apparent in the life-story interviews with Lisa's eight siblings, Helena, Edwin, Jean, Claudette, Jim, Yvette, Marilyn, and Edith.[1] It had not been lessened by the parents' death a couple of years before these conversations took place. On the contrary, the siblings were concerned about the future of the home after the parents died. Despite this dedication to the family home, most of the siblings lived far away from it in the British and U.S. Virgin Islands, as well as in Great Britain. As they related their life stories, however, it became apparent that they did not see a contradiction between living far away and remaining attached to the home, because during their long sojourn they had maintained close ties, sending frequent remittances that helped improve the family's material condition and its social standing in the community and returning to visit whenever possible. Indeed, some of the siblings who had emigrated noted that their move away from home had allowed them to do more for the home than would have been possible had they stayed behind. The journeys might have removed them physically from the home, but this had only reinforced their ties to, and identification with, their home and place of origin in Nevis, and some were convinced that it was only a matter of time before they would return. While they might not want to live in the physical structure of the home itself, they were hoping to live nearby on a plot of the land their parents had purchased.

This loyalty to a distant home on Nevis can be seen to be rooted in the African Caribbean people's long search for a place of belonging in a society of extreme subjugation. Nevis is one of the Caribbean islands where this sub-jugation lasted the longest and involved the most extensive efforts to control the body and soul of the black population. Colonized in 1628 by the British, Nevis was turned into a plantation society based on African slaves by the middle of the 1600s. While the plantation system was weakened with the abolition of slavery in 1834, it managed to survive well into the twentieth century by instituting a sharecropping arrangement (Hall 1971: 114). Little land was therefore available for sale to the emancipated and their descendants, except for small plots unsuited for plantation agriculture, and most of the black population was forced to remain as sharecroppers on the plantations or to eke out an uncertain existence in marginal areas (Frucht 1966: 71). When the sugar plantations finally collapsed in the early twentieth century, the British crown purchased the old estate land and sold it to the local population in a major land-settlement program that aimed to create a population of peasant proprietors (Frucht 1966: 42, 85). The land sold to the local population was described by the geographer Gordon Merrill as "worn out" after three centuries of monocropping. In his opinion, the land-settlement program had come way too late and had had "little to recommend it" (Merrill 1958: 107–108, 112; see also Olwig 1993b: 98–99). When the government closed the last public sugar-processing factory during the 1950s, cotton became the main cash crop, but drought and insect infestations made this an unreliable source of income (Olwig 1993b: 140). By the late 1950s, the island's economy had become limited to various subsistence activities, supplemented with the occasional sale of fish on St. Kitts.

While the land-settlement scheme was a failure from an economic point of view, the local black people experienced it as a significant improvement in their social condition, because it allowed them to acquire land, build homes, and settle in their own villages. This enabled them finally to leave the plantations and develop their own communities of small farmers, based on social relations, economic activities, and cultural traditions developed during and after slavery. It also conferred on them a social identity as landowners and small farmers who could be recognized as proper citizens in the wider society. This recognition, however, depended to a great extent on their ability to live up to social norms propagated by British missionaries.

The Methodist missionaries arrived in Nevis during the 1780s to work with the slaves (Olwig 1993b: 69–74). During slavery, their missionizing activities concentrated on imparting the Christian religion to the slaves to "bring their conduct under its salutary control, and thus at once to promote their present happiness, and to fix the peace and security of the colonies upon their surest foundation" (missionary report no. 1821, as quoted in Olwig 1993b:74). After the abolition of slavery in 1834, however, the Methodists hoped that their followers would be able to settle with their families on their own land, thus becoming "a fount of industry, good order, and domestic comforts, as the peasantry of Britain" and had visions of such peasant proprietors as the foundation of the free society (missionary report no. 1834, as quoted in Olwig 1993b: 101). The plantocracy was less sympathetic to this cause, however, and prevented such settlements. The Methodists, joined by Anglican priests and, later, other Christian missionaries, nevertheless continued to preach the moral superiority and social respect due to those who lived in a home based on holy matrimony, with the husband and father functioning as provider and head of household and the wife and mother as nurturer and moral guardian of the family and home. They thereby instituted a powerful model of proper citizenship based on an economically self-sufficient household with a male-headed nuclear family. When during the 1930s and 1940s the black population finally was able to purchase smaller parcels from the ruined plantations, this signaled the establishment of a post-plantation society on Nevis, where the black population finally might acquire land and a home and gain a position of respect in society. The impoverishment of the local society meant, however, that this newly won right to recognition and respect rested on an extremely weak economic foundation. The Smith siblings' preoccupation with the home as a project that through mutual caring, sharing, and personal sacrifice would confer recognition and respect on the family in society, as well as a firm place of belonging, should be seen in the light of this particular historical context. While the historical details differ, much of the Caribbean has experienced similar social and economic development, where respectability and acceptance in the society was associated with the adoption of a set of sociocultural norms beyond the material means of the vast majority of the local population. The life stories related by members of the Smith family therefore resonate with the experiences of many Caribbean families of lower-class background.

THE FOUNDING OF THE FAMILY HOME

The Smith family's home came into official existence in 1942, when Patrick Smith married Miriam Marshall and settled with her in a two-room wooden house built on a plot of land that Patrick had purchased in Richmond Village. The couple already had two children, Helena and Edwin, who had lived with Miriam in her parents' home. In the local community, marriage and the acquisition of a house—two preconditions for the establishment of a respectable home based on holy matrimony—signaled the end of a long process of courtship. This took its formal beginning when Patrick received formal permission from Miriam's parents to marry their daughter. Patrick's sister, Jenny, explained how her own courtship had taken place:

> He said he loved me. I said that he should write my parents a letter. So he asked about their names, and I told him, and then he went and had a letter printed for them. He went to a man to have this done. This man printed invitations and so. Some people who were not good at writing had others do it. When my father got his letter, he asked me whether I knew the man. I said yes. And after the second child we got married.
>
> [Why did you wait to marry?]
>
> He didn't have the finance. He had to repair the house. The two of us worked together to repair the house, and then we married.

In a small community such as that of Richmond Village, the families involved would have known each other well, and they probably would have known about the young couple's relationship, as well. However, by writing a proper letter that addressed the woman's parents by their full and correct names, rather than by the informal nicknames known in the village, the young man requested the parents' formal acceptance of his relationship with their daughter. Having gained their permission to court the daughter, marriage could follow later, when he had the means to acquire his own house. This does not mean that marriage was unimportant. Quite the contrary: The ideal would have been to marry before having children. Marriage, however, required having a proper home, and it therefore had to be postponed for those who were of lesser means. Marriage, in other words, signaled that a young couple had established an independent social and economic unit to be reckoned with in the wider society. The close association between marriage and ownership of a house has been noted throughout the Caribbean (Abrahams 1983: 148; Blake 1961: 138; Clarke 1970 [1957]: 78; Rubenstein 1987: 249–50; Smith 1962: 114) and interpreted as a legacy from the colonial system, in which "legal, Christian marriage" became "a sign of status" in the local hierarchical system (Smith 1982: 131). The complicated system of courtship described by Patrick's sister shows that the local community had developed its own version of this marriage ideal that fit its limited economic means. By recognizing a formal letter of intent of marriage as a kind of marriage contract, it was possible for a young couple to enter into a sexual relationship and have children before they had the financial means to acquire land and a house of their own and thus become legally married.

With their marriage and establishment of a home, Patrick and Miriam settled down in Richmond Village, which emerged when old estate land was parceled out and sold to the local population during the twentieth century. Miriam's family apparently lived on the outskirts of Richmond Village in a small area of tiny plots that had developed near a ravine cutting through the plantation areas, whereas Patrick's family came from a relatively isolated village located on rocky land unsuited for large-scale agriculture (Olwig 1993b: 97, 1995). When land became available in Richmond Village, Patrick's and Miriam's parents purchased plots and moved there. Patrick himself purchased two lots in Richmond Village before he married: a small lot within the village proper, where he built the family home, and a three-acre lot on the lowlands between Richmond Village and the sea, where he could cultivate the land and keep his animals. When Patrick later inherited land from his grandfather, he was not interested in it, regarding it as having little social value because it was located in a remote area where nobody would want to live.

The house that Patrick and Miriam erected in Richmond Village was in a central location. It was right on a village street, close to the main road leading into the village and near the local school and the mission church. This was a good spot, because, as Nathaniel, Patrick's younger brother, explained: "It is more important to be to the front. You come off the road to the house. To the back you feel you are pushed back. It is higher to be on the road. Nobody wants to live to the back." According to Edwin, it was the man's responsibility to acquire a plot of land and build a house: "The man must provide land and a house for his wife, and it would not be right for a man to build a house on his wife's land and take the land away from the family when he should be providing his own."

Patrick could only afford to build a small house. Indeed, by modern standards the two-room dwelling inhabited by the large family of ten children might be regarded as providing a rather inadequate setting for a good home. This is not, however, how the siblings remembered their childhood home. Most of their family life was not confined to the house, which would have been uncomfortably hot during the day, anyway. They remembered having spent much of their free time on open pastures, where they gathered after school to engage in sports or just play. When they were at home, they usually stayed in the "yard," a fenced-in area surrounding the house that served as a kind of extension of the house, because it was here that many domestic activities, such as the caring for small children, washing, and cooking (on a coal pot) took place. The yard was also the area where the members of the family spent most of their time together, and some of the fondest childhood memories concerned the moonlit nights the family enjoyed in the yard, as in this recollection by the youngest sibling, Edith: "There was no electricity or cable or radio. At nights we would sit outside on a stone in the moonlight. They [the adults] told Anancy stories. We [the children] sang and played games."

The family life that did take place within the house was structured in such a way that it was able to accommodate a great number of children and at the same time present a nice home that could be respected in the local community. Yvette described the intricate logistics of it:

> It was a two-room house. We had the chamber, where there were two beds. There was a curtain separating my mother's and father's beds from the biggest children who were the fortunate ones to sleep on a bed. . . . The other room was the hall, where we entertained. It had chairs, table, a china cabinet where my mother kept her things so that when guests came, they did not eat and drink from everyday things. So that she could entertain with something nice to drink and eat out of. That same hall was converted at night into a bedroom. The old clothes and so— what there was—we spread out on the floor and put a big sheet over them to make like a bed. At early morning we would get up and put the clothes outside to sun so people didn't know that we slept there. In the afternoon, we took the clothes in, but we put it under the bed until we were ready to sleep. Even when people were there in the evening, we would wait until they were gone, and then we put out the clothes. We might fall asleep on the bed, and then we would move up to the bedding, when the guests had left.

Even in the smallest and seemingly most crowded house, family life thus was organized in such a way that it was possible to maintain a back stage of privacy and limited means, and a front stage of acceptable appearances and some degree of material affluence. Keeping a respectable home was an important mark of social standing in the local community (Abrahams 1983; Olwig 1993b, 1995). The careful separation of the parents and children when sleeping; the importance attached to the children's education; the attempt to hide the poverty of the family (and hence the implied limited success of the father according to the model of the male-headed household); and the maintenance of a room where guests could be received in material comfort can be regarded as aspects of this ethos of respectability.

MAKING A LIVING

The older children recalled the family's being involved in several different economic activities, some of them oriented toward the market economy. Helena, born during the early 1940s, described a whole range of economic activities:

> We grew cane, and there were two factories. My father sold some cane to the factory, so we had wet sugar, and we went there after school to get the skimming, the cold juice from the sugar factory. Father sold the cane to the government, but the ground food [vegetables] was for the family. We also grew cotton, and we cleaned it to sell. The clean cotton we sold, the bad we ginned to stuff into pillows and bedding. We had also bed grass for the bed. We made our own bed.
>
> [Did you work in the field?]
>
> Yes, I prepared for planting the vines, the tannia, pumpkin, tomatoes, whatever. Just like you see me have a garden here.
>
> [Did you also work with cane and cotton?]
>
> Yes. We would pick the cotton in February [or] January, then clean it and sell to the government.

By the 1950s, when Yvette grew up, sugar cultivation was no longer possible with the closing of the sugar factory, and she remembers her father primarily fishing commercially, as well as for the home:

> My father used to go fishing. He went out to sea, and if it was a good catch, he would go on to St. Kitts to sell the fish. We had to go to the bay, and he would send fish for the home, and then go back out to the boat to go to St. Kitts. The donkey

we brought up to water. And the next morning we carried back the donkey and tied it so that he could go back with the sails and what he needed for the boat.

Despite the many different economic activities in which the family engaged, it experienced great difficulties making a living. This was not just because the three acres of land owned by Patrick offered a limited material basis of life, but also because the economic foundation of the island society was crumbling. The only kind of paid employment that could be found on Nevis was intermittent task work in agriculture or domestic work. Both were poorly paid and associated with low social status, and the Smiths seemed to make a point of working on their own. When I asked Helena whether she worked for others, she replied:

> I never worked out. Just to help my father, mother, and myself. . . . Once a girl offered me a job to work for people. I had to walk to an estate where the water was and then bring it back home and wash the clothes. When I had finished, they paid me fifty cents, and I said: "Keep the money. If it is so little, I would rather do it for nothing!" So I would rather work for myself.

Although the family was struggling to make a living, Helena was too proud to accept the unreasonable remuneration she was offered for her hard labor. By saying that she preferred giving her labor to being paid so poorly, she also implied that she would have been better off if she had been remunerated within the moral economy of informal and, in principle, egalitarian exchanges of help that operated among fellow villagers rather than within the formal and hierarchical system of direct exchange of labor for wages that characterized relations between estate owner and worker.

Helena's insistence on being treated on an equal and fair basis and her refusal to accept what she perceived to be an exploitative work situation must be seen in the light of the historical context within which the village emerged on Nevis. As noted, Richmond Village was a community of former plantation laborers, or descendants of such laborers, who would have known only too well the forms of exploitation inherent in relations between those who controlled the economic resources and those who had to work for others. By acquiring their own land and becoming small farmers, people in Richmond Village were asserting themselves as independent villagers to be shown respect in the wider society. An important basis of this respectability was the ability to maintain a livelihood of independent small farming and fishing activities, and the keeping of a decent home. Those who had to stoop so low as to work for others for miserly wages demonstrated that they were not able to live up to the ideals of respectability, and they therefore risked losing the esteem of their fellow villagers.

The family managed to make ends meet most of the time, but there were occasions when it just did not have any money. As a last resort, the mother sent Helena to seek help at her parents' home:

> My mother used to send me to them if we had no money. So I would go there and spend some time with them, and then my grandfather would say, "Isn't it time that you go back and tell you mother that you didn't get what you came for?" He said this so that my grandmother would hear it and think that we did not get any money. But I knew that as I passed him on my way out, he had money in his blue zephyr bag, and he would open it and give me some money. Grandmother had what we called cherry trees—it is a cashew tree, and she had baskets of nuts. You would roast them, pick off the skin and eat them. She gave us a little, but he would give more. . . . I get the feeling that they were fair people and that maybe they were upset that my mother married a black man. And she might think that it was my father's obligation to provide for the family, not theirs. Outside of that, they were nice. My grandfather might not be rich, but he had money. He was one of the first with a radio, and we would listen to cricket and hymns on the radio.

Children are often used to run errands in Caribbean villages. Miriam, however, sent Helena to her parents not so much to deliver or pick up something for her, but to make a request that she would rather not make herself.[2] When a woman married, it was expected that her husband would be able to support her and provide her with a home. The inability of the husband to support his wife and children therefore reflected badly on the family. Rather than humble herself and beg money from her parents, Miriam therefore preferred to send her oldest daughter. She seems to have done this frequently enough that the grandparents knew the purpose of Helena's visits and had developed a routine to deal with the requests.

Whereas the family received some help from Miriam's parents and could count on them when times were hard, it received a rather cool welcome from

Patrick's parents, despite the fact that the paternal grandparents were relatively well off because they received remittances from several of their daughters who had migrated to Curaçao, where they were working as domestic
servants. Lisa recalled that the paternal grandparents would "hoot" their
grandchildren when they came for a visit and demand that they stay outside
the house. Yvette remembered the visits to these grandparents as demeaning:

> They didn't like to see us there. They said that we did things, so we would be sent
> home. If they ate, they didn't give us part of the food. They would send us out to
> pick arrowroot bush, and they would put a little spoonful of food on the arrowroot
> and make us eat it off the arrowroot. I will never forget that they made us eat out of
> that dirty arrowroot. They had more than my mother's parents because they had
> children in Curaçao who sent boxes.

By treating the children in an unkind manner and giving them miserable
handouts on dirty arrowroot, the grandparents just barely recognized their
grandchildren as kinsmen with whom they had an obligation to share their
food. The grandparents' failure to share the boxes from Curaçao was a particularly sore point in the siblings' accounts of their relations with the paternal grandparents. Lisa related:

> They got this big box, and we as children went by them to see what was in the box,
> but they said that they did not open it at that time. And the next morning when we
> came, we saw this big box outside with paper. They told us that only paper was in
> the box. Now that we are big, we know that things are wrapped in paper. But then
> we wondered why they sent all this paper for them.

Yvette was of the opinion that the grandparents did not want to acknowledge their poor grandchildren because they aspired to higher status in the
community:

> Some believe that they are better if they have more. That is what I think they
> thought. We were underneath. They went to the Mission [the Wesleyan Holiness
> church] and had friends from Gingerland who went there to eat. Grandfather was a
> good cook. He cooked up a storm. When we lingered there for the scraps, we were
> chased away. They didn't want their friends to know that we were their grandchildren.

By depicting the paternal grandparents as unkind and selfish people who sought higher status at the expense of close family members, the siblings used them as a negative backdrop against which they described their own childhood of sharing and caring.

A SHARING FAMILY

The notion that family is based not only on a biological tie but, just as significant, on the bonds that are formed through growing up together is a strong theme in the life stories that the Smith siblings related. Even though there was more than a fifteen-year age span between the eldest and the youngest siblings, they spent their childhood in the same home and shared many experiences of seeking to maintain a respectable family home in the village community, despite the limited resources available and the large number of children to provide for.

In their life stories, the siblings emphasized that their parents instilled in them the importance of "looking out" for one another. Indeed, it was through a relationship of sharing and caring that kinship was constituted. While the existence of a biological tie was regarded as an important basis of a kin relationship, a biological tie was not enough in and of itself to establish a kin relationship. If the sharing and caring that go into kinship are conceptualized in terms of mutual relations of rights (to receive) and obligations (to give), people who have a common biological tie but fail to engage in such relations will fail to be proper kinsmen. Examples of this were the paternal grandparents who, rather than help their own grandchildren, preferred to entertain strangers to gain a name in the community. Another example of poor "kinsmanship" pointed to by the siblings was the biological father of their maternal grandfather. According to the siblings, their mother's father was quite light-skinned and had black, straight hair, and some people described him as a white. His "whiteness" derived from his father, who was believed to have traveled from Europe, possibly Ireland, to Nevis, where he had a son with a local woman. Apparently, he abandoned his wife and son soon after. After she died while the son was still young, he was reared by relatives who mistreated him and did not send him to school. When I asked Marilyn about her maternal great-grandfather, she said that she preferred to ignore him and remove him from her family tree: "I have never been interested in my great-grandfather. If he couldn't treat my grandfather well, I am not interested in him, and as far as I am concerned, my family starts with my grandfather."

While miserly treatment and neglect represented a disregard, or even denial, of kinship, as in the case of Patrick's parents and Miriam's grandfather, generous sharing and "looking out" for one another constituted the essence of kinship. Indeed, the siblings' accounts of family life when they grew up are suffused with the morality of sharing and caring that they saw as constitutive of kin relations. Considering the poverty that they had to endure, the siblings saw such relations as the main reason why they succeeded in their struggle to create a good life for themselves. Marilyn explained:

> To me it [the family] means a special bond. A treasure. It is knowing you have somebody there that looks out for you, and you can look out for them. It is sharing and caring. My mother used to say, "It is hard to break a bundle of sticks." If you take each stick apart, you can break it. She said this to stress the importance of sticking close together as a family, and I value that.

Looking out for one another, in other words, was not only a moral obligation for each person within the family; it also created a united family that was invincible. But if individuals tried to make it on their own, they would be easily broken. Miriam also admonished her children to be generous and help other people, according to Edith:

> She told us to remember to give a portion to seven, and also to eight, because you don't know where you will be when you are in need. Treat everybody equally. Suppose you don't give [to] that person, and it might be the one to help you! Try to be fair; don't side with anybody. The person you side with might be the one to "diss" you, turn on you, and the one unfairly treated may be the one to help.

As an example of the family's sharing and caring, Lisa described how the older siblings helped the younger ones get ready for school. Some of the older siblings formed a special relationship to younger siblings and assumed special responsibility toward them. As the youngest sibling, Edith benefited from this: "Carol and Claudette were the fourth and the fifth, and they took me as their own. They carried me places, bought me things. Claudette bought me shoes, clothes, and socks for school. She plaited my hair and put ribbons in the hair and took me to school. When she was away, she sent clothes." Similar relationships also developed between the siblings and Patrick's younger sisters, Sally and Eva, who lived nearby and seemed to have had good relations with their brother's family. Yvette remembered that she and her twin sister, Marilyn, received special attention from two of their aunts:

> My mother said that when I was born, Sally said that I belonged to her, and Eva said that Marilyn belonged to her. They helped when they were here. And when grandmother got a box from Curaçao [sent by Sally and Eva], there would always be two dresses or two pieces of material for me and Marilyn.

There often was little to share within the home, however, and the siblings therefore actively sought to develop relationships with people outside the home who had more to share. Their visits to their grandparents' home must be seen in this light but usually failed to generate more than the absolute minimum of food. The siblings were more successful when they visited their godparents. Godparents often were chosen among villagers who were considered better off. Not only did they have more to give, but they were also more willing to do so, because they would be demonstrating their relative affluence by giving something to the less fortunate villagers. This was unlike grandparents who would not receive wider social recognition but merely drain their resources by sharing freely with their many grandchildren. Yvette recalled the generosity of Marilyn's godmother: "The first time I ate butter and bread was at that lady. She shared with us. She was Marilyn's godmother. We used to walk through her yard to and from school, and then we called her, until she heard us and said, 'Wait here!' That meant something was coming." Edith also described her godmother with affection:

> My godmother had a shop, and every time it was a holiday she would bake a cake or a tart for me and give sodas. And for Christmas and birthdays she bought me things and gave. If I was hungry, I could ask Miss Jones. When I passed, she gave. I was more fortunate than the others. I would get at least two breads and a drink, and I shared the bread with my sisters. All took a bite and was satisfied.

These descriptions show that the children developed special routes between school and home that involved walking through yards or passing by houses where they knew they could call people who might give them something to eat when they were hungry. The children emphasized that they went there together or shared with the others if they received something on their own.

Jean did not confine herself to making brief visits to relatives and close friends of the family. She also developed a more permanent attachment to a particular home with which the Smith family does not seem to have had a prior relationship but which was located near the Smiths' house. She did so by offering to help two elderly women who were living in a house by themselves:

> I didn't depend on my mother. I used to come home from school, and as soon as I had changed my clothes, I went by two ladies' where I would clean and cook food for them. And then I would eat there. My mother had nothing to cook for us. She had it hard with ten children. When my father went away, things got a little better

> [How did you get to spend so much time with the two ladies?]

> I went there one afternoon and asked if they wanted help. And so I helped them and got money for my peanuts and sugar cane. They lived close by. I was seven, eight, nine years old when I began to do this. When one of them died, I went and helped the other one until she died.

Jean explained her independent maneuvers by saying that she found it difficult to get along with her younger siblings: "There used to be a lot of fighting between me and the smaller ones." However, it was apparent that she set herself somewhat apart from her siblings by spending so much time in the house of the two ladies.

In her analysis of children's role in kinship processes on Pulau Langkawi, Malaysia, Janet Carsten (1991) argues that children both divide and unite houses and the kin relations associated with them. New houses come into being when a couple has one or two children and the mother and children move away from her parents' house to join her husband in a separate house. Through the sharing of cooked food, relations of close consanguinity are created, and siblingship formed through co-residence as well as co-eating is regarded as basic to kin unity. At the same time, children move between houses—either on temporary visits or through more permanent fostering arrangements—and in this way serve as important mediators of exchange relations between houses that may blur the boundaries between discrete households and reunite kin separated in different houses. Children are able to both divide and unite houses because they are not fully formed in the sense that they have not yet engaged in sexual or marital relations and therefore have not "directly participated in, or incorporated, the division which affinity introduces into the unity of the sibling group" (Carsten 1991: 439).

There are important similarities between the ideas and practices of kinship that Carsten describes for Langkawi and those expressed in these life stories. In the Nevisian village, as in Langkawi, children played an important role in the formation of new houses, and kinship was conceptualized in terms of a group of the siblings who grew up within the house and shared the substances of life. Similarly, the children were regarded as important mediators creating, or reinforcing, exchange relations with other houses. Ties were expected to be particularly strong with the houses of grandparents to whom the parents had formerly belonged, or with the houses of godparents with whom the parents had established, through the children, a formal religious relationship of co-parenthood. Furthermore, the children seem to have had a special ability to mediate between houses because of their status as children who did not yet have their own home for which they were responsible.

In their accounts of their childhood, the Smith siblings only described themselves as mediators in the social order in the sense that they—as yet unfinished human beings—moved between different homes and helped maintain ties with kin relations that had been divided by marriage and the subsequent creation of separate households. When they visited relatives and godparents and offered their labor to elderly people, they obliged the receiving homes to give them something to eat and drink that they could share with their siblings. They thereby helped their parents maintain the appearance of keeping a decent home and a successful family life, although the material basis of the household was extremely limited. The children, however, had to be very careful about how they moved around. Thus, there was a fine line between visiting and offering to help kinsmen, godparents, and friendly neighbors and blatantly begging for food and hence displaying the inadequate material basis of the home. Sociable and helpful children would make the family more respectable in the local community; begging children would undermine the respect the family worked so hard to maintain by keeping a nice home. This does not mean that kin relations were only utilitarian and could be reduced to those ties that served to maintain the home. It means instead that family, or family-like, relations were acknowledged and maintained through the sharing of the substances of life and that the home was an important symbol of the unity—and respectability—of the married couple and their children in the local society.

MOVING INTO THE SOCIETY

While the Smith siblings dwelled on family relations when talking about growing up in Richmond Village, they also noted the significance of the church and the school, public institutions that brought them into the wider society. These institutions were the primary promulgators of the notions of respectability that were linked with the local middle class that emerged in post-emancipation Nevisian society (Olwig 1993b). They therefore were associated with social mobility. The village church was owned by the Pilgrim (later Wesleyan) Holiness church, an offshoot of the Methodist church that began to missionize on Nevis early in the twentieth century and erected a church in Richmond Village (Olwig 1993b: 123–24). Patrick and Miriam belonged to the Anglican church located outside Richmond Village on the main circum-insular road, but they let Patrick's sisters take the children with them to the Pilgrim Holiness church in the village. Marilyn thought that, as children, they probably would not have been able to go to the more upper-class Anglican church because the family did not have the means to dress all the children properly for this church: "I went to Pilgrim Holiness because my father's sisters belonged there. When they went to church, they took us along. In the village, we didn't have to dress up for church or wear shoes. We could go barefoot. We might stray if we had to have money for dress and shoes." Marilyn was one of the few siblings who remained a member of the Wesleyan church and emphasized the importance of the church. Most of the other siblings eventually joined other denominations, such as the Baptist church or the Jehovah's Witnesses, and they no longer identified with the church that they attended as children. Religion therefore had become a divisive rather than a unifying factor in the family, and this may be one of the reasons that most of the siblings spoke relatively little about the role of the church during their childhood.

The significance of the school, and education in general, was underscored by most of the siblings. Sending all of the children to school was, as Lisa emphasized in the introductory quote, an important element in the family's struggle to make a good life for itself in the village. It would have been tempting for the parents to keep the children out of school to help with the farm work. Patrick and Miriam had very little education themselves because they had to help their parents. However, they wanted their children to do better than they had, as Yvette explained:

> School was a must. No matter how much work, we had to go to school. My father and mother were not totally illiterate, but they wanted their children to do more. They insisted on school. We had chores before school in the morning. We had to help with the land or the animals and still be home on time so that we could go to school. Only cotton-picking time, at the end of the school term, when it was mostly playtime anyway in school, we might skip one or two days to help pick and clean the cotton.

As was the case with the church, the children were able to attend school in the village, even if they did not always have the expected school clothing. Marilyn said: "I remember going barefoot to school, and we would pull the coalpit bush—the real name is colita—or paper around the feet to make shoes, so that they would not burn."

Yvette explained that she and Marilyn did so well in school that they were able to capitalize on their brains: "There was a girl in town—they were rich— she went to the village school. She was a dunce, dull. We did her work for her, but she had to pay: orange or pineapple juice, sweet biscuits." Marilyn here makes clear that when dealing with a wealthy girl from town, they did not practice the more generalized system of exchange used among the poor villagers, who helped one another with the expectation that their help would be returned some time in the future. Rather, they resorted to a more calculating system of direct exchange, where a favor had to be paid—in this case, with goods that they would not otherwise be able to afford.

Marilyn noted that she finished the seventh standard, the highest grade in the village school, and therefore could have continued at the high school in town, but the family's financial situation did not allow this:

> You could go to high school, but you had to pay for the subjects and the books. My parents couldn't afford it, so I couldn't go. So I don't have a secondary educa-

tion. After a while, they changed the system with the high school so that every-body after twelve [could] go without paying. If I had done that, I might have been premier today!

Several of the other siblings did not complete primary school but opted to leave early to find gainful employment. While they contributed to the up-keep of the family by doing so, Miriam did not like it. She would have preferred for them to get as much education as possible. If they left school, they should know it was their own decision. Helena recalled, "My mother said, 'Don't tell anybody that I stopped you and make you leave the school.' So I don't tell anybody, but I thought it was necessary to leave school. I wanted to work my land—I had a piece—to get money on my own."

When they left school, they realized that the economic and social oppor-tunities on the island were extremely limited. Helena was "sent to a lady to go to needle school there" but found that she ended up spending all morning caring for the woman's children and cultivating the land in her "ground," leaving little time to learn sewing before she had to return home in the afternoon to help her mother. She never learned to sew. The main kind of work that could be found on Nevis was intermittent task work in agriculture or domestic work. Both kinds of work were poorly paid and associated with low social status, as Helena experienced when she was offered a job washing for others. Marilyn was of the opinion that domestic work, the main kind of employment available for women at the time, invariably meant being taken advantage of: "I have seen how it is done. You work for somebody and give your hours. But there is no job description, and you end up doing every-thing. And if they entertain friends, you have to entertain the friends also. And there is no extra pay. To me, that is taking advantage." Marilyn therefore preferred to work at a grocery store in Charlestown. Although the hours were long, and the pay was low, she knew at least what kind of work she was expected to perform:

> I worked from 7 [A.M.] to 5 [P.M.], Monday through Friday, and on Saturday from 7 [A.M.] to 9 [P.M.], until I approached my bosses and said that I could only work until 7 [P.M.] because it was hard to get a ride back to Richmond Village so late in the eve-ning. . . . I worked for Johnson like a little slave. I couldn't leave on the dot at 5 [P.M.]. It might be later. If people came through the door, I might work until 5:30 [or] 6.

It was not much easier for young men to find work. Edwin, who also left school early, had hoped to earn a living as a joiner, but had to give it up because he earned no money while learning the trade:

> I found that the bosses back home would not pay any money, because they were teaching you a trade. So I found it hard to survive. I worked all day; still I had to get dinner money from my mother. She had a lot of children to support, and it was hard for her to have me be dependent on her. So I had to find something. I went fishing, because this was the best-paid job in the islands.

CONCLUSION

The families that moved to Richmond Village from estate villages or marginal rural settlements during the 1930s and 1940s were hoping for a better life in the society of peasant proprietors that was emerging after the collapse of the old plantations. By acquiring their own land, they sought economic independence and social recognition in local society, and by sending their children to school they aspired to some measure of social and economic mobility for the family in the future. Most were not able to realize these aspirations. The introduction of small farming on Nevis came about because of the decline of large-scale plantation production, and it offered an inadequate basis for the support of large families with few economic resources such as those who settled in Richmond Village. All Nevisian smallholders suffered from the economic decline of the island, and rather than becoming respectable members of the local society, the villagers seem to have receded further into the margins of the crumbling British colonial society.

When the siblings left school and experienced how difficult it was to make a decent living on Nevis, out-migration for economic opportunities abroad seemed to be the only viable way ahead for most of them. When they emigrated, they did not leave behind the family's struggle to maintain a respectable home in the local community, because this struggle was an important basis of the notion of relatedness that defined the siblings as a family. Indeed, the siblings' life trajectories abroad were guided by their strong desire to support and further improve the family home where they had grown up, as well as to acquire homes of their own in the local community.

When I began to do fieldwork on Nevis in 1980, virtually all families in Richmond Village had a large number of close relatives living abroad. For the villagers, emigration had become the best way out of their poverty as the local economy declined, and it therefore did not seem to be a question of whether or not to leave the island but, rather, when and how it might become possible. Thus, a questionnaire I administered in 1981 among children in the sixth grade showed that more than 70 percent were hoping to leave the island (Olwig 1987:159).[1]

The orientation toward the outside, which characterized Nevis as a whole, should not be interpreted to mean that people wished to abandon Richmond Village—or Nevis, for that matter. People traveled to obtain the economic means to return and settle as respected members of the local society. The Richmond Village people, in other words, were oriented toward the global arena of opportunities to improve their position in the local Nevisian community (Olwig 1993b). They were here drawing on a long tradition of outmigration that began after emancipation of the slaves during the 1830s and included moves to large-scale sugar plantations on other Caribbean islands, to fruit plantations in Central America, gold mines in South America, canal work in Panama, and work in the industrial and service sectors on the U.S. East Coast. There were few emigration possibilities during the depression of the 1930s and the war years of the 1940s, but after World War II, new economic opportunities opened up in Curaçao, Great Britain, the U.S. and British Virgin Islands, Dutch St. Martin, and, finally, the United States and Canada.[2]

When the Smith family began to migrate during the early 1960s, England was on the verge of closing its borders, but the Virgin Islands and St. Martin were beginning to admit labor migrants. For this reason, only the oldest son, Edwin, moved to England, whereas the other siblings migrated to the Virgin Islands, except for the youngest, who went to St. Martin. They found in these destinations job possibilities that allowed them to improve their economic situation, but also harsh social environments where discrimination against blacks and foreign nationals was the order of the day. This inhospitable reception strengthened the siblings' commitment to their Nevisian family home and thus their sense of belonging on Nevis. The complexity of local and global relations constituted an important framework within which the Smith siblings recounted their life stories and their continued relations to the family and to Nevis. In this chapter I examine how the Smith siblings emigrated with the dual agenda of helping the family home where they had grown up and acquiring the means to establish homes, and families, of their own in Richmond Village. The narratives show that, as the siblings prolonged their stay abroad, it became increasingly difficult for them to maintain this dual purpose of their migratory move and thereby to sustain a sense of home in Nevis. This tension, which touched a central nerve in their notion of relatedness as a family group, is a central theme in the life narratives and the lives that they portray.

> I came out feeling that I would return after six months with enough money to set up my own business and acquire my own home. As a young person, if you have a nice home, children will look up to you, and you can marry any nice girl from a decent family. You will be respected. If you also have money, this, of course, will add to it. So I had the goal to get enough money to acquire a home. But this did not happen as fast as I thought it would. I got stuck, and I have been here for thirty-five years, and I still have not built my own home on Nevis. . . . My other goal was to have enough money to purchase a fishing boat, because fishing was one of the best-paid jobs on the island. When I left, fishermen had the best jobs and the best houses. So those were the two goals that I had, the two most important things for me.

The perception of migration as a sojourn undertaken to achieve specific goals abroad and return as quickly as possible could not be stated more clearly than in Edwin's description of his decision to move to England in 1961 as a young man of nineteen. His journey did not turn out to be a brief six-month English interlude, as planned. When I interviewed him, he had lived almost two thirds of his life abroad, yet he maintained that he was only temporarily in England—he had gotten stuck and was hoping eventually to return. This strong return ideology was also present in the other siblings' narratives of their migratory movements abroad.[3] As in Edwin's life story, the focus on return was closely connected with their having left to obtain the means to improve life on Nevis, not to create a new life for themselves in the migration destination. While Edwin was most concerned with obtaining the means to build a house and to provide a secure economic foundation for his new family, his sisters were not so concerned about this, because it would be a husband's primary responsibility. They were rather keen to earn an income that would enable them to send support to the family that they left behind. Edith put it this way: "I went to do what I had to do. . . . I worked to care for my mother and to help my sisters with their children. They had small children, and I tried to accommodate everybody."

The sisters' main reason for migrating was of such a nature that it was difficult to set a specific goal that had to be reached before a return was desirable. There would always be family left behind that was in need of help, and their return therefore depended to a large degree on their marrying men with the material means necessary to establish viable homes on Nevis. While the brothers and sisters emphasized different reasons for migrating, they recognized the significance of both sets of goals. Thus, a man who only worked for his own good and did not help the family that he left behind would have failed to maintain good relations with those to whom he was hoping to return. A woman who did not in some way aspire to obtaining a house would only be able to return to the family home that she had supported, and this, as shall be seen, could be problematic.

The two migration goals were integral aspects of a more general notion of migrating to "better one's condition," which revolved around gaining the respect of others in society. Helena explained,

Here we try to save so that we can extend the "bettering of our condition."

[What do you mean by "bettering your condition"?]

If you were twenty years old and you didn't do anything and you were just back to that home that you left there, you did not better your condition. But if you remodeled and expanded the house and got a cistern, you bettered your condition. I got my home and I built a cistern, so I did better my condition. I have a child born here. If the child stayed when I leave, I want to leave a house for that child here.

[So bettering your conditions is mostly about the material improvements?]

You are already what you are inside, the real you. The material, physical you, that is what people look at. But it is important to have both.

"Bettering one's condition" primarily refers to outward appearances, to that which "people look at." It is, in other words, what is examined and, hence, judged by others. By bettering one's condition, one may therefore gain others' recognition and respect. This bettering is primarily judged within the Nevisian community, whether it is the Nevisian community in Richmond Village or the Nevisian communities in the migration destinations and the global community of relations that connects these various places. Thus, when the family in Richmond Village receives remittances, it will be able to improve its material standard of living and thereby its position of respect in the Nevisian community that extends between Richmond Village and various migration destinations. The migrants will benefit from this, because it will be known that they are the ones who have underwritten these material improvements.

While the two goals were closely related, they were somewhat at odds with each other, because it would be difficult to send substantial amounts of support to the family home and, at the same time, save money to acquire a home of one's own. There is therefore somewhat of a tension between the two goals of helping the family and bettering one's own condition. This potential tension was heightened by the fact that individuals' migratory moves were only possible because of assistance received from the family, whether in the form of economic assistance when purchasing the ticket, a place to stay on arrival, or help with finding a job. Edwin, as shall be seen, traveled to Britain with his girlfriend and her sister, who was joining her future husband in Oxford. When he wanted to move to an area with a larger Nevisian community, his uncle helped him settle in Leeds. Patrick was encouraged to go to the U.S. Virgin Islands by his brother and aunt, who had already migrated there and offered him a temporary place to stay when he arrived. Some of the money for Patrick's ticket came from Edwin's remittances, which were, in part, repayment of money that Patrick had lent him for his ticket. Patrick later sent a ticket for Claudette, and she lived with him in his apartment. When she had children and married a migrant from another Eastern Caribbean island, they all moved to a larger apartment. Helena, who was living with her husband, provided a home for Jim and Jean when they arrived, and she had found employment for them before they left Nevis. When Lisa arrived, she stayed with her father and Claudette, keeping house for them and helping to look after Claudette's children while Claudette worked. Yvette was sent for by her husband, who had worked in the Virgin Islands for a number of years. Edith, who went to St. Martin, received money from Jim to tide her over until she was able to manage on her own when she experienced difficulties finding a job. Migration was therefore a family project and entailed important obligations toward the family, yet at the same time, it involved individuals who sought to establish lives for themselves.

The potential conflictual relationship between individual ambition and collective goals is apparent in the siblings' life trajectories. Thus, despite the strong return ideology that characterized their life stories, only three of the siblings moved back to Nevis. They returned despite the fact that they had not achieved the sort of betterment that Edwin described. Yvette, who migrated to the U.S. Virgin Islands to join her husband, who was working there, moved back to Nevis within a few years because of marital problems. Edith returned after sixteen years in Dutch St. Martin to help care for Miriam, who was then seriously ill. Jim was commuting between work in the U.S. Virgin Islands and family life on Nevis. The other siblings were still abroad. The life stories reflected the long period in which the siblings had remained loyal to obligations and emotional ties to the family in Nevis while dealing with the social and economic opportunities and restraints that they encountered abroad in the best way possible. The life stories also revealed the siblings' growing awareness that as they prolonged their stay in the migration destination, they developed new networks of relations there and a firmer sense of familiarity with life abroad, while they experienced a growing feeling of having lost touch with Nevis. It was therefore increasingly difficult for them to maintain the sense of home on Nevis, cherished abroad, when they actually visited the island. This had become particularly apparent after Patrick's and Miriam's deaths, which took place a few years prior to my interviews with the siblings.

MIGRATING FOR A HOME

England   When Edwin left in 1961, he was the first of the siblings to move away from Nevis and the only one to travel to England.[4] He arrived in Britain at the tail end of the massive Caribbean migration to England that began in the early 1950s and ended in 1962 with the passing of a law that in effect prevented further immigration to Great Britain, except for family reunification. Caribbean migration to Britain peaked in the last years before free immigration from the British Caribbean colonies was stopped, and during 1960 and 1961 more than 5,000 persons immigrated from the three islands of St. Kitts, Nevis, and Anguilla (Byron 1994: 52).[5] Edwin traveled to England with Syvilla, his childhood sweetheart from Richmond Village with whom he had a son, and her sister Francine, who was marrying a man from St. Kitts living in Oxford:

> Syvilla's parents sent her here [to England], and I decided to come along, so we came here together on the same boat. We went to Oxford, but there were few black people in Oxford, so I didn't feel at home. I wrote to my uncle, and he told me that most of my schoolmates were here [in Leeds], so one Sunday morning I packed up and went here. A week later, Syvilla followed me. We started to look for a place to live. We had one child, Roger, and we left him behind with his grandparents [Syvilla's parents]. We couldn't bring him. We were young; we didn't know the situation here. We sent for him later, and he came along.

An important motivating factor in Edwin's decision to go to England was to prove his worth as a husband and father: "Syvilla's parents knew that I had nothing, so they were prepared to send her away. And I was determined to show that I could look after her and to prove them wrong. And I worked hard to prove a point." For Edwin, proving his worth entailed both providing for Syvilla and their child, who stayed with Syvilla's parents, and sending regular remittances to his own family. Furthermore, it meant saving money so that he could acquire a house and boat on Nevis. These ambitions proved to be

exceedingly difficult, if not impossible, to fulfill, and Edwin explained his
unrealistic expectations in the light of the many encouraging stories that he
had heard about the colonial mother country:

> We had heard fantastic stories about England, like how money was growing on
> trees in the back yard and all you had to do was shake the tree and the money
> would fall down. Or the streets were paved with gold. People were very disap-
> pointed when they came here. They thought that the English were the godliest,
> most honest and righteous people on earth. When I grew up, there was little
> contact with English people. There was not even a dozen white people on Nevis,
> and they were very isolated and lived at places like Mt. Pellier, where black people
> could not afford to go. So we were overjoyed to go to England. It was a great
> thing—it was the next best to going to heaven.

The hyperbolic tales of money trees and streets paved with gold reflected
Caribbean perceptions of England as the fabulously wealthy country of
origin of the upper-class plantation owners—and hence, as a place of un-
imagined riches available for the picking of immigrants. Similar accounts
have been documented in studies of other Caribbean migrants in Britain. In
her study of Barbadian migration, Mary Chamberlain (1997: 72) refers to
the "imperial mythology, the 'sacred geography' of empire" that led many
Caribbean people to regard Britain as a very special migration destination.
The migrants she interviewed emphasized their strong exposure to British
culture and history in Barbadian society as the reason for their high regard for
Britain. Edwin turns this around, however, by stating that being a poor black
person from Nevis, he had met few Englishmen and therefore was in no
position to judge the truth value of the many stories that circulated about
Britain.

The fantastic stories about Britain were in stark contrast to their descriptions of the actual encounter with British society. Syvilla recalled:

> When I came here, it was a horrible place. It was different to what I thought. I
> didn't know there were slums and chimneys with smoke coming out of them. I
> thought they were factories, but I was told that they were what made the houses
> warm. The houses here were disgusting; England was filthy. I cried for months to
> go home. I was depressed. It was easy to get in, but hard to get out.[6]

The disappointment that they experienced during their first encounter with Britain continued as they began to look for work and a place to stay. Edwin likened their life to that of refugees: "Life was hard, there were no rooms to rent, and we had to struggle from place to place. The facilities were bad, the people were arrogant, and we had to move on. We were like fugitives, moving from one place to another. Finally we got a corporation flat." It was easier to find wage employment, but most of it, as Edwin explained, involved "a lot of work, but little money." Syvilla emphasized that there were certain jobs that she just was not willing to take: "It was my parents' decision to have me go to England. They did it for me to make a better life for myself. I would not come here to clean for anybody else, be a servant and housemaid. I would have starved before I did that."

After a few years both Edwin and Syvilla succeeded at getting fairly well-paid jobs that they liked—Edwin in the leather tanning industry, Syvilla as a nurse's aide. Still, little money was left when they had paid their living expenses, and even less when they also had sent money to their families in Nevis, as Edwin explained:

> Every month I sent money to my mother from England. Life was hard, the wages low, yet I had to put money aside for my parents. And what I sent went a long way. My father also sent from the Virgin Islands, not just money, but also boxes of food and clothing on the boat. It is good if you can move and help the less fortunate.

Sending remittances was more than a matter of providing the necessary means of subsistence to the family, because, as Edwin noted, the family received both money and boxes of food and clothing from the father, who migrated to the Virgin Islands a few months after Edwin had left. It was also a question of remembering the family left behind and maintaining ties to the place where he hoped to return in the near future.

After many years of hard work—and little hope of obtaining a secure financial basis with which to return to Nevis—Edwin visited Nevis for the first time in 1975, bringing with him one of his daughters:

> I brought Caroline with me. The first week she was all in the fruit trees, then the next week she kept asking when we were going back. She was too young to go; it was a waste of money. She was only seven years old, too young to remember. And

she could not understand what [her cousins] were saying to her, and didn't like to stay alone with them, only with my sister, so I had to take her along wherever I went.

This experience made him change his plans for returning:

When I went back in 1975, I felt that there was nothing for the kids there. There were better opportunities for education in England than back home. I realized that if I went back home, it would only be Syvilla and I, and we would go when we had retired. So I decided to get my own home [in England]. You couldn't bring up kids in a council house. And if you keep paying rent for a council house, you will leave empty-handed when you want to go back to Nevis. I purchased the first house in 1976.

Edwin's decision to purchase a house in England reflected his realization that Nevis was a foreign place to his children, who had grown up in England, and that it therefore would be difficult to take them back to Nevis. Furthermore, he revised his migration goals because his plan no longer was just to acquire a house and a fishing boat, but also for his children to become well educated. Moving them to Nevis at a time when they were going to take advantage of the superior educational opportunities in Great Britain therefore made no sense. Purchasing a home in England would reflect well on his achievements in England and give him respect in the wider community of relations linking Nevisians in England with close relatives and friends living in Nevis as well as other migration destinations. However, Edwin maintained his original plan to return—eventually—to Nevis and explained that the money gained from selling his house in England would provide needed capital for the final return. He therefore purchased a run-down house in Chapeltown, the West Indian section of Leeds, and fixed it up. When I visited the family in 1996, it was apparent that it was strongly oriented toward the West Indian "community" in the Chapeltown area of Leeds, where there is a heavy concentration of Caribbean immigrants.[7] Edwin was involved in organizing a dinner for senior citizens at Christmas and regarded this dinner as an important way in which to honor the elderly people who had come first to Britain, clearing the way for later migrants like himself. To raise funds for the dinner, he organized bus trips to the seaside during the summer. While the trips were open to everybody who would pay, they were announced on posters in the Chapeltown area or on the local radio, and they therefore attracted local Caribbean residents. Most of all, however, Edwin, as well as Syvilla, participated in a large number of funerals of Nevisian immigrants, especially if they came from Richmond Village or were related to a close friend from Richmond Village. Some of them involved long bus trips organized by relatives or friends of the deceased who lived in Leeds.

With their close involvement with the Nevisian community in Leeds, which included a number of friends from Richmond Village, Edwin and Syvilla had to a great extent re-created a Nevisian life abroad, and one might therefore think that they had, in effect, settled permanently in the West Indian ethnic community in England. This was not how they saw their situation; nor was it the way in which their children liked to see their family in British society. While Edwin and Syvilla remained dedicated to Nevis and were an integral part of the Caribbean community in Chapeltown, they had mixed emotions about being Caribbean people in Britain, and they were well aware that their children had ambivalent feelings toward the Caribbean—and people of Caribbean background. Thus, the family had moved to a new house in a more upscale neighborhood just outside Chapeltown. As Edwin explained, "The area got a bad name, and the children didn't want to stay there. So we sold and moved out." Edwin and Syvilla were also keenly aware that their children were not as oriented toward Caribbean events as they were. Some children of West Indian migrants, Syvilla noted, were hesitant to visit Nevis because of what they had learned in school about Africa and other places in the Third World. She remembered that one of her daughters did not want to go to the Caribbean the first time she took her along because she was worried that Nevis would be just like Africa where, she had learned in school, people live in primitive huts: "She said that she did not want to live in a grass hut in the jungle, and I had to tell her that we were going to live in a real house. It might not be brilliant, but it was a real house." While Edwin and Syvilla had helped build up and sustain a Caribbean community in Leeds, they fully realized that in the public eye the community was associated with Chapeltown, which was regarded as a social and economic problem area in Britain. Identifying with this community therefore did not give them a position of respect and recognition in British society.

At the same time that they did not feel fully accepted in Britain, Edwin and Syvilla had never given up on their plan to return to Nevis, and neither had their friends in the Caribbean community. When I visited them in the 1990s, the goal of returning, which formerly had been rather remote, was becoming a more realistic possibility. During the 1990s, an increasing number of Nevisians had begun to move back to Nevis as they reached retirement age and were able to return with their British pensions. According to Margaret Byron (2000: 164), the Commonwealth Caribbean Population and Housing Census of 1991 listed 657 persons who had returned to St. Kitts and Nevis from Britain, 358 persons (or 55 percent) of whom were of "pensionable age." When I visited Edwin and Syvilla in 1996, several Nevisians in Leeds had moved back to Richmond Village, including Edwin's paternal uncle, who had built a large, three-bedroom house for himself in the village. Edwin and Syvilla were approaching retirement age, and it was apparent that they would have to make a decision on whether or not to move back in the near future. There were no longer any major obstacles to returning, because with a British pension, they would not have to worry about earning an income on Nevis. Furthermore, the proceeds from the sale of their house in Leeds would be more than enough to build a new home on Nevis.

Edwin worried about whether he would be able to build a satisfactory home, because after many years of hard work and respectable family life in Great Britain, not just any home would do:

> I know now what I would like my house to be like, and I think that I can build something that I can enjoy. This is what I have worked hard for. I would like people to come and admire my house, and I would like to sit on the veranda and be comfortable, having a drink. I would like a nice bungalow, not all under one roof, but maybe a drop roof. I want three bedrooms—spacious—a dining room that opens into a sitting room. I want a drive-in, a big lawn, and a flower garden. The house that I have now is rubbish compared to what I would like to have at home. I would also make an orchard with a lot of fruit trees.

While he emphasized the joy that he would experience once he had built a home in Nevis and moved back, he was clearly having second thoughts that had to do with unpleasant experiences on Nevis during visits on the island:

> No matter where I go, Nevis is home. I have lived more years here—from the age of nineteen to fifty-four, which is what I am now—but I still feel Nevis is where I

want to go back to when I retire. I feel more secure there. The place is poor, and there are no facilities, but it is nice. It may not be as pretty as some of the neighboring islands, but any place where you can go to sleep at night without locking your door is nice. Some of the people in Nevis are critical of people who have been away, especially if they are from England. People from America and the Virgin Islands are better treated; they don't get so many remarks. I think it has to do with the way the British government has treated South Africa and other places like that. I can understand the dissatisfaction with that, but why do they have to take it out on us? The people there do it out of ignorance. I find it hard to take, so I keep a low profile. I try not to talk about politics when I am in Nevis. Nevis politics can get you into a lot of trouble, so I try not to get involved in it. But anybody can feel free and happy to go to Nevis. You never have to worry about people sneaking up behind you, doing something to you. Nevis is the nicest place on earth.

When I left Edwin and Syvilla in Leeds, they were busy packing for a six-week summer holiday in Nevis. Toward the end of the visit they would see most of Edwin's siblings, because Jim was getting married to a woman in Richmond Village, and Edwin would then be able to discuss with them the possibility of acquiring a house lot on the land that his father left for his children. He and Syvilla would also be able to look into what sort of a house they might be able to build and investigate various practicalities concerning their return to Nevis.

The Eastern Caribbean   Soon after Edwin left for England in 1961, his father, Patrick, moved to the U.S. Virgin Islands, leaving behind his wife and children, to whom he sent remittances. When he had found a job and an apartment, he sent for Claudette, and gradually most of the siblings relocated to the U.S. Virgin Islands. By the time Edith was ready to leave Nevis, it had become impossible to travel to the U.S. Virgin Islands due to the institution of new visa restrictions, and she therefore went to nearby Dutch St. Martin. During the early 1970s, Patrick returned to Nevis after eleven years of employment on St. Thomas because of several accidents, one of them work-related, that incapacitated him. While he would be seriously handicapped for the rest of his life, he had succeeded at improving the material condition of his family considerably, as had been his goal. Moreover, he had secured its economic future, because he would receive monthly Social Security checks from the United States for the rest of his life. He therefore had accomplished his migration goal, albeit at a rather high price.

In some ways, Nevisian migration experiences in the Virgin Islands were radically different from those in Britain. Whereas it was possible, until 1962, to move freely into Britain from the British Caribbean, migration within the Eastern Caribbean was regulated by complicated immigration rules tied to the political affiliation of the individual islands. By the time Britain was closing its borders, the U.S. Virgin Islands had instituted temporary visa programs to allow for the importation of labor needed in the rapidly developing tourist economy. Thus, the Smith family was able to seek employment in the U.S. Virgin Islands under a labor-certification program that enabled employees to hire foreigners on temporary contracts for specific kinds of work and required that that they be offered working conditions and wages as specified under American law. This meant pay at least at the minimum wage, full Social Security benefits, and a guaranteed forty-hour workweek. The opportunity to obtain work at American wages attracted thousands of Caribbean workers, especially from the smaller islands in the English-speaking Eastern Caribbean, including Nevis.[8] They arrived on tourist visas and had to find employment in the American territory that would qualify them for a labor certificate, locally called a "bond," before the tourist visa expired. Those who found no employment before their tourist visas expired went to the nearby British island of Tortola—less than an hour by boat from the American islands of St. Thomas and St. John—and re-entered on a new tourist visa. The British Virgin Islands and St. Martin developed similar programs with temporary work permits for foreign workers.

The migrants who went to Britain were traveling to an entirely different social, cultural, and geographical environment, although many nourished the notion that they were moving to the British mother country. Furthermore, Britain was far away and involved a long and expensive journey. It was therefore difficult for migrants in Britain to travel back to the Caribbean, and many, like Edwin, were not able to visit their island of origin for many years. Those who traveled within the Eastern Caribbean found that their migration destination was in many ways quite similar to their home island, even when the place was ruled by another nation. Furthermore, they were able to visit their place of origin annually or biennially, since this involved a relatively brief and inexpensive journey. The migrants who went to Britain made up a small minority in a large white population, whereas those who traveled in the Eastern Caribbean went to areas with a black-majority population. Furthermore, they traveled to places that had long been subject to a great deal of Caribbean immigration, and many of the local people therefore had a mixed Caribbean background. While the migrants often received a rather hostile welcome initially, especially in areas like the U.S. Virgin Islands, where the local population was soon outnumbered by immigrants, there was no racial divide between immigrants and the majority population such as that described for Britain, Canada, and the United States.[9] These differences play an important role in the migration experiences of members of the Smith family and their possibilities for achieving their overall goal of "bettering their condition."

The siblings' life stories show that, while the labor-certification program enabled inhabitants of the impoverished British West Indian islands to take advantage of the many wage-labor opportunities in the booming tourist economy, it opened up a system of exploitation that took advantage of the migrant laborers. Claudette's narrative illustrates some of the problems involved:

I worked at a guesthouse and a home.

[Did you like it?]

I didn't, but I had no choice. I couldn't leave for other work unless I had the proper paper.

[Did they take advantage of your being kind of stuck there?]

I wouldn't say that. But the pay was small. And when the government raised the pay, they said that they would have to cut the hours, because they couldn't afford to pay me. But it was only eighty to one hundred dollars a month. They said they couldn't afford [it], but they could. . . . They cut my hours, but I had to do the same work, so I had more to do in less time.

When Claudette changed work, she encountered similar problems, and she noted that she was always underpaid while she worked on a bond. Her siblings experienced similar problems. Helena worked for years for the same employer for less than minimum wages but decided to accept the situation because she developed a close personal relationship to her employer and thought that the informal help she received from this employer more than compensated for the poor wages. Jim, who was employed in construction, found that many contractors were not able to offer steady work and that he had to supplement his official but periodic income in the building industry with other kinds of unofficial work, such as gardening for wealthy American residents. Yvette, who had entered the U.S. Virgin Islands on her husband's visa, never succeeded in obtaining labor certification on her own, largely because new labor certificates were not being issued during the 1970s when she arrived. She was therefore confined to doing informal domestic work for various people at whatever pay they could afford to give.

To avoid the kinds of exploitation encountered when being bonded by an employer, Claudette decided to make an agreement with a neighbor to bond her, that is, sponsor her for a labor certificate—while she looked for work elsewhere, explaining that she "felt safer being on her [neighbor's] bond and not being dependent on [an employer] for a bond." Claudette seems to have worked out this system while she had small children and was staying on her husband's bond. It allowed her to negotiate her own working conditions without having to depend on her employer for a bond, but it also meant, of course, that she was undocumented and therefore did not pay taxes, just as the employer did not contribute to her Social Security. When the immigration authorities began to demand to see receipts from payment of income tax and Social Security before renewing the bonds, her neighbor could no longer sponsor her bond. This did not affect Claudette's employment situation, however, because her employers had never been involved in bonding her, just as they had never asked to see any papers, deducted any taxes, or made payments to her Social Security:

> So I just stayed here. When they [immigration] caught up with me, they took me to their office and questioned me. By then I had three children who were born here, and they decided that it would be too great a hardship if they had to go to Nevis. So I was allowed to stay.
>
> When I was working at the store, people didn't know whether I had papers or not, because I had been in St. Thomas for such a long time. But the migration went to check at the different stores, and when they checked me, I had no papers to show, and that was it. I worked at the store for about three or four years with no papers.

[Did that worry you?]

Oh, yes. In the first place, I couldn't go home to see my parents, because I wouldn't be able to come back in. So I could go no place. I could just stay here, and I was afraid that I would get hauled in any time, and then I would not know what would happen.

While Claudette still had a bond, she visited her family on Nevis at least once a year, taking her children so that they might get to know their family on Nevis. With no legal documents, this was not possible anymore:

The worst part of the visa problem was that I could not go places when I felt like it. One of my biggest concerns was if my mother and father died. I would have gone anyway. One night I dreamed that my father died and that I went. I called to tell him about it, and he said that my stomach was too full when I went to bed!

Claudette was undocumented for three to four years in the sense of living and working illegally in the U.S. Virgin Islands, but she remained undocumented for another five years in the sense of being accepted by the immigration authorities on humanitarian grounds but having no visa of her own. During this period, she was allowed to work, but she could not leave the American territory. She received permanent immigrant status only when the United States instituted a program to grant permanent visas to all individuals who had stayed for many years in the U.S. Virgin Islands with no, or only temporary, visas. Many other Nevisians, including Helena and her husband, Kevin, benefited from this program, because they did not succeed at converting their temporary visas to permanent resident visas due to the low annual immigration quota for British dependencies in the Caribbean.[10] Only Jim, who was married for a short while to a woman with permanent immigration status, managed to obtain an immigrant visa.

Yvette and Jean did not stay long enough in the U.S. Virgin Islands to benefit from the amnesty program. When they experienced visa problems, they decided not to stay, largely because their legal problems were closely related to marital difficulties. As noted, Yvette had traveled on her husband's bond, and she was not able to obtain her own bond but had to do domestic work in the informal economy. When her husband began to drink up his wages, she became entirely dependent on this limited income to support herself and the three children living with them at the time. Still, she had to stay with him because she was dependent on his visa. When he lost his visa, she finally decided to leave:

> He drank on the job, and the boss found out because of the poor work he was doing and let him off. He looked for another job. Drank more. He was on a bond. The immigration picked him up, but he was not doing anything illegal. We . . . were told that we could stay and have a hearing. If we won the hearing, we would get a visa. If we lost, we would have to leave. I told him to stay for the hearing. But I had to get some freedom, so I went home. He also went home.
>
> [If you had got your own bond, would you have stayed?]
>
> I don't know. I was embarrassed about his lifestyle. It was like being up against a wall. I am not sure whether I would have stayed.

Jean also learned that being dependent on a husband for a visa was problematic. When she married a Virgin Islander with whom she was having a child, she stopped having her own bond and went "on his time."[11] Apparently, her husband did not file for permanent immigration status for his wife, and when they divorced after a short-lived marriage, she lost her visa and had to leave the U.S. Virgin Islands. Rather than go back to Nevis, she opted to move to the nearby British Virgin Islands, where it was relatively easy for nationals from the British West Indies to find work.

At the same time as the siblings experienced severe difficulties in maintaining their status as certified alien laborers in the U.S. Virgin Islands, they encountered hostility and name-calling from the local population. Claudette recalled: "I never took them on, and they never came out and called me. But I heard them talk about island people—how they came here and wanted to take jobs and wanted the best. Some had good jobs, and then St. Thomians would go to immigration to complain about it to make them leave and go back." Helena's oldest daughter, Cynthia, also remembered being met by name-calling when she first arrived, but it stopped when there was a newcomer to pick on: "When you had been there for a while, a new one came so they would forget about you."

Emmanuel, Helena's son, remembered being put in his place when the local Virgin Islanders thought that he did too well:

I graduated as valedictorian of the [junior-high school]. . . . I remember being called *garrat*[12] [a derogatory term for a "down islander"] and alien, and that people were asking how somebody who was not from the island could be given those credentials. They failed to realize that I worked hard for it, that I had earned it. . . . As I was not from here, I didn't get any scholarship. But I had spent most of my life on the island, yet others spoke up about it. Then at the last minute they gave me two hundred and fifty dollars.

Later, when he became a teacher at the same school, he encountered hostility when he disciplined children of Virgin Islands parents: "The parents would say on the street, 'Who is he to think that he can do that?' " Not only the Virgin Islanders put him down, because when he looked for work to help finance his college education—illegally since he was on his parents' "bond"—fellow Nevisians who had achieved the coveted permanent immigrant status exploited him:

I had to work in the summer. I had no scholarship—what could the two hundred and fifty dollars do? It could hardly purchase books. I am not sorry that I had to work during the summer. If I worked for it, I would enjoy it more. I got into construction work. At that point in time—I was about eighteen years old—you could go and ask for work. I started out with a person from the same place that I was from. . . . But I didn't like the way he operated. I felt I was working and not getting an honest wage. When I did get pay, it was little or nothing. I saw people go out of the bank with a lot of money, and I got twenty-five to fifty dollars. I was ill-treated.

Emmanuel essentially described a local pecking order in which the more settled wanted to uphold special privileges in relation to the recent arrivals. As long as people kept to their place within this order, they would be accepted, but if they worked too hard and attempted to move beyond their place, this was disapproved of. When his family received permanent immigrant status, he was no longer subject to discrimination, and he added that he thought that hostility toward people from the other islands was no longer so important: "We are moving beyond that; most individuals have some kind of foreign link." Whether or not discrimination against outsiders as such was disappearing, Emmanuel and his family by then had become so established in the local community that they no longer felt the brunt of it. They had become incorporated, at least to a certain extent, into Virgin Islands society where, as noted by Emmanuel, most of the population had family ties to other places. Being a foreigner here was mainly a question of relative status in the socioeconomic system.

IMPROVING THE FAMILY'S STANDING

One of the reasons that the members of the Smith family were able to endure all of the racial, legal, economic, and social problems they experienced in the migration destinations was that they had migrated with a clear goal of improving their own, and their family's, standing in the Nevisian community, not of settling and improving their individual situation in the migration destination. As noted, this goal revolved around sending economic support to the family at home on Nevis and, especially for the men, saving enough money to build a home and have a secure economic foundation in Nevis. As family members stayed on in the migration destination, the main efforts seemed to be concentrated on improving the family home.

The first person to send substantial remittances to the family home was Patrick, who was the first to migrate to the Virgin Islands. Yvette remembered well the improvements that the family enjoyed when her father began to send remittances, "I guess he struggled there for a while, but when he settled there our life became easier. There was more to eat; we got better clothes; life was easier." The improved material standard of living involved not merely more comfort for the family, but also visible signs of improvement that would make others recognize that the family had "bettered its condition." It is apparent that Patrick's remittances were used largely on the home, an important material manifestation of improvement. Marilyn, the only sibling who never migrated, recalled: "My father expanded [the house], and we had more room and nicer things. We were among the first to get a TV. Everybody in Richmond Village used to come at night to watch TV. It was like a little movie house."

While Patrick lived and worked in the Virgin Islands he visited his family as often as possible and thus enjoyed the improved material standard of living—and the higher status that this conferred on the family in the village. Furthermore, he made sure that all of the children became acquainted with the place where he spent most of his time: "He came every year; he made it a point of duty to come here at least once a year, and mother also went there to him, leaving us. And at some point, we all had an opportunity to visit him in the Virgin Islands." Although Patrick emigrated, he nevertheless very much remained part of the home, with his regular remittances of money, food, and clothing and his frequent visits. The domestic unit was essentially extended between Nevis and the Virgin Islands, with some family members rearing the young siblings and looking after the house and the land in Nevis; the father providing for the family by working in the Virgin Islands; and frequent visits between Nevis and the Virgin Islands.

As the older siblings began to work abroad and send remittances to the home on Nevis, the household was extended further to include them whether they lived in the British and the U.S. Virgin Islands, St. Martin, or Britain. New members were also added to the home in Nevis, because several of the siblings left children behind when they migrated. Helena left three children with her mother for a few years until she and her husband were settled in the Virgin Islands. Jean left a daughter when she migrated to the Virgin Islands. Later she sent back a son and a daughter when the father of the children moved away from the Virgin Islands and she found it difficult to work and care for them on her own. Jim left two sons on Nevis when he migrated and later sent a daughter born in the Virgin Islands to the family home on Nevis when he did not like the way in which his daughter was being reared by the mother, a national of another Eastern Caribbean island. When Yvette returned to Nevis, her seven children spent a great deal of time in their grandparents' home. Finally, Marilyn, who stayed behind, lived in the home with her three children. Thus, the household functioned as a tightly knit system of social and economic exchanges between providers in the various migration destinations and child rearers and home keepers in Nevis. Similar relations developed between other Nevisian migrants and their home base on Nevis, and extended households therefore were an integral part of a wider Nevisian community of social and economic relations that developed between family homes on Nevis and relatives working in various migration destinations (Olwig 1987, 1993b).

A central theme in the siblings' life stories concerned the various ways in which they, from their particular vantage point, had contributed to this extended household and its material manifestation, the home on Nevis.

Helena, who had emigrated to join her husband, emphasized that he had
been considerate toward her family:

> My husband has been a very good husband and father, and he took care of all of us.
> Whatever money he worked for was *our* money, not just his to use. So we sent
> money for my mother that we left the three children with, and we went back every
> year and wrote often. And it never was an empty letter, even if I only could afford
> to put a five-dollar bill in it, so that I knew that she would have a good meal for
> herself and the children.

Edith depicted her life in St. Martin as revolving primarily around helping
her family. She even bought a large gas stove for Lisa, who at one point ran a
little store in Richmond Village:

> I just had to get it. When I saw it, I said, "That would suit Lisa." It had a double
> oven, and Lisa had a small shop, so she would not have to go by the stone oven to
> bake, and in the rain she could stay indoors. It cost me a lot. I saved the money up
> and borrowed some from the boss, and I paid her back every week until it was paid
> off. If I needed something, I would ask her to lend the money to me, and I would
> pay back. I knew my sisters had little money, so I sponsored their school things—
> Jim's and Jean's children I sponsored. Sometimes I wonder how I did it, but I did. I
> didn't think about me, I only thought: "The school is open, and there is something
> that they need."

Lisa, who spent a year with her father and Claudette on St. Thomas after
she finished school on Nevis, explained that she decided to return to Nevis to
help her mother rear her siblings' children who lived in the family home:

> I just felt sorry for my mother with all that portion of work. It was too much for
> her alone.
>
> [Which children did you look after?]
>
> All who were born on Nevis. Yvette's seven, Marilyn's two, Jim's three, Jean's
> two. All of them. All were cared for in my mother's house. Benjamin came when
> he was three months. Lucinda came when she was not walking yet. When I
> carried Roy and Debbie to Nevis, they were two and three. They all grew up

there. I am glad that I was able to help. I have no regrets about helping out with them.

Marilyn, who remained on Nevis, emphasized that she alone stayed behind and cared for her ailing parents, especially her father, who was seriously ill for many years:

> When I talk about my mother and father, I talk about them with a certain amount of pride. My father was in his bed for eight years. He couldn't do anything to help himself. Although it was like that, I am not going to take all the praise for looking after him. My mother did a lot, but at a point she couldn't. I had to do it. At times it was rough, because I had to work and I still had to look after them. I didn't have a husband to give me anything, and my parents needed looking after.

The siblings' contributions helped make possible the improvements in the material standard of the home on Nevis such as the expansion of the house and the purchase of a TV. This reflected well on all family members, whether they lived in the U.S. Virgin Islands, the British Virgin Islands, St. Martin, or Britain.

While the siblings received recognition for their contributions to their parental home, they would also be expected to obtain their own house, especially if they married and had children. Since a main purpose of acquiring a house is to gain others' respect, the house, as noted, is built not just to be lived in, but also to display the "bettering of one's condition" within a community of significant others. This means that young migrants who wished to gain others' respect by acquiring their own home might do so by building a house on Nevis rather than in the migration destination where they would be working and living with their family. Thus, a good house in Nevis would better their position in the wider translocal Nevisian community to which they belonged just as well as one built in the migration destination. During the 1970s, when Helena and her husband, Kevin, had accumulated the funds to construct a substantial and modern house, they built it in Richmond Village. They did so even though they already had a small, traditional wooden house on a plot of land that Helena had acquired through her paternal grandfather and had no immediate plans to return to Nevis. The family of six lived in a small rented wooden structure in a crowded area in the

Virgin Islands and visited the large, modern home in their village of origin on
Nevis for about one month every two years. The rest of the time their house
on Nevis was empty. They did not rent out the house while they were away,
fearing that the occupants might damage the home, the symbol of their
achievements abroad.

Helena and Kevin were by no means the only Nevisians to organize their
lives in this way. When I first did fieldwork in Nevis during the early 1980s,
migrants were building new houses all over the island, despite the fact that
they did not intend to return to Nevis in the near future and spent little time
in the houses. These houses gave the owners respect in the local community
and affirmed their ties to it. Apart from its symbolic value, the house also had
concrete practical value, because it provided a material home in Nevis where
the migrants would be able to live if they were to move back. Having a secure
home base on Nevis was of practical importance for those who did not have
permanent immigrant visas in the migration destination and who therefore
might be deported if they, somehow, failed to qualify for a renewal of their
labor certification. This, as has been seen, was for many years a real worry for
members of the Smith family who migrated to the U.S. Virgin Islands—and
with them the thousands of immigrants from the British dependencies who
had moved to a foreign destination in the Caribbean. Thus, it would be a
risky venture for them to invest in the migration destination, given their
insecure legal status. Furthermore, most of the migrants could not afford to
purchase property in the highly inflated tourist economy of the migration
destinations because they had to accept poor working conditions, being
dependent on their employers for the renewal of their temporary labor
certification.

By the late 1990s, the situation of Helena's family had changed radically. As
soon as he obtained the desired immigrant visa, Kevin was able to work on his
own, and within a number of years he and Helena had saved enough funds to
buy land in a fairly upscale area of the U.S. Virgin Islands. When I saw them
in the mid-1990s, they had recently finished building a large, modern house.
The house demonstrated their ability to "better their condition" in the affluent society of the U.S. Virgin Islands as well as in the village in their Nevisian
place of origin. Their success was well known in the translocal Nevisian
community and the house therefore improved their status in Nevis as well as
in the U.S. Virgin Islands.

While building a modern house on Nevis constituted a socially accepted and economically realistic way of displaying one's betterment within the extended Nevisian community, it meant that many migrants lived most of their lives under quite poor material circumstances in the migration destination. Some, according to Jim, even lived in substandard housing to save as much as possible. This, in his opinion, reflected badly on the migrants:

> There are a lot of broken-down homes in the Virgin Islands where the rent is eighty-five American dollars a month, and some people from different Caribbean islands live in them so that they can save money. I don't do that, because I have to carry a certain pride when I travel there [in the Virgin Islands]. When I am there, I will get dressed to go out and go to church now and then. And I can still support the family.

Here, Jim is introducing another perspective on personal betterment: the importance of personal appearances in the migration destination as well as in the place of origin. From his point of view, saving for a house in the place of origin does not lead to any betterment if it entails accepting subhuman working and living conditions. Betterment must also be reflected in everyday behavior, and a migrant therefore must have a decent place to live and wear proper clothing when going out or attending church.

Social recognition through personal appearance has been described as an important aspect of Caribbean public life associated with going to parties; participating in various celebrations, such as Carnival; attending church; and having white-collar or "pink"-collar employment (Freeman 1993, 2000; Manning 1981; Miller 1994; Olwig 1993b). In his analysis of clothing in Trinidad, Daniel Miller (1994) argues that certain styles are associated with the respectable sphere of the church and the home and are connected with the enduring relations of family and religious institutions. Other styles, however, prevail at parties, Carnivals, and other celebrations outside the home and signal the more transient relationships of temporary sexual unions and personal acquaintances. It is apparent in Jim's statement that it was rather more important for him to "go out" than to "go to church," yet he mentioned both, just as he emphasized the importance of living in a proper home and being able to support the family. He therefore sought to balance the individual as well as the family-based aspects of "betterment" against each other so that he did not engage in more fleeting relationships of parties and other public festivities at the expense of the more enduring relations of the family, the home, and the church.

Proper appearance can easily be a drain on the migrants' limited material resources, making it difficult to save money for house building, especially if there are also several children to support. Indeed, during his many years as a migrant in the Virgin Islands, Jim had not built his own home there or on Nevis. This was partly because he did not have the funds, partly because his relationship to the mothers of his children had been fairly short-lived—perhaps because he valued informal sociability in public places more highly than a formal domestic relationship with a wife. However, during the mid-1990s, he had built a house for the mother of his last child, who was living on Nevis, and with whom he had had a steady relationship for a number of years. It was not Jim, though, but his girlfriend, Wendy, who paid for the materials for the house on the basis of her hard-earned savings on Nevis: "The house was built with money that Wendy had saved. I built it for her, but since we were not married, I could not build the house on Smith land, because she would have no right to live on the land on her own." By doing all the construction work on the house that Wendy wished to build, Jim made the relationship more permanent and respectable, but she kept her independence by insisting that the house would be hers—at least, as long as they were not married.

Most of the Smith siblings had found it difficult to strike a balance between fulfilling obligations to the family, saving money for a house, and maintaining a proper appearance, all important aspects of "betterment," largely because they just did not have much money to go around. Several of the sisters ended up spending most of their resources on the family, leaving them with no home of their own. This was the case for Lisa and Edith. They were in the paradoxical situation that they had devoted a considerable part of their life to the parental home, yet they did not have any children of their own and had never married. This put them in a vulnerable position. Lisa, as noted, returned from St. Thomas to help her mother care for her siblings' children, and she in effect ran the family home for many years. She did not leave the home again until the late 1980s, when she felt the children were old enough to manage on their own, and joined her boyfriend, who was working in the British Virgin Islands. She enjoyed her job as a supervisor in a shop but looked forward to going back to Nevis as soon as she had accomplished her goal: "My goal is to accumulate money to get a house and a business someday so that I will be the owner and not the supervisor of the shop. But my first priority is to get a home."

Lisa did not expect that she would be able to meet these goals during the next ten years, almost twenty years after she had migrated to the British Virgin Islands, because her earnings were small and the cost of living high. Besides, she wanted to be sure that she did not return too early: "You know, not all the limes become big, yellow limes. And I want to become a big, yellow lime in good health. I prepare to go back home. I left to get away and to prepare to get something for myself: 'Mother has, father has, blessed Lisa if she has something of her own.' " Lisa here might be referring to her sister Edith, who had moved back to Nevis to care for her ailing mother after sixteen years of wage employment in St. Martin. Edith returned before she had what she might call "something of her own," largely because she had spent most of her resources on helping her siblings with their children. When her mother died a few months after her return, she found herself back on Nevis with little money to establish a life for herself there. She concluded that she should have saved more funds for her own purposes: "My thought was more about helping my sisters with their children. But I realized that I had to think about myself."

Some of the siblings were wondering what kind of "betterment" they had really achieved by migrating. Claudette noted: "You go back home, and you see everybody working and happy. And you are here rushing, paying rent, and you have nothing. Everything is kind of hard. Who knows whether it is better there?" Claudette is describing her life in the Virgin Islands as one long struggle that left her with "nothing" to show for it, because she still had to pay rent every month and work hard for her living. Meanwhile, back on Nevis everybody seemed to be doing well—they were "working and happy." For Claudette, a return to Nevis was a remote possibility:

> I would have to win in the lottery to go back. If I had the money, of course, I would build a big house and go live there. I would be away from the rush. Here you must leave the home at seven to reach your work by eight. I would need a nice place where I can relax, no mansion.

Indeed, Claudette had stayed so long in the Virgin Islands that she was no longer certain whether she wanted to return to Nevis to live. She added:

> I would build over here [the Virgin Islands] and there [Nevis] and go as I please.
> But if I could only build one house, I would build here first.
>
> [Why?]
>
> This is where I live and feel comfortable now. When I go to Nevis, I go for three or
> four weeks and I am ready to go back. I have my children and grandchildren here. I
> spent most of my life here. Here is home. I was born in Nevis, but I have spent
> more time here than there. My sisters who live there are busy working. And I don't
> have my mother and father to chat with any longer.

Even if she had no home of her own in the sense of a separate material
structure that would be a visible sign of her achievements as a migrant, she
had developed a home in the Virgin Islands in the sense of social relations and
an everyday life that made her feel comfortable and at home. These social
relations revolved largely around her children and grandchildren. With her
close relationship to her children, Claudette was rather better off than her
sister Jean, who had migrated from Nevis a few years after Claudette.

Like Claudette, Jean had seen few material improvements in her life, but
unlike her older sister she had not succeeded in establishing stable social
relationships that might give her a firm sense of home where she was living.
She had her first child when she was sixteen, but the father left the island, and
she never saw him again. Jean's mother therefore suggested that she go to the
U.S. Virgin Islands to provide for her child. Soon after arriving in the U.S.
Virgin Islands she married a Virgin Islander and had a child with him. When
they divorced after a brief marriage, she moved to the British Virgin Islands,
leaving the child with its grandmother in the U.S. Virgin Islands. She then
had two children with a man from St. Lucia but lost contact with him when
he moved to the United States. Being alone, she convinced her mother to
take these two children into the family home on Nevis: "At that time I didn't
feel that I wanted to go back to Nevis to live. I didn't feel like it. When I had
my first child, my mother didn't like it. And it was worse with four children. I
preferred to stay on my own." In the British Virgin Islands she had three more
children within a few years and did not manage to find full-time employment. Jean felt that others, including some of her siblings, "judged" her
because of her failure to care for her children (six of her seven children were
reared in the homes of various relatives) and her lifestyle (she liked to go to

parties). She was the odd one out in the family and noted that it had always been that way because she did not get along with her siblings when they grew up together in the home. When I asked her about her relationship to the family, she emphasized that she had a close relationship to Lisa, the only sibling who lived in the British Virgin Islands, but saw little of the other siblings: "It [family] means relationships, and that is what I don't have. I have my sisters who I don't call and they don't call me. I chose to live here; they chose their place. And I don't have a phone, that's it. We don't write." The sense of not having close relations to her family was painful to Jean, and she saw as an important reason for her problems the fleeting relationships that she had had with men—caused, she felt, by men taking advantage of her. These short-lived relations had left her struggling on her own, unable to care for the seven children born of the relationships, let alone send help to the family that she left behind in Nevis or acquire her own house.

Whereas several of the sisters who had stayed abroad were uncertain about what they had achieved abroad, Yvette, who decided to return to Nevis when she ran into visa problems, was satisfied with her life. This does not mean that she had an easy life, because she had to work extremely hard to support the family. Rather, she had a sense of accomplishment at what she had achieved, given her bad situation when she returned to Nevis:

> After we were back home, he [Yvette's husband] drank more until he was dead. Life was hard for me. What money he had, he drank. The money he brought back from the Virgin Islands he gave to a fellow to buy molasses to boil rum so that he had rum to drink. I left with my children to look after them on my own. All we brought from the Virgin Islands he moved to his mother's house. I had to take him to court for it. He sold the land and tools he had and drank up the money he made from it. All I was left with was the six children and the misery in my life.

Yvette found domestic work in one of the government buildings, but to keep her cash requirement at a minimum, she also kept animals, grew vegetables in her garden, and burned charcoal for cooking. Despite the hardship that she endured, she put her children through secondary school. She even purchased her own house when a small house was offered at a favorable price.

Yvette fully acknowledged that she would not have been able to manage if the rest of the family had not helped her. Her father had helped with the down payment for the house; the family home looked after her small children while she worked at wage employment; and her siblings abroad remembered her when they sent remittances to the family home:

> My sisters and brothers in one way or another have played a part in my children's life. When I was struggling, Lisa was here, Edith was here partly, and Marilyn was here. The others were away. They knew I was struggling with no help. Every so often my mother would say to me, "Edith said to give you this," "Helena says that this is for you," "Edwin asked me to give this to you." The need was there, and they always made sure to send something. Not just money, but also food, clothes.

Yvette thought back on her life with a certain amount of satisfaction: "I don't think I have done too badly. I raised them single-handedly. I see how other youngsters are. My kids have done fairly well. I find that I pat myself on the shoulder—I did fairly well."

The siblings' life stories made clear that the extending and receiving of help, and the grateful acknowledgment of this help, made the family. Yvette realized that in many respects she had been on the receiving line because she had reared her children on her own. She was thankful for the help and thought she had administered it well, because she had provided a good home for her children. Jean, by contrast, was less certain that she had been a good member of the family, because she had not established a home for her many children but depended on others to rear most of them. Furthermore, she had lost contact with all of her siblings except Lisa, who lived close by and visited her regularly. Though she was worried about her status in the family, none of the siblings condemned her in conversations with me. Rather, they noted that she "had tried her best" and had struggled to manage on her own. The notion of relatedness that shaped the family therefore was not so much an idea of having to give certain things or contribute so much to others as a sense of showing concern over others and helping if at all possible. It was a sense of concern for the well-being of a certain group of people, because the well-being of the individual depended on that of the whole group. This well-being involved everyday matters such as looking after children and the elderly in the family and obtaining the material means of living, as well as attempts to improve the social status of family members.

The significance of the family's working together as a group, and thus asserting both the closeness and the achievements of the family, was clearly demonstrated at Jim's wedding. This celebration became an important occasion in which the family members demonstrated their willingness and ability to work together. It also, however, showed that the family unity was vulnerable because individuals had developed somewhat different understandings of family relations after many years of living under quite disparate social and economic circumstances.

JIM'S WEDDING

I arrived on Nevis two days before Jim's wedding was to take place and found Marilyn, Yvette, Claudette, Jim, Lisa, Edwin, and Syvilla at Jim's house busily preparing food for the celebration. Marilyn and Yvette, the masterminds behind food preparations, were directing the cutting up and spicing of goat meat. "It is impossible to have a wedding without goat meat," they explained and looked with obvious pleasure at the hectic activities around them. Marilyn added, laughing, "If there is something the Smith family can agree to work on together, it is *food!*" They noted that Claudette and Cynthia, Helena's daughter, had done most of the shopping for the wedding celebration on St. Thomas; Jim had paid the bills; and Wendy had approved everything in Nevis. Claudette and Cynthia had bought chicken, ham, turkey, and roast beef, other important items on the wedding menu, and purchased liquor, tinned beer, and soft drinks. They were responsible for the head table, where there would be bone china, glass, stainless steel cutlery, cloth napkins, and a tablecloth with lace. The bride and bridegroom would even drink out of real champagne glasses, whereas the rest of the wedding guests would use paper plates, plastic cutlery, and paper on the table. Claudette and Cynthia were also in charge of the color scheme (peach and light green) and the selection of all the items that fit into this scheme. This included the printed programs for the church ceremony, the corsages that would be pinned on wedding guests, the small boxes in which the cake was to be served, and the little scrolls with the bridal couple's thanks that would be distributed at the end of the wedding feast. Finally, they had sent a catalogue with wedding gowns to Wendy and ordered the outfit she had chosen. Last, but not least, they had selected the wedding rings. The wedding preparations continued the following day with the cooking of more food, preparing of bouquets for the bridesmaids, and cleaning and decorating of the church where the ceremony was to take place. When all the food was prepared for the wedding reception, they had cooked seven goats, three turkeys, two hams, and fifty pounds of rice.

The wedding celebration began with the ceremony at the Wesleyan Holiness church in Richmond Village, festively decorated for the occasion with peach-colored and white balloons and matching crepe flowers. It continued with a sit-down dinner for more than two hundred people in a hall rented for the occasion. The siblings had never held a large wedding feast on Nevis, and everybody was eager to make it a great success that would reflect well on the family. It was apparent that Jim was asserting himself in the community of relations that extended between major migration destinations abroad and Nevis. The wedding guests included many friends from the Virgin Islands, where Jim had worked for about thirty years, and the celebrations were very much designed to give a taste of local culture to those who had traveled from abroad to attend the wedding, while demonstrating the family's mastery of modern ways. There was the traditional goat soup and the string-band music performed by a local group, called real "culture" by several in the family, as well as modern, imported goods such as the carefully color-schemed paraphernalia, the well-decked head table, and the bridal car, all of which followed latest fashions abroad. The local food emphasized the family's identification with Nevis and grounding in the small village where they had grown up; the imported goods reflected the modern global arena where many family members had lived most of their lives and showed that the local family knew the latest styles and fashions.

The wedding reception was followed, the next afternoon, by a large, informal party held in the yard by Jim's house for all of the villagers, most of whom had not been invited to the formal reception. At this party there was a great quantity of food and drink, freely served to all who came, and there were no set schedule of events, speeches, and formal seating plan. Again Jim's sisters had helped cook the food—goat soup, grilled chicken, corned pork and dumplings—and Jim had made sure that there was plenty of liquor. This party emphasized Jim's generosity, his close relations with friends and neighbors, and his firm grounding in the local village. By holding two wedding celebrations, Jim, and the family, asserted his respectability in the global fields of relations and the wider Nevisian society outside the village while acknowledging their rootedness in the village and showing that they regarded themselves as part of the local community.

Jim himself embodied the close interrelationship between the local and the extended community. He had grown up in the family home in the village but spent most of his adult life working in the U.S. Virgin Islands. It was his many years abroad that enabled him—and that made it mandatory for him—to put on a wedding of this magnitude and lavishness in his home village on Nevis. He noted afterward:

> More than twenty came from [the Virgin Islands]; more than two hundred came for the wedding. I made the wedding large to make the girl happy. My family said that they would help, and they did. I knew they would help, so I went for it. We started to plan the wedding at Christmas [about eight months before], and I went back [to the Virgin Islands] and worked hard. I paid for ushers' and bridesmaids' clothes. . . . The majority was happy with the party, like my friends from the Virgin Islands were very happy. . . . Don't even ask me how much the wedding cost, because I don't know.

Some of Jim's siblings noted that they would not have spent so much money on a wedding, but they all agreed that the wedding had given the family a good name in the community. This was not only because of its lavishness, however, but also because the success of the wedding had demonstrated that the siblings and their children could unite to organize and stage such a large event. This was important because after the death of their parents a few years earlier, the siblings had lost a central locus in the family. When Marilyn exclaimed, "If there is something the Smith family can agree to work on together, it is food!" she was not just joking about the great pleasure that most family members took in preparing and eating good food. She was also expressing great joy that so many family members had joined up from far and near to participate in the staging of Jim's wedding. When I interviewed Marilyn after the wedding took place, she described the family's accomplishment in radiant terms: "Because all pitched in and did what they could, the end product was splendid. It was a work of art done by the family."

It was quite apparent, however, and noted by some of the siblings, that some close relatives in the family had not participated much in the wedding preparations and done little to help in the final staging of the reception. Edith hardly seemed to take part in the activities, and Helena and Jean had not come for the wedding, despite the fact that both of them lived fairly close by in the Virgin Islands. When I talked to these three sisters several months later, Jean and Edith expressed the feeling that their family on Nevis did not care for them and ignored them. For this reason, Jean explained, she rarely visited Nevis and she did not intend to move back. Edith felt that, for some reason she could not explain, she had a tense relationship with her sisters on Nevis. Therefore, she chose to keep to herself most of the time. Helena simply explained her absence from her brother's wedding by stating, "I did not go to Jim's wedding, because I thought there might be some confusion [arguments or disagreements]. Many felt that my father's will was not right." Helena's premonition proved right. The good family feelings generated by the wedding celebrations were not strong enough to keep unity and peace within the family when it came to settling the inheritance of the family home and land. This inheritance did not merely concern the distribution of scarce resources among the siblings. It also, and perhaps more fundamentally, involved the negotiation of rights of belonging rooted in a family home that had essentially functioned as a "transnational household." The problems that Jean and Edith experienced vis-à-vis their siblings on Nevis were most likely related to their rights in this home, though in very different ways.

A CLAIM OF BELONGING

While the siblings were gathered on Nevis, they tried to come to an agreement concerning how to divide the property that had been left by the parents, but failed. It seemed that their disagreement revolved around who really had a moral right to inherit the home and the land. According to Nevisian custom, those who care for people in their old age will inherit the home and the land owned by these people. The heirs will typically be the children of the deceased, although they may also be more distant relatives or people who are not related to the deceased at all. When some of the children have migrated—a situation quite typical in Nevis—there are two different ways in which offspring customarily take care of their parents: (1) they stay behind with the parents, run the household, and care physically for the parents should they become ill and disabled; (2) they travel abroad and send part of their earnings and various goods to the parental home, in this way providing the economic basis for its continued existence. Usually, at least one child stays behind while the rest leave to help provide economic support.

Since the 1960s, the Smith family home, as noted, had involved an extended household with a division of labor based on wage employment in various migration destinations in economically developed areas outside Nevis and the provision of care for children and the elderly on Nevis. The family home functioned successfully while the parents lived. At their death, only Marilyn, Marilyn's three children, Edith, and two adult grandchildren were living in the home. While some family members continued to send periodic presents of money and goods to the home, the household was no longer the natural center of intense economic and social-exchange relations involving relatives living in geographically distant areas. Indeed, the siblings expressed a great deal of uncertainty concerning their continued ties with the home. This was not just because they had lost their parents, but because the parents had left a will making Marilyn the sole heir of the family home and a quarter acre of land surrounding the house. The rest of the land by the house, about half an acre, and the three acres of land located at a distance were to be divided equally among all the siblings.

The favoring of Marilyn in the will, as far as inheritance of the family home was concerned, created tension among the siblings. Several expressed the opinion that all had contributed to the welfare of the family home and that they therefore deserved an equal claim in the family property. Edwin explained that some years before his death, his father had offered him, the only married son, all the land. He had declined, he said, because this would not be fair, since all the siblings had helped support the home and the family there. He added that if certain people were to be singled out for having been especially devoted to the family home, one could not merely single out Marilyn but would also have to include Lisa and Edith. Lisa had worked full time in the family home and kept it in splendid order for many years, until she finally left for the British Virgin Islands, and Edith had sent a great deal of support back to the home and given up her job in St. Martin to care for her mother. He therefore argued that if Lisa and Edith were not to have a share in the house, they ought to divide the rest of the land next to the house, leaving the less attractive land in the bush to be shared among the rest of the siblings. Most of the siblings were in sympathy with this suggestion but noted that the will did give Marilyn a legal right to the family home and surrounding land, as well as a ninth of the remaining land. Marilyn, for her part, felt that some of her siblings had no understanding of all the work she had done, mostly on her own, caring for the parents when they were old and disabled. She was the only one to remain in the family home, whereas most of her siblings had left when they were young, lived virtually their entire lives abroad, and just sent whatever they could spare to help the family home. Furthermore, some of them had not even done this. She was therefore not willing to reduce her claim in the land or to share the family home with others. To do so would be to admit that she did not deserve her inheritance.

At a more fundamental level, the discussion of land concerned the siblings' right to be included in the family legacy and the sense of belonging on Nevis that this afforded. Everybody knew that the amount and consistency of contributions to the family home from the siblings abroad had varied a great deal, as had the siblings' dependence on the household. As long as the parents were alive, and the family home functioned well, the family had emphasized unity rather than the variation in individual contributions. When the parents died and the family property was to be divided up, some of the siblings began to measure and compare these contributions. This made, ironically, both Jean and Edith feel excluded from the family home. My guess is that Jean felt unwelcome in the family home because she knew that she had given little to it, whereas Edith sensed a tension in relation to her sisters on Nevis because she had no legal right to live in the family home, despite her extraordinary contribution to the welfare of the family on Nevis. She continued to live in the family home, having no other place to stay, but she had a strong desire to have her own home: "That is the one time I would be on my own, independent. I wouldn't have to pay rent or ask, 'Can I borrow the key?' I don't have to knock on a door when I come back for somebody to open it."

The inability to reach an agreement on how to divide the land meant that those who wished to acquire their own homes on Nevis would face even greater difficulties doing so, because they had no land. Lisa would have to prolong her stay in the British Virgin Islands to earn enough money for the land purchase; Edith would be forced to stay longer in the family home, where she did not feel welcome, or rent a place of her own; Jim would have to leave the house he had constructed for his wife on land he had "rented from strangers"; Edwin would not be able to build his large, modern home on his father's land. He explained, however, that he had reached a point where he would prefer to build on purchased land so that he could avoid further discussion of the land issue with his siblings. Lisa, by contrast, who had lived for many years in the family home as an adult, was strongly attached to the place and noted that she was the only one, besides her father, who had actually cultivated the land.

For those siblings who did not wish to build a house on Nevis, the inheritance problems had little practical importance. Nevertheless, the demise of the family home meant that they had lost what they considered their natural grounding in Nevis. Both Helena and Claudette saw this as an occasion to reorient themselves and, finally, to settle in the Virgin Islands. Helena, who had just moved into the large, modern house that her husband had succeeded in building after more than thirty years in the Virgin Islands, decided to relocate her Nevisian roots in this home. She explained that she had planted a "provision ground" by her house that reminded her of the family home in Nevis as she remembered it when her parents were alive:

> My father had a breadfruit tree, grapefruit tree, orange tree, tangerine tree. Since he became sick and went home, he had it for the children and the grandchildren, and it bothers me that they don't take care of it. We should have cherished it in memory of him. I plant around the house here to keep in touch with him. I could say, "We live in [this well-to-do neighborhood in the U.S. Virgin Islands]; we don't want a ground." But I am proud of where I came from, and what I am. . . . The ground I have here keeps me in touch with my parents and the life I had with them.

Claudette, who was a single mother and had no possibility of building her own home, was not able to re-create her Nevisian family home in the form of her own house and land in the Virgin Islands. She found in her children and grandchildren a new home in the Virgin Islands. Furthermore, she maintained her Nevisian ties by joining a club formed by Nevisians who had attended the same village school and wished to help the school in various ways. It organized social events to raise funds to improve the facilities at the village school. This helped Claudette transform her personal roots in her home village on Nevis into a broader identity rooted in a village-based Nevisian ethnic organization.

CONCLUSION

The Smith family described itself as originating in a small village of poor people who were struggling to establish themselves as respectable members of the local society. Their sense of relatedness was grounded in this shared struggle and the tight network of exchanges of help between the siblings and their parental home in which it resulted. For the siblings, having a well-organized and materially affluent family home in the village of origin therefore was both an important demarcator of the family's position of respect in the local society and a symbol of the loving and supportive family relations that they maintained.

The devotion to the family home in Nevis was somewhat contrary to the siblings' desire, and need, to establish their own home base. For the men, the acquisition of houses of their own was a precondition for the "bettering of their condition" that was necessary to achieve a position of respect as full adult members in their home community. For the women, remittances to the family that would enable it to improve its social and economic standing might give them social recognition in the local community. The longer they stayed away, however, the less secure their place in the family home became, especially after the death of their parents. Since the opportunities abroad often did not match the migrants' expectations of substantial and quick earnings, it was difficult for them to return and establish their own homes. At the same time, their prolonged sojourn abroad made it increasingly difficult for them to sustain a sense of belonging in Nevis, where their frame of reference tended to be more narrowly confined to the family home and the small rural village in which it was located. This problem became acute when the migrants' parents died and the migrants lost the family home that had constituted an important material and emotional link to their community of origin, making their position in this community even more tenuous. Several of the emigrant siblings were therefore reaching a point of no return, where the only viable solution was to establish new homes abroad. From the vantage point of these homes, it would then be possible to celebrate their place of origin as a more abstract, symbolic place of cultural identification.

PART FOUR ....

....

....

....

.... THE FAMILY LEGACIES

M igration studies have rightly emphasized that the family plays an important role in migration. It is misleading, however, to treat the family as an
established organization that engineers migration and provides the backbone
of transnational communities that connect migrants in different parts of the
world. The family does not exist in and of itself, even if there may be a social
ideal and societal institution called the family. The family as a phenomenon
emerges as individuals, through concrete "statements and practices" (Carsten
2000: 24), develop a notion of relatedness that they identify with "family." In
the previous chapters I have shown how the siblings, through their narratives
of shared childhood in a particular family home, generated a sense of relatedness that defined and demarcated them as a family. An important aspect of this
notion of relatedness was the understanding of the family home as a social unit
that gave them a certain social and economic status in the wider society. The
maintenance and improvement of the social position of this home therefore
was an important aspect of family life. As the siblings grew up and were able to
avail themselves of opportunities outside the local community, migration for
social and economic improvement became common practice. When they

migrated, the siblings did not leave as individuals pursuing only their own personal interests, because their concrete acts as migrants reflected on their family and its position in society. Leaving thus did not entail a rejection of the family, but an act confirming and supporting the notions of relatedness that constituted the family, because leaving was for the social and economic improvement of this family as well as for members' own personal development.

When the groups of siblings from the three families moved to disparate areas of the world, they departed with particular goals for social and economic improvement, defined by the cultural values and social norms associated with their family home. These values and norms influenced the ways in which the siblings responded to the varying conditions of life and possibilities for improvement encountered abroad. The siblings were exposed to a migratory regime that, at varying historical conjunctures, presented different opportunities for, and barriers to, geographic, social, and economic mobility. It is apparent that some were subjected to severe discrimination that had deep personal consequences. Despite this, the siblings were careful to describe their experiences in such a way that their sense of personhood, as defined through the values and norms of their family network, remained intact. Nevertheless, as the three sibling groups turned into dispersed family networks anchored in widely different places, they developed increasingly different practices and understandings of the notion of relatedness that defined and underlined their family relations. Furthermore, those siblings who did not enjoy the kind of "improvement" in the migration destinations that they and the family might have hoped for revised their goals, as well as the social and cultural significance of these goals. At the same time, most of the siblings founded their own family homes and thus constituted their own social units in relation to the wider network of relations of the siblings and their descendants. As a result, the feeling of belonging to the same family and place of origin in the Caribbean became increasingly abstract for some. These family dynamics are the subject of this comparative analysis of the siblings' migratory journeys, the lives they lived abroad, and the ties they maintained with their place of origin.

THE JOURNEYS

Members of the three families had a very different point of departure when they left their Caribbean islands. Some journeyed as graduates of prestigious secondary schools who entered foreign universities, and others went as early school leavers who primarily had their labor to offer. Some left from an economically comfortable, if not wealthy, home that provided leadership in a local community and associated with the higher levels of colonial society, and others left from a much more humble home that struggled to manage in a poverty-stricken village that had been more or less abandoned by the British colonial system. Some traveled to further their own careers, with support from the family, whereas others traveled primarily to work and send support to the family left behind.

These socioeconomic differences naturally placed the family members at very unequal vantage points in terms of negotiating the opportunities and constraints that they encountered in this engagement with the wider world. This, of course, is reflected in their life trajectories. The family members who traveled directly to foreign institutions of higher learning in the Caribbean, the United States, and Britain moved within the same Western academic environment that they had become familiar with during their several years of education at secondary schools in the Caribbean. For them, migration meant relocating in another setting, but not necessarily a shift to a totally different cultural environment. The family members who moved on their own from a small African Caribbean village to a Western metropole, where they had to find jobs and places to live by themselves, had to deal with a completely new social, economic, and cultural environment in which they were unprotected against the hostility of the local population and exploitation by unscrupulous employers. By contrast, those who had no obligation to send remittances to the family left behind—and even received support, whether in the form of a scholarship or boxes of food and money from home—were able to concentrate their time and effort on furthering their own career goals.

It is not surprising that the three groups of siblings displayed different social and economic profiles when I interviewed them many years after they had first left their Caribbean islands of origin. The siblings in the Muir family had held various white-collar jobs and were living in, or moving into, middle-class suburban neighborhoods or villages. They had settled permanently abroad, and only one had returned to Jamaica: William, who had purchased a small hotel in Jamaica. Most of the siblings in the Gaston family completed university educations in a profession or received other forms of advanced education, and several had brilliant careers within their fields. Seven had returned to Dominica, where they had become a highly respected family of professionals, whereas four remained in the United States and Canada, where they lived in primarily white, upper-middle-class neighborhoods among professionals. The Smith siblings had been employed in domestic service, construction work, merchandising, and factory work. With the relatively low pay they received, and with much of their earnings being remitted to the needy family in Nevis, it had generally been a struggle to make ends meet, and only two had succeeded in acquiring their own homes abroad. Three had returned, but not to an economically independent life in substantial homes of their own.

The three families' varying social and economic backgrounds provide a useful framework within which to account for individuals' migratory moves, career trajectories in the receiving societies, and possible return to their islands of origin. However, families should not simply be reduced to categories for providing background information on social and economic factors in migration processes. In the context of migration, Caribbean families can be viewed as units tied together by societal ambitions and moral obligations; these forces encourage individuals to pursue physical and social mobility, while remaining loyal to the family (cf. Chamberlain 2005; Glick Schiller and Fouron 2001). In Caribbean families, this has led to the development of extensive networks that constitute both a centrifugal and a centripedal force. Thus, family networks help individual family members move away to various destinations of social and economic opportunity.[1] At the same time, the networks offer belonging and identity, rooted in a shared place of origin in the Caribbean, to those individuals who through their own social practices and displays of moral worth show that they are members of a particular family. Thus the family does not just organize and structure migration, up-hold moral prescripts, or offer a source of belonging. The family is constituted, maintained, and modified through practices and narratives that generate those notions of relatedness that define family relations (Carsten 2000). In a Caribbean context, as noted, these practices and narratives are intimately linked with movements for social and economic improvement. A study of individuals' narratives of their family background in the Caribbean, their migratory moves, the lives they have lived in different places, and their notions of belonging that are grounded in the Caribbean therefore must be an investigation of the ways in which a sense of relatedness has been constructed and reconstructed through time. The close interrelationship between migration and Caribbean family relations becomes apparent when examining the nature of Caribbean notions of relatedness.

At a general level, the Caribbean family has been described as flexible and able to explore shifting opportunities and to adapt to different situations of constraint (Rubenstein 1987: 233–34). This flexibility and adaptability is seen as based on a "folk model" that all kindred "ought to live loving" and therefore to extend mutual help and support as the need arises (Olwig 1985; Rubenstein 1987: 233). Because of this, Linda Basch, Nina Glick Schiller, and Cristina Szanton Blanc argue, Caribbean people have been able to use "family networks of kin to provide access to resources" and to sustain family relations that link kin in place of origin and migration destination (Basch et al. 1994: 238). From a somewhat different perspective, Raymond T. Smith (1988) has documented the existence of wide-ranging family networks that consist of a large array of variously related persons. Caribbean family relations, however, have also been seen to be influenced by another "folk model" that upholds the superiority of the nuclear family based on legal marriage and living in an economically independent, male-headed home (Alexander 1973; Douglass 1992; Olwig 1993b; Smith 1996; Wilson 1973). Whereas the former model emphasizes extensive and open-ended networks of relations that share resources, the latter leads to the disassociation and demarcation of the status of a small group of people (Douglass 1992). Rather than seeing these as two contradictory models, I argue, they should be seen as an expression of the dual character of family relations. This duality may be particularly apparent in places like the Caribbean, where limited resources and structural barriers constrain the quest for social and economic mobility, and where migration therefore offers an attractive way out. Thus, though the wide networks of relations help individuals migrate and sustain those individuals in the early phases of settling in a foreign place, it is the desire to increase the status of the smaller family group that motivates the migratory move. Migration therefore involves a contradiction between dependence on and solidarity toward the extensive web of kin and kin-like relations and separation in relation to these people to consolidate and demarcate the achievements of a smaller kin unit tied to a particular family home. This tension between two different principles for family relations constitutes an important driving force in Caribbean migration processes, and it has a great impact on how individuals experience migratory moves. The complex interrelationship between diffuse communities of relations that facilitate mobility, on the one hand, and a small family unit associated with a particular home representing individuals' status in society, on the other, is apparent in the narratives of family origins.

FOUNDATIONAL STORIES

When the elder generation of siblings related their life stories, they took their point of departure in their childhood homes on their Caribbean islands of origin, where they had been born and reared. As they constructed their life stories, their narratives of childhood in that home served as a foundational story that rooted them in a particular sociocultural context in the Caribbean. This context gave special meaning to the lives they had lived and placed them within a social unit of personal relations with which they identified. As they constructed their life stories, they adapted them to the family's foundational narrative at the same time that they highlighted certain aspects of the foundational narrative to support their individual life stories. In the process of doing this, they created distinctions, affiliations, and discontinuities in the family's past that conferred on them, and their family, a particular status and identity.[2] Each family network developed a somewhat different foundational narrative, with its concomitant notion of relatedness and place of origin within the Caribbean.

The Muir Family   In the Muir family, the narratives put great emphasis on the family's background in the colonial British parish capital of Falmouth, where it had obtained a position of respect in the light-colored middle class of colonial Jamaican society. The siblings emphasized their family's European heritage and noted that their paternal grandfather had come from Scotland to Falmouth, where he established the shipping and fishing business carried on by their father. They described how this brought them into contact with people from the outside world, such as the European captains who occasionally dined with the family. They also referred to their maternal grandfather of Portuguese background. The grandmothers were described in vaguer terms as local or mixed, and little was said about their family history on the island. It was apparent that Emma had little regard for the "backward" village "in the bush" where she grew up, and the only aspects that she emphasized of her childhood in the village was her rearing in the Baptist church and her mother's strict upbringing, both of which gave her an excellent basis for entering the more sophisticated urban environment of colonial Falmouth. None of the siblings made any reference to the fact that Emma had been born and reared in one of the earliest free villages to be established after emancipation of the slaves, and apparently most of them had never visited the village, even though it is located a few miles from Falmouth, where they grew up. This aspect of the past seemed to have been "forgotten" in the family. The only links to the rural hinterland that the siblings mentioned were those they maintained with their maternal grandfather, who was the manager of an estate outside Falmouth and with whom the brothers often spent their holidays. As far as the countryside was concerned, the family therefore emphasized its ties with the estates, not the villages of small farmers. The family therefore inscribed itself within the privileged light-skinned, European history of Jamaica and cut its links to the black, African Caribbean history associated with the lower levels of Jamaican society.

Yvonne Davis-Palmer notes the desire to forget aspects of the past that are regarded as undesirable in her study of another early Baptist free village in Jamaica. She describes how some of the villagers wished to forget that they were the descendants of slaves, associating this past with "backwardness" and "failure" in society (Davis-Palmer 2005: 57). Davis-Palmer refers to such forgetting as "closure" and defines it as a "process of ending or sealing elements of the past, which includes the act of a person or group consciously forgetting." Such conscious forgetting may be difficult, when living in the village, and one of the villagers stated: "Remembering is easy; forgetting is a far more difficult path to traverse. I have no desire to communicate along those lines. I am a part of this village. I belong by my actions, not by remembering. I prefer the past buried and forgotten. It is one death rite which should be observed and I intend to keep it" (Davis-Palmer 2005: 57). The villager, however, found it difficult to gain recognition on the basis of her present "actions" rather than her historical roots. Emma Muir solved this problem by leaving the village, and the history that it represented, and seeking acceptance in the wider colonial society that Falmouth represented.

In their narratives of their early lives in Falmouth, the siblings emphasized the family's middle-class, or even upper-middle-class, position in the colonial society of Falmouth. They described their father as a person who employed other people to work for him, whether in stevedoring or fishing; the substantial, two-story family home and the two or three servants employed to keep the home and grounds in good order; the family's respectable social circles, which included employees in the colonial administration and people involved in various organizations at the Anglican church; the education of several of the siblings at well-known private secondary schools; and the "proper" manners that the siblings learned to master. The siblings acknowledged that the family fell on hard times when shipping decreased but explained that this occurred because Jamaica experienced a period of a general economic decline, not because the family suffered downward social and economic mobility. Emma's successful development of her own business when her husband's economic ventures faltered did not fit entirely into the accepted pattern of gender roles within the middle class, where women were expected to devote themselves to the home and the church. Indeed, some of the siblings referred to the store as the "family's" business rather than "Emma's" business; others stated that Emma had gone into business after their father died.

The cultural values that the Muir siblings described as theirs were similar to those described for Jamaican upper-class families by Lisa Douglass (1992). The Muirs' reluctance to disclose any family secrets to outsiders, such as the keen anthropologist, is similar to the desire to maintain the privacy of the family that Douglass found among the families she studied. This can be seen as reflecting the ambivalent attitude toward "outside" relations found in the middle class, as well as in the upper class. At a more general level, it may also be related to a desire to control the privacy and proper nature of the socially respected family in relation to the wider network of kin that included a range of relatives of varying social and economic status (Douglass 1992: 22–23). The gender roles cherished in the Muir family home also resemble those depicted for upper-class families. The daughters were to be turned into proper ladies with good manners, most notably illustrated by two of the daughters' being sent to a private boarding school that, they explained, also served as a finishing school. This emphasis closely resembles the "*culture* of femininity" that revolves around a "continual process of personal refinement" whereby upper-class women distinguish themselves from women of the lower classes (Douglass 1992: 246). Mastering this culture, Douglass argues, is "particularly important for a woman whose class is not clearly revealed by her color"—that is, for women who can be identified as of colored background (Douglass 1992: 247).

The Muirs maintained an image of themselves as a respectable family belonging to the better layers of society in colonial Falmouth, but the social and economic basis of this status was insecure. This was partly because the family had recently established itself in this society, and partly because Jamaica, like the rest of the world, underwent a period of economic decline beginning in the late 1920s in which the family's shipping business suffered. The difficulty the family experienced maintaining its status in Jamaican society becomes apparent in the migration narratives. Thus, the siblings described the moves abroad as both a consequence of their middle-class ambitions for further education that was not available in Jamaica and as a solution to the problem of finding acceptable social and economic positions in a hierarchical colonial society. In their accounts of their migration experiences abroad, the siblings described their family's background in the respectable, lighter-skinned layers of Jamaican society as providing a natural basis for mixing with the middle class in the migration destinations. It was apparent, however, that this attempt at mixing ran into severe obstacles, such as racial barriers that prevented family members from settling in white neighborhoods in the United States or limited job opportunities for people from the colonies in England. Their mixing therefore took many forms. In the United States, it tended to mean holding well-paid jobs that allowed them to live in large, well-maintained family homes in black neighborhoods and sending their children to private schools. In Britain, it meant maintaining the appearances of a middle-class lifestyle of respectability under much more modest material circumstances, at times aided by more affluent members of the family. This generous help within the group of siblings was combined with careful management of the information flow within and outside the family to keep a lid on those aspects of family life, past and present, that challenged their image of respectability.

The Gaston Family Whereas members of the Muir family emphasized the family's relatively privileged class position in Jamaica, members of the Gaston family downplayed this aspect of their background as much as possible. Indeed, in their life stories there was little reference to class in the sense of a system of social and economic inequality. They emphasized that they had grown up in a poor, remote village where they, as the children of the head teacher, had been part of the local community. They pointed out that the family house was located in the middle of the village and that the family had kept a store where villagers congregated to chat and have a drink. The family was also part of the rural community by virtue of the fact that their maternal grandparents were peasant proprietors living in the countryside outside the village, and the siblings recalled having visited them frequently with their mother, enjoying the simple life they led. Finally, the parents had been active in the Catholic church in the village, which served as the center of the local parish.

The siblings also acknowledged that their family had a special status in the village because of the father's position as headmaster of a school but stated that this did not give them great material benefits; nor did it place them in a higher class. It instead gave them certain moral and educational advantages that obliged them to set a good example for others. They had done this through hard work and dedication to education. The siblings elaborated on all the work they had performed as children growing up in the village: the cultivating of the land in the mountains; the keeping of the school garden when the other schoolchildren were on holidays; the tending of the store and picking up of supplies; the strenuous walks up and down the mountains, where the family cultivated crops for the home; the long treks to the port, carrying foodstuffs to be sent by boat to the elder siblings in Roseau. This work, they explained, was necessary to keep the large family going, given the modest income earned by a head teacher and the high ambitions he had for his children. In keeping with this image of the family as one of modest means but dedicated to hard work, the siblings said little about the people they employed to help them. Hired hands in the fields are only briefly mentioned, and there are merely references in the life stories to the domestic help employed in the home. The term "servant" is never used.

The siblings also said little about the fact that the family was relatively light-skinned. In the Dominican context, being from one of the French villages, such as Sainte-Anne, would have been equal to being light-skinned. Light color did not in and of itself confer high status in the colonial society, and the siblings dwelled on their experience of low status as villagers who spoke English with a French creole accent when they described their move to Roseau. It was apparent, however, that with secondary educations they were able to occupy positions in civil service and banking that would not have been easily available to people with darker complexions.

The Gastons' tendency to downplay those aspects of their childhood that had to do with their privileged position in society finds a parallel in the Swedish life stories examined by Orvar Löfgren (1989). Löfgren shows that in the course of the twentieth century, Swedish society changed from being a highly stratified class society to a social-welfare society characterized by a strong egalitarian ideology. This was reflected in the life stories related by elderly Swedes who had grown up in Sweden when the country was still a strongly hierarchical society. They, like the Gastons, did not elaborate on their class background, especially if they came from the upper classes. If they did, their references to class tended to be descriptions of moments of embarrassment when, as children, they had encountered special situations that made them aware of the system of inequality that once dominated social relations. In the Gastons' narratives, relations of inequality in the village were noted primarily by the younger siblings when they described the embarrassment they had experienced in connection with the father's increasing drinking problem. When the father was drunk, he lost the controlled, civilized manners of the middle class and adopted the "uncultured" ways associated with people of the lower class. This embarrassment was worsened by the father's habit of telling his children about their shortcomings in relation to this class system when he had had too much to drink: the darker skin color of some of the siblings, the poorer educational achievements of others, and the friendships and dating relations with people of lower-class background of yet others. If class relations were a source of embarrassment in the village, and therefore generally de-emphasized, the siblings did not hesitate to describe their encounter with the upper classes in Roseau when they arrived to attend secondary school. Since they were at that time at the lower end of the social hierarchy, they thereby confirmed their identity as humble villagers. In this way, they portrayed the family as part of the people and underscored that it was discipline and hard work, instilled in them by their father, and not special privilege that had led to their impressive educational and occupational careers.

With their family background, it was only natural that the family members should migrate for further education. Indeed, the siblings who traveled to Roseau, and later abroad, for education did not offer special explanations for their moves. Rather, they regarded them as a natural extension of the kind of life that their father had taught them to live in Sainte-Anne. Similarly, those who returned to Dominica emphasized that they had put their education and special skills to good use in Dominica, and that serving the country, rather than the desire for social and economic mobility, had been their driving force. Even though the Gastons had become one of the most prominent families in the new nation-state of Dominica, this was therefore not something that they bragged about. Although these siblings did not talk much about the family's prominence, those who had more modest occupational and educational careers or who had not returned to Dominica were quite aware that they had not made the same contribution to their country of origin—or to the family's image, for that matter. They therefore emphasized that they had served in other ways, either through their profession abroad or through their devotion to the family and the Catholic church. By doing so, they drew on another important dimension of the family legacy: the dedication to moral and religious matters that the mother especially had represented. This dimension was also cherished in the family, even if it had not brought the same prominence and recognition to the family as the educational achievements.

The Smith Family   Like the Gastons, the Smith siblings described their family as one that had a background in a poor village of mostly black small farmers, where it was necessary to work hard to make a living. Unlike the Gastons, the Smith family had to contend with much more meager resources, having to survive entirely on the parents' small farming and fishing activities. The Smith siblings therefore did not celebrate their modest background as a state belonging to the past that had taught them the great value of hard work and discipline. In their accounts, poverty was instead a condition of life that exposed the weak to exploitation. This was perhaps most dramatically illustrated by the European great-grandfather who had abandoned their black great-grandmother, leaving her with a child. As a result of this ancestor, some of the siblings had a relatively light, or "clear," complexion. This had not given them any privilege, however, and family members did not mention race and color as issues of special significance in the village where they grew up.

If anything, poverty had taught them that it was necessary to gain strength by uniting as a family, and family unity was a central, organizing theme in the siblings' life stories. When the parents toiled in the fields from early morning, the siblings helped and cared for each other, and when only meager rations of food resulted from the parents' hard labor, the siblings developed various ways of looking for food outside the home—not just to take care of their own needs, but to share whatever they gleaned from these explorations with the rest of the family.

In the siblings' narratives, the moves abroad were described as an integral aspect of the strong relations of caring and sharing that characterized the family home. The siblings stated that they had migrated with a view to sending support to the family home left behind and to returning as soon as they had gained the resources necessary to build their own houses and settle there with spouses and children as respectable members of the village community. When the siblings began to migrate for wage employment, several left children behind with the grandparents. Some of the children joined their parents within a few years; others spent their entire childhoods with the grandparents. These children were described as having stayed behind, or as having joined the family on Nevis, while their parents worked abroad and continued to be active members of the family home by sending remittances and visiting as often as they could. The family home expanded, so to speak, to include not just those physically present on Nevis, but also those who were working in a migration destination and supporting the family. It was described as a loving and caring home where all the grandchildren felt at home, with grandmother Miriam as the central figure.

Among the siblings, only Jean challenged the cohesive image of the family. She recalled that as a child she had not gotten along well with her siblings and preferred being in other people's homes, even the home of strangers. She thereby placed herself outside the united family. This accorded well with her view of herself as somewhat of an outsider, a position that was underlined by the limited support she had given to the family home. Thus, when I interviewed her, she stated that she had lost contact with most of the family and that she was not really part of the family any longer. Another important aspect of the family unity was the siblings' notion of migrating with a view to returning to Nevis. In their narratives, their prolonged stays abroad were described as being caused, to a great extent, by their desire to continue to help the family left behind, and the acquisition of homes in the migration destination was depicted as an investment that would provide them with the funds to build the substantial homes on Nevis that would allow them to return permanently. It was therefore not a sign of their having given up their plans to return but, rather, another strategy toward meeting this goal.

The notion of family unity received a concrete manifestation in the family home. In their narratives, family members emphasized that since its establishment during the 1940s, the home had been a focal point in the family network, receiving remittances from relatives abroad and rearing two generations of children, many of them the offspring of migrant family members. The material improvements on the home, the children's well-being, and the frequent visits by the migrant relatives showed that the family remained united. This gave them a position of respect in the local community. The family members noted, however, that this unity was threatened after the death of the parents, who had been key people in the network of social and economic relations among the relatives and central anchoring points in the family home. Those who were beginning to revise their views on whether returning to Nevis was as attractive as they had thought explained that the parents' death, and the inheritance of the family home by one of the siblings, had been a turning point in their decision to reconsider their plans. They explained that, with the death of the parents and the division of the family home, their most important tie to Nevis had disappeared and there was therefore less reason for them to return.

MIGRATION FOR BETTER OPPORTUNITIES—GENDER PERSPECTIVES

The three foundational narratives focus on the emergence of a family unit associated with a specific home in a local society. While the family home is embedded in larger webs of kin ties, these ties are not emphasized as significant in and of themselves. Rather, they provide the social context within which the smaller family group is seen to have emerged and constituted itself. The Muir family pointed to relatives who had given an important moral and cultural basis of the family (Emma's mother), connections with the upper-class society of planters (Emma's father), and the economic basis of a good standard of living (James's father), but it said little about other kinsmen. This set the stage for migratory moves that would enhance the social and economic status of the family. The Gaston family focused primarily on the father, a man who through his exceptional qualities moved beyond the peasant life of his own family, as well as that of his wife, and the notion of making oneself through hard work and discipline emerged as a strong defining feature in this family. This provided the basis for migration for further individual achievements that would reflect well on the family and created an understanding of migration as a way to obtain the means to further help and support the family left behind. The Smith siblings centered their narratives on the parents, who were dedicated to maintaining a decent home with a united family. They did so, however, not just by describing the parents' and their own struggle to maintain the home, but also through contrastive descriptions of ungenerous relatives who, they said, did little for the family, despite their relative affluence. The strong sense of commitment to the family home generated by a childhood of struggle provided a motivation for leaving both to support the home and to obtain a more secure basis for establishing homes of their own.

The foundational narratives related by the siblings had a dual purpose. Their description of the sense of relatedness that characterized the smaller family unit worked to root this unit in a specific social and economic context in the Caribbean. At the same time, however, they pointed to the need for the siblings to migrate to honor the moral values and social norms that characterized the family. While migration was associated with improvement in all of the families, the ways in which such improvement was sought or accomplished through migration therefore varied a great deal. These overall differences, however, are not so clear-cut when the siblings' life stories are examined through the prism of gender relations, which reveals some of the tensions between ideal and practice in the three families' attempts to improve their position in society.

Gender had a strong influence on migratory moves in the three families. In the Smith family, men migrated to amass funds to build their own houses and invest in businesses that would make them economically independent, although they were also expected to send remittances to the family. Since it was the man's job to obtain a home, the women could devote themselves to sending remittances to the family left behind. In the Muir and Gaston families, an advanced education was described as an important overall migratory goal. However, it was apparent that, whereas the men regarded education as a means of furthering their careers, the women were not expected to be career-oriented. Thus, while women in both the Muir and the Gaston families traveled for further education, once they had married, they were supposed to follow their husbands and give up their careers when there were children to raise—even those who were better educated or received higher wages than their husbands. This perception of women as the guardians of the home and nurturers of family relations accords well with the nuclear-family model based on marriage that is associated with the upper classes in the Caribbean, where the man is seen as the breadwinner and the women is regarded as being devoted to the home. From this perspective, women's education is valued mainly as a mode of ensuring that wives are well mannered, capable of running proper homes, and "good arbiters of 'high culture' " (Anderson-Levy 2001: 197). Furthermore, women's wage employment is regarded as extra money, not as an income that provides the necessary material means for a household.

The nuclear-family ideal, based on different but complementary gender roles in the family, did not match the social and economic situation of the three families. In the Muir family, only Amanda, who had married a medical doctor and moved to one of the Windward Islands, where it was possible to keep domestic help, devoted herself to being the "centralizing woman" described by Douglass (1992: 217)—that is, the woman who is "central to the daily life of family" but lets the husband represent the family in the wider society. Her sister Jessica continued work as a nurse in London, except during the years when she reared her son, as did their elder sister Sylvia in New York, who also was employed as a nurse for most of her life. Their careers appear to have been generated by a combination of economic need in the family, especially in the early years of settlement, and their own desire to work. Their sister Margaret, who had married a British minister before she finished secondary school and who never obtained further education, was not so well prepared for the labor market and had to take unskilled employment when she left her husband.

In the Gaston family, it was apparent that the father gave greater priority to the sons' than to the daughters' education, partly because of economic constraints and partly because the daughters were useful in the family home. The eldest daughter, Anna, was not sent to secondary school in Roseau. She received an education as a locally trained schoolteacher and stayed behind in the family home as an assistant at her father's school and a helper in the household until she left for England. Similarly, when Nelly did not obtain a scholarship for secondary school, her father refused to pay for further school-ing. She attended secondary school only because her godfather paid the fees. By contrast, her brother Mark, who similarly did not obtain a scholarship, was summarily sent off to secondary school and strongly pressured into per-forming as well as possible. These gender differences had a great impact on the migration trajectories of the siblings. Thus, when Anna and Nelly emi-grated, they had to seek employment in factory work and domestic service. After marriage, Anna spent some time in the home rearing the children, but Nelly opted for night work so that she could be in the home with the children during the day and still earn an income that could contribute to the household economy. Janet and Mary received secondary education on schol-arships, but when they finished, both of them worked for a while in Roseau, partly because there were no other opportunities for them and partly because it allowed them to help the remaining family on Dominica. When Mary refused to marry a local man from the better classes in Roseau, her father was disappointed. Both Janet and Mary ended up acquiring further education on various scholarship programs, and when they married, they resumed their professional careers as soon as their children were in school.

The sisters in the Smith family emigrated with little educational back-ground, and they had to take whatever work was available, realizing that the family home in Nevis, as well as the families they were forming abroad, depended on their wage earnings. Several of them were forced to leave their children for short or long periods of time with the children's grandparents on Nevis so they could continue to work full time. They therefore became an integral part of a large, extended domestic unit where the providers lived in various migration destinations, whereas those taking care of children, the elderly, and the family property lived in the family home. Helena enjoyed a stable marriage in which she benefited from her husband's support. She was therefore able to acquire a home in Nevis, as well as in the Virgin Islands. The other sisters who were single or divorced ended up with no homes, having no husbands to build them.

While women were regarded as being especially responsible for the family in all of the families, the implications of this responsibility were quite dif-ferent. In the Smith family, the notion that women are responsible for the home translated into both economic and social obligations toward the home of origin, as well as the household of residence, because of the structure of family relations. Since they had to split their resources between two places, acquiring homes of their own was much more difficult, especially if they were not married and therefore could not rely on husbands to help them. This is an important reason that several of the Smith sisters did not acquire their own homes, despite many years of work abroad. In the Muir and Gaston families, women's central role in the family meant rearing the children and being responsible for the functioning, and appearance, of the home. Only Amanda, as noted, adopted this role fully as the wife who supported her husband's career, the mother who reared their children, the housewife who kept a good home, and the responsible woman who helped in the community. Janet and Mary were proud of the contributions they had made to the well-being of the family. However, they had no regrets that they had also pursued their own careers. Indeed, Mary insisted on this even though her husband had a job that made him more than capable of being the sole breadwinner of the home.

The fact that the women's migration trajectories were shaped by gender roles that tied them to the family while the men appeared able to pursue career goals might give the impression that the men were free to live their own lives while the women had to subordinate themselves to the wishes of the family. This could not be father from the truth. Men were also subjected to strong family expectations. When they sought higher education and strove to attain good white-collar jobs, the men in the Muir and the Gaston families were adhering to family values that had been imparted to them from childhood. Even though he had a fine career as a successful businessman, for example, William Muir regretted that he had disappointed his family by not completing an education in medicine and thereby fulfilling its ambition to have a doctor in the family. He felt that he had let his family down because, as he explained, he had not "accomplished" what he "had set out to achieve." This meant, I suggest, that he felt he had not been the dutiful son that his parents deserved. Mark Gaston was proud of having finished a degree in ophthalmology but added that he was sorry that his parents had not lived long enough to see his great achievements. If they had, he implied, they would have realized that he was a worthy son who had lived up to family expectations to receive an education in one of the professions. Edwin Smith was happy that he had been able to send remittances to his parents and, at the same time, create a nice home for his wife and children in England, thus proving that he was a good son as well as a fine husband and father. When the men acquired an education or held a good job, when they purchased a home of their own and supported the family well, they did this not because it was the "natural" thing for them to do, but because they were living up to social norms associated with specific notions of gender roles in their family. As in the case of the women, the men's migration goals therefore were also very much defined by the family network's expectations and ambitions. However, the expectations of men—education, marriage, and the establishment of a family in a home of one's one—were closer to those of modern middle-class norms in the Caribbean, as well as in the Western migration destinations, than were the expectations of women. Those women who devoted themselves to the family—whether that left behind in the Caribbean or that in the migration destination—had greater difficulty experiencing the social and economic improvement that was the overall goal of migration.

RECOGNITION IN THE MIGRATION DESTINATION

An important issue that had a bearing on whether the siblings felt they had enjoyed any improvement in connection with migration had to do with how they were perceived in the migration destinations and the avenues of social and economic mobility that this offered them. Caribbean immigrants' reception and integration in the United States, Canada, and Britain has been investigated in a large number of studies in the past thirty years. "A consistent finding of these studies," Oswald Warner has noted with particular reference to research on North America, "is that Afro-Caribbean immigrants perceive that they often encounter and have to overcome upward mobility barriers that are racially based" (Warner 2006: 6). It may seem surprising that Caribbean migrants should make particular note of the existence of racially based barriers, because they come from societies with strong systems of inequality structured along systems of racial differentiation. Warner provides several explanations for this seeming enigma in a North American context. First, the racial hierarchy that Caribbean people encounter abroad is quite different from that of the Caribbean in that it tends to categorize people in either–or terms (either white or black) rather than according to a color gradient, as in the Caribbean. Many therefore find themselves in a new, usually lower position in the system of inequality of the migration destination. Second, Caribbean migrants are well acquainted with the North American ideology of equality, which maintains that all who work hard can enjoy social and economic mobility. For this reason, they are not prepared to encounter racialized hierarchies in North American societies but expect to enjoy the American dream. Such expectations, Oswald adds, are often nourished by knowledge of individual migrants who are seen to have "made it" abroad. Third, there is a long culturally ingrained tradition in the Caribbean of regarding migration as a means of social and economic improvement. The realization that such improvement is not possible will thus go against understandings of migration that are fundamental to Caribbean culture and society (Warner 2006: 7–10).

My life-story-based interviews show that, while the siblings encountered many racially based and other barriers to social and economic mobility, they did not always choose to emphasize these barriers. This, as Warner's analysis points out, is because experiences of discrimination are grounded not just in the objective consequences of social constructions of inequality but also in cultural understandings of social orders, movement, and individual improvement. These understandings, in turn, will be influenced by individuals' place in the systems of inequality in the society of origin and the receiving society and the avenues toward recognition and mobility that this affords them. Thus, I would argue that whether or not individuals interpret and act on the obstacles that they encounter as problems caused by racial discrimination depends to a great extent on what they gain by regarding themselves as racialized subjects. This, in turn, is dependent partly on individuals' particular background in the racially based hierarchies of the Caribbean and partly on the specific historical and societal contexts within which they encounter racial barriers in the migration destination. Many of the siblings therefore did not elaborate on issues of racial discrimination unless they saw themselves as actively involved in dealing with these issues. Rather, they sought to emphasize those avenues of inclusion and acceptance that allowed them to find a place in society.

Members of the Muir and Gaston families were quite light-skinned, and in a Caribbean context they would have been viewed as almost white. In the United States, however, members of both these families were classified as "black" on par with American blacks. This was quite different from the way in which the Muir siblings perceived themselves, because with their background in the colored middle class of the British colonial society of Jamaica,

they identified with middle-class (white) American society and acted accord-
ingly. They settled in middle-class neighborhoods of white professionals, sent
their children to white Catholic schools, and took the "stiff upper lip" approach, as one of the cousins noted. When they and their children experienced difficulties in gaining acceptance in American society, they created a
circle of family and friends of the same Jamaican background with whom
they maintained their social norms and cultural values as members of the
respectable middle class. The only Muir sibling to fully acknowledge problems of a racial nature was William. He explained that he had realized that as a
person of color it would not be possible for him to become fully accepted in
American society and that he would have to maintain his quality as a foreigner to escape being categorized as a black, and therefore lesser, person.
This had made him decide to move back to Jamaica:

> The [United States] has room for foreigners. It amazes me to see a black Spanish-
> speaking person be more accepted than a well-educated black American. The
> latter is not accorded the same treatment. . . . There is some respect, but the person
> is not socially accepted.
>
> [How were you foreign?]
>
> My way of speaking, and the culture. . . .
>
> [You didn't feel accepted?]
>
> I was not genuinely accepted.

In William's narrative, the existence of a racially based system of inequality
therefore was acknowledged because it was linked to his decision to return
to Jamaica. In this way, he underlined the significance of his position as a
middle-class, or upper-middle-class, Jamaican who refused to subject himself
to poor treatment in American society.

The Gaston brothers who moved to New York did not experience the sort
of racial discrimination at a general societal level encountered by the Muirs,
partly because they spent the first several years in a university environment
and partly because they migrated about twenty years later. With their strong
feeling of loyalty to ordinary Dominicans, grounded in their village background, they identified with the cause of the black Americans, and Robert

even participated in the Civil Rights Movement. He did so as a student, however, joining activities organized at the university, and not as the victim of discriminatory practices, and he regarded this as part of his development of political consciousness. Both Alan and Richard referred to having experienced racism at the level of interpersonal relations. Alan noted that, when he began to date a white American woman, she was disowned by her parents, leading him to marry her. This hasty move, he explained, was a major reason he ended up divorcing her. Similarly, Richard referred to discriminatory practices within the church, noting that they were a reason he had left his Catholic order. In these two life stories, as in that of William Muir, racial discrimination thus became causes of specific decisions, often linked to unusual acts, not reasons for lack of achievement.

None of the Gaston siblings mentioned having racial problems in Canada when they moved there during the 1960s, during the early stages of Caribbean immigration to the country. On the contrary: When Nelly's family moved to a wealthy, white suburb of professionals, it claimed to have been fully accepted. Nelly's husband, Adam, did note that people stared at him when he first arrived because there were so few black people in Toronto at the time, but he did not describe this as a problem. In Britain, some of the light-skinned Muir and Gaston family members seem to have passed as white, to a certain extent. Mark Gaston joked that he had no difficulty finding a place to stay in Bradford as long as his black-skinned Dominican friend did not accompany him. Henry and Jessica similarly emphasized that they had not experienced any racial problems in British society but added that if people did make snide remarks, they attributed them to ignorance. Mark's sister Anna, who was darker in complexion, also did not point to racial problems in Britain but described her relations with friendly English employers, neighbors, and family friends in glorious terms. The Smith family painted a much more negative picture of racial discrimination in British society and described how they were denied places to stay and decent employment and were generally subjected to derogatory remarks.

The Smith family probably *was* exposed to a crude and blatant form of racial discrimination from which the Muirs and the Gastons may have been shielded because they were fairly light-skinned and well versed in English culture, including the King's English. The Muir and Gaston siblings' denial of having experienced any significant racial discrimination, however, should not be accepted entirely at face value. Anna's children had insistent, if some-what vague, memories of their father being involved in a racial incident, and one of them even thought that this might have been one of the reasons they had moved to Canada. Similarly, while Henry brushed off the seriousness of the "racial abuse" he had encountered and emphasized that he had experi-enced no real problems becoming accepted in British society, his wife and children had another story to tell. They related that he had resigned from a low-level civil-service job that he obtained in Britain after demobilization and took a better-paid job as a welder because he had not received the promotion to a better remunerated position due to him. And when he met his English wife, his in-laws did everything they could to prevent their daughter from marrying a "colored" Jamaican. The Muirs' and Gastons' refusal to acknowledge any serious racial problems in British society therefore represents a desire to give a more favorable impression of their easy accep-tance in British society than actually was the case. This agreed with their understanding of themselves as well-educated people of Caribbean middle-class background who moved with ease in the wider world.

The Smith family's story of hardship probably did not just reflect the family members' actual experiences of racial discrimination in Britain, but should also be seen in the light of their self-image as a family who came from a socially and economically underprivileged background and therefore had to struggle to improve their lot in life. Indeed, a comparison of the life trajecto-ries of Henry Muir and Edwin Smith in terms of objective social and eco-nomic indicators would probably show that they had done about equally well.[3] Both had ended up as relatively well-paid skilled laborers who had been trained on the job. Both married, acquired houses of their own, and raised large families. Whereas their socioeconomic integration into British society was similar, the cultural contexts in which they settled were dissimilar. Henry had married an English woman and settled in a white village, where he had become accepted as the cultivated gentleman grounded in good English manners that he was. Edwin, who had grown up in an African Caribbean village on Nevis, where the British presence was extremely lim-ited, did not feel comfortable in the all-white English environment of Ox-ford, his initial destination when he migrated to England. He therefore moved to Leeds, where there was a large community of immigrants from St. Kitts-Nevis. For Henry, downplaying the difficulties he had met as a Caribbean person of color supported his story of full acceptance in the village where he settled. Elaborating on the plight of racial discrimination would have meant emphasizing those aspects of the migration experience that had denigrated him and violated his sense of personhood rather than those aspects that validated his sense of achievement and social worth. For Edwin, however, stressing his struggle against racism underlined his choice to identify with the African Caribbean local community in Leeds where he had lived for most of his life, and thus his sense of self as a person of black Caribbean background demanding social recognition. By doing so, he may represent the views of many of the migrants of primarily lower-class background who moved to Britain during the 1950s and early 1960s or to the United States and Canada beginning in the 1960s.

The issue of race is complicated by the fact that some family members migrated to areas where they were subjected to forms of social exclusion that were not structured along racial lines. Thus, the members of the Smith family who migrated to the U.S. Virgin Islands were subjected to severe discrimination, even though their physical appearance was not different from that of the local population. This discrimination was caused by their status as outsiders and their concomitant legal status as foreign workers with temporary visas or no documents. Their position as outsiders was further underlined by local Virgin Island perceptions of them as interlopers who took good jobs from the local people, only to send all their earnings back to their island of origin. While they were stigmatized in public discourse and offered poor working conditions at less than minimum wages, especially during the early years of immigration, Helena's relationship with her employer shows that close, family-like relations could develop between individual employers and employees. Helena's employer, a member of the old middle class in the Virgin Islands, systematically underpaid Helena, but at the same time, she showed great interest in her family in Nevis and extended various forms of help to the family that went well beyond what could be expected from an employer–employee relationship. She therefore essentially had been incorporated into the Smith family's network, where she figured as one of the economically and socially better-situated people who were respected and given special consideration but who could then, in turn, be counted on in times of need. This was possible because the local Virgin Islands employer and Helena shared an understanding of Caribbean family networks and saw an advantage in regarding their relation of inequality in terms of the moral obligations and rights inherent in family relations. When a close relative of Helena's employer realized that she had been underpaid for many years and offered to pay back the money owed her by the family, Helena declined, preferring not to turn the relationship into a strictly contractual one involving only economic remuneration.

NARRATED LIVES AND PLACES OF ORIGIN

The disparate ways in which individuals perceived their migration experiences underscore that life stories reflect not just lived lives but also lives as experienced by people from the vantage point of the particular time and place in which they are situated in their lives. William, who moved back to Jamaica, where he enjoyed a comfortable and respected life in the upper levels of society, preferred to describe his sojourn in the United States as a profitable and interesting experience but one that, in the long run, was unacceptable and therefore not possible to continue. Henry, who stayed on in Britain, was keen to emphasize the good aspects of the lifetime he had spent in that country. Edwin, who was still dreaming of a return to Nevis, maintained a much more skeptical stance toward British society. His sister Helena, who had finally acquired a comfortable modern home in an upscale neighborhood in the U.S. Virgin Islands, looked back on her migratory move with great satisfaction. Nelly, who enjoyed her retirement in a nice home in a Canadian suburb surrounded by family, was equally desirous of painting a generally positive picture of her life in Canadian society. Benjamin, who dedicated his life to working in his profession in Dominica, did not dwell on his experiences abroad and only briefly noted the foreign universities where he had obtained his medical training. To a certain extent, these disparate descriptions of individuals' life trajectories reflect important differences in migration experiences that have to do with the broader social, economic, cultural, and personal contexts within which individuals' migratory moves took place. These experiences, however, were perceived and represented in the light of the notions of relatedness that fostered and supported migratory moves within the three family networks. The life narratives therefore were about not just lives lived in different parts of the world, but also about individuals who constructed, and made sense of, their lives from the perspective of their position in a particular family network.

The varying migration experiences described by individuals in the three family networks, and the ways in which they are related and given meaning within the framework of family narratives, have important implications for how individuals define and identify with the Caribbean. As already noted, the three foundational family narratives in and of themselves pointed to different places of origin. The Muir siblings referred with pride to their respectable family background in colonial Falmouth and the cultural values that it instilled in them, but they ignored the family's "black" roots in Refuge. The family home in Falmouth was still owned by a branch of the family. Emma lived there on and off until she was well into her nineties, and the siblings stayed in the home when they visited from abroad. It was apparent, however, that the old home and the sleepy town had their heyday in the colonial period and that they provided a limited basis for belonging in the modern-day, independent Jamaican nation-state, where, as Diane Austin-Broos (1994b: 11) notes, the notion of race "has changed, not least through the accumulation of symbolic capital by black Jamaicans." The Muir siblings' Jamaican identity, in other words, was grounded in the past, and they had no intention to return to their Jamaican origins.

While the Muirs had "forgotten" their rural origins, the Gastons emphasized their origins in the French creole village of Sainte-Anne. The siblings who returned to Dominica, however, settled not in rural Sainte-Anne but in the capital, Roseau, where they could work within their professions and contribute to the development of the new country. None of the siblings expressed any regret at the loss of the family's village home when it was sold.

The Smith siblings had strong emotional ties to their family home in the African Caribbean community of Richmond Village. They had not only grown up together in the home but had also provided considerable support to the home and returned for visits as often as possible. Their Nevisian identity was therefore very much associated with the home, and the village in which it was located, and those who had remained abroad had only limited contact with the wider society of the modern nation-state of St. Kitts–Nevis. When the home was inherited by one of the siblings, those who remained abroad lost their most direct and concrete source of belonging on Nevis. Some still hoped, eventually, to move back and settle in their own homes on Nevis; others decided it was time to settle permanently in the migration destination.

The disparate ways in which the three families constructed their Caribbean origins led to very different sources of belonging and identification rooted in the Caribbean. The Muir family's Jamaican identity was rooted in the colored middle classes who had had a privileged position during the late-British-colonial period, and it was cultivated in the private circle of close family and friends. The Gaston family's Dominican identity was associated with the independent Dominican nation, where several members of the family had made a name for themselves through public service, and confirmed through close relations to these relatives and visits to the island. Color played less of a role here, perhaps because color is less of a factor in Dominican society. The Smith family's Nevisian identity remained grounded in the old family home village of origin. As the village became an increasingly remote place for those who had lived most of their lives abroad, they redefined or relocated this place of identification and developed new sources of belonging that celebrated aspects of this home. Helena developed a garden by her new house in the Virgin Islands that reminded her of her parents' home, whereas Claudette joined a Nevisian organization in the Virgin Islands that sought to help the local village school that she had attended as a child. Edwin and Lisa, however, continued to hope that they would be able to build—and eventually settle in—homes of their own in their village of origin.

STUDYING MIGRANTS

Research in the social sciences tends to reflect contemporary societal concerns in terms of both the topics investigated and the theoretical approaches applied. Migration studies are an excellent example of this. Recent reviews of migration research demonstrate how topics of investigation and analytical approaches within this field of investigation have changed through time in accordance with societal views of migration and migrants. In a British context, migration research developed when the country experienced massive immigration of people from declining British colonies in search of work in the reconstruction of postwar British society. As a result, Mary Chamberlain (1998: 6) states, the migrants were "seen to be primarily black and colonial, poor and dependent." Early migration research, working under the assumption that these new arrivals would become assimilated into British society, concentrated on "charting migrant settlement profiles" and "hypothesizing on the nature and practice of racial prejudice and discrimination." As assimilation policies began to be questioned, researchers moved toward studies of "racial prejudice and discrimination" and offered "social, cultural and historical explanations of, for instance, underachievement by, in particular, West Indians." With the introduction of the notion of a multicultural society, this research orientation, in turn, gave way to a focus on "ethnicity, on its impact on politics, on nationhood, on new cultural—hybrid—formations and finally on the meanings of identity and the nature(s) of subjectivities," most notably "subjectivity and gender" (Chamberlain 1998: 7).

In a North American context, where migration has played a key role in the foundation and further development of the modern nation-states, early studies, as Nancy Foner has pointed out, "emphasized the way immigrants were assimilating and becoming American; ties to the home society were often interpreted as 'evidence for, or against, Americanization' and, in many accounts, were seen as impeding the assimilation process" (Foner 2000: 185). As ethnic diversity and cultural pluralism became accepted features of American society, migration scholarship moved toward investigating transnational relations between immigrants' receiving country and country of origin: "Once ignored or reviled, transnational ties are now a favorite topic at conferences and are sometimes even celebrated in today's multi-cultural age" (Foner 2000: 184).[4] In recent scholarship, there has been increasing criticism of the great focus on the ethnicity of migrants and their descendants and its impact on integration processes in the receiving society. This concern with ethnicity, it is argued, is similar to the "culture-of-poverty" arguments advanced during the 1960s, in which the culture of poor people is blamed for their socially and economically disadvantaged position in society (Pierre 2004). As the nature of modern society has become subjected to critical investigation, North American migration research has also begun to critically examine the technologies of governmentality whereby the receiving countries attempt to shape immigrants into new citizens (Ong 2003).

While these approaches to migration represent different theoretical perspectives and interpretations that highlight various aspects of the migration process, they have a common frame of reference in the receiving country. Thus, they study immigration, not migration; forms of incorporation into a migration destination, not life trajectories unfolding in a wide variety of places throughout the world; cultural expressions of minority populations, not the cultural contexts of life that people seek to establish within various socioeconomic environments. In this analysis, I have sought to shift the focus of study from the point of view of the receiving country to the perspective of those who move by exploring the role of migration within a Caribbean framework. This may be interpreted to represent a return to regional ethnography that can have only limited interest to those who are not area specialists. I suggest, instead, that it means abandoning national frameworks of investigation defined by contemporary social concerns and cultural politics and returning to in-depth research on the relationship between physical movement, social position, and places of belonging on a global scale. Such fundamental issues are a vital concern to the comparative discipline of anthropology in general and, in particular, to the more specialized area of migration research, especially as it is tied to basic research on different ethnographic areas. In the next chapter, I will extend this ethnographically informed approach as I analyze how the second and third generations in the three family networks construct places for themselves in societies where most of them are defined in terms of a categorical "other" originating elsewhere.

When the first generation of siblings narrated their life stories, they did so with reference to notions of relatedness generated by their shared childhood in specific family homes in the Caribbean. Though the siblings experienced different life trajectories that had taken them to different parts of the world, they sought to account for these differences in such a way that they fit into a collective family narrative that, to a great extent, constituted their "Caribbean" identity. In the siblings' narratives, their Caribbean roots, family background, and personal history thus blend imperceptibly.

When the siblings' children narrated their life stories, they had a varied point of departure.[1] They were born and reared in different parts of the world, ranging from immigrant areas in the gateway cities of major migration destinations to middle-class suburbs and rural communities, as well as various cities, towns, and villages in the Caribbean. Furthermore, as adults their lives differed significantly, and defy easy categorization. The second generation in each family network included financially secure, well-educated individuals, as well as relatively uneducated individuals who were struggling to manage with limited means. And it included nuclear families, single parents with children, and singles, as well as extended families of various kinds. This chapter explores how, from their differing vantage points in various parts of the world, the cousins and their children have experienced their family networks and the relatedness that they involve. What significance can common origins in a distant family home in the Caribbean, and the social norms and cultural values with which it is associated, have for people who live such diverse lives?

The analysis of the life stories related by the cousins and their children shows that the family networks meant many different things to different individuals, not just because they lived in disparate areas of the world, but also because their personal circumstances of life varied a great deal. Generally, however, the family networks were valued because each had a foundational story linking individuals with a common ancestral place of origin in the Caribbean while pointing to expected futures for succeeding generations. The networks thus provided a community of belonging that accounted for individuals' personal Caribbean background as it gave meaning and purpose to their present-day lives. While some lived up to the family's expectations, others were less successful. The cousins in the second generation therefore experienced the family network as a variegated field of social relations where some relatives had a central position and others were more marginal. This led some to reject the family or, more commonly, to adjust the notion of relatedness that defined the community of belonging. The significance that individuals attached to the family networks therefore depended to a great extent on whether they were able to see their own life stories as meaningful in relation to the network's foundational stories.

For the vast majority, being part of the family network was not entirely a private matter, because they lived in societies where their physical appearance bestowed them with a social identity (Jenkins 1996) as part of a minority. They were defined as either a racial group ("blacks") or an ethnic group (for example, "West Indians" or "African Caribbean"). The personal link to a Caribbean place of origin in the form of concrete family relations and a family history provided a means whereby they could give the externally imposed social identity personal meaning and form. This enabled them to escape the "colonization, massification, or anonymization of the human subject" that often takes place when identity is conferred on people merely by virtue of their being associated with a certain "nation or a group" (Cohen 1996: 803). Most of the cousins and their children were thus keen to maintain a sense of belonging in the community of family relations that rooted them in the Caribbean. The family's foundational stories, and the futures that they staked out for family members, played a key role in the family members' attempt to create their own identity as "Caribbean."

THE FOUNDATIONAL STORIES HANDED DOWN

Most of the cousins learned a considerable amount about their family through the foundational stories related by the parents, who had grown up in the family home. Mary Gaston's daughter, Louisa, described her childhood in New York as one where her mother's stories about growing up in the family home in Dominica were daily fare:

> Mom talked constantly about the family in terms of what she didn't have, like electricity. Her dad was blind, her mother died, and she had to take a boat to school. Ben was mean, and Janet and Ina raised them. Dad didn't talk much, but his brothers and sisters did. I loved the fact that we were West Indian.
>
> [Why?]
>
> I wanted to be different and unique. We had a family, and that was so much better than what others had—the closeness, all these people to call mine.

In the Gaston family, the cousins often spoke about the family home as rather poor, with many children inculcated with the values of "education," "discipline," and "hard work" who had "to fight for what they have now." In the Muir family, the cousins described the Jamaican family home as well established and respected in the local community at the same time as they were careful not to identify with the class- and race-based hierarchy of colonial Jamaican society. Thus, I often heard such statements as: "My grandfather and grandmother carried a lot of respect. They were not poor people. They built up respect. Grandmother treated people equally, although her husband was called 'mastie' by the servants. When you are in Jamaica, people know the Muir family." Education that reflects personal qualifications, not inherited privilege, was projected as the primary means whereby the family might consolidate, or even improve, its position in Jamaican society.

In the Smith family, many of the cousins had grown up in the family home and experienced it at close hand. When they talked about the home, they were therefore relating their own childhood experiences. Their narratives, however, fit the overall Smith family foundational story of a poor but caring and sharing family. Miriam, the grandmother, figured centrally in the cousins' stories, such as this one:

> We were so many in a small house, but we had good relations, we got along. We made jokes. We would fight, but that didn't stop us. I slept with Benjamin at night, so I could be vex with him at night, I had to sleep with him. . . . We were all in the home, and grandmother was mother for all of us. Nobody worried about their original mother. . . . They had only grandmother. But it didn't make a big difference, because grandmother gave to all.

Most of them also emphasized that aunt Lisa played a central role in the home: "She was very serious about us. She always tried to do the right thing. She was the one who was responsible for our growing up. She would dress us, get our clothes together, comb up our hair, until we were old enough to manage. She was like my mother, and I got to love her." Among the Smith cousins, stories of the family home therefore were accounts of the sense of relatedness they developed by living, joking, fighting, sleeping in the same bed together, and sharing the mother-like figures of the grandmother, who "gave to all," and Lisa, who was "responsible for their growing up." But, as will be seen, they were also stories of expectations to lead decent lives and make the most of new opportunities.

Most of the cousins in the three family networks, who grew up outside their Caribbean place of origin, developed close relations with family members and an understanding of their origins by virtue of living in one of the major Caribbean migration destinations surrounded by relatives and close family friends. This was especially the case for those who lived in New York, Toronto, Leeds, and the Virgin Islands. Some of the cousins also spent extended periods with their family on the island of origin. In the Muir family, the cousins in the New York area stayed for several summers with their grandmother in her home in Falmouth, and in the Gaston family, the children of Christopher, Mark, Benjamin, Janet, and Robert lived with their parents in Roseau for at least part of their childhood. In the Smith family, many of the cousins, as noted, were reared in the family home on Nevis, and those who lived in the Virgin Islands spent many of their summer holidays on

Nevis. The mesh of family relations within which most of the cousins were reared meant that they grew up sharing firsthand experiences of their family's place of origin and knew the relatives living there well. This provided an important setting for maintaining the foundational family narratives that gave the cousins a sense of their origins as well as goals for their own lives.

POSSIBLE AND EXPECTED FUTURES

Narratives not only account for past lives but point to possible, or even expected, futures (cf. Bruner 1986; Ochs and Caps 1996; Whyte and Whyte 2004). The foundational family narratives described a smaller group of relatives born and reared in a family home who had taken it upon themselves to migrate for improvement of self and, thereby, the family. This had resulted in the dispersal of the family. It was apparent to the cousins, who were born in the lands of social and economic opportunities, that they were expected to continue the family tradition of seeking improvement. If they did not do so, the foundational narrative would lose its meaning, or they would become peripheral in the family network as others took it upon themselves to carry on the tradition.

In all of the families, the second generation of cousins realized that doing well in school and receiving an education were highly valued means of improvement. The Muir cousins were well aware that an important migration goal for the parents was further education, and that the family was disappointed when William did not succeed in becoming a medical doctor. They realized that they were now expected to fulfill family aspirations because the parents had sent them to the best private schools available and made sure that they stayed inside studying while neighboring children were outside playing. The educational mission was a success because most of the cousins attended college and received an education in a range of professions, including the highly coveted one of medicine. An important aspect of this success was the family's inculcating in the cousins that they were bound for further education, not unskilled labor, even when the surrounding society might have had different expectations of black children. Thus, Kathy was devastated when her high-school counselor told her that she was suited only for agricultural work, but still went ahead and applied to a number of colleges and got accepted to all of them with scholarships.

Louisa emphasized the significance of having a family that saw further education as a goal. She explained that the many family members in the Gaston family with a higher education had been an important source of inspiration for her: "Such great people, doing things, succeeding. When things were bad in college, all these people had succeeded and had it so much harder than me. It was part of my motivation." In this family, where the eldest generation had done so well, further education was not so much a goal as a "natural" expectation that went with being part of the family.

The Smith family had a far less privileged background as far as education was concerned, because none of the first generation of siblings who migrated had attended secondary school, and several had not even finished primary school in the village. Education therefore was not specified as a migration goal by the Smith siblings. However, they knew that education was a chief mode of social and economic mobility, and when they discovered the educational opportunities abroad, they encouraged their children to avail themselves of them. Edwin, for example, noted that a main reason he had decided to stay in England rather than return to Nevis as planned was that he wanted his children to benefit from the educational opportunities in England. Several of the Smith cousins underscored that they had taken full advantage of the possibilities for further education that opened up for them. Susanna noted that when she began to work after finishing secondary school in Leeds, she was the only employee who accepted the employer's offer to pay for college courses. She completed several years of study for a diploma in catering. Her brother and sister in Leeds similarly continued their education while working and ended up with university degrees. In the Virgin Islands, the cousins attended the local university, and several received their bachelor of arts degrees. Though their parents had encouraged them, they had nevertheless not benefited from the kind of support that the Muir and Gaston cousins had received. Some of the cousins therefore described their educational achievements as the result of a struggle where they had to work their way through college and, in some cases, had not been able to pursue all their educational ambitions. This emphasis on struggle, of course, was in keeping with the family's foundational narrative.

Not all of the cousins, however, had entirely positive experiences with education. Especially in the Gaston and the Muir families, some of the cousins felt that they had been subjected to heavy pressure to study particular subjects. Kathy recalled that the family ambition that she become a medical doctor prevented her from attending a high school for the creative arts and pursuing a career in dance. Louisa joked that she had the choice to become either president of the United States or a medical doctor and therefore settled on the latter, more realistic option. Several of her cousins in Britain, the United States, and Canada stated that they had been expected to study for a profession in law, medicine, or the technical sciences and that they felt they had failed the family when they chose other career paths. Insofar as a further education seemed no longer to be merely a possible future but, instead, an expected life trajectory, these cousins were essentially given the understanding that being a proper family member equaled receiving a university degree in certain accepted fields.

The notion of what constitutes a proper family member can be viewed as an aspect of the dual nature of Caribbean family relations. As discussed in chapter 7, this dual character has been described as being characterized, on the one hand, by open, wide-ranging networks of relations, exploring various social and economic opportunities, and, on the other, by small social units working for higher status in society. The cousins who did not live up to the expectations in their particular family sensed that they had disappointed their parents, who feared that their branch of the family would be relegated to the periphery of the family network as the successful children of the other siblings validated and asserted the high status of the family. As Peter Gaston expressed it, if they did not do well, they felt that they were "letting somebody down."

The fear of failure and marginalization was experienced even more strongly with regard to another central dimension in family relations: sexual relations and marriage. In the Caribbean, a "respectable" family home based on holy matrimony is an important marker of middle-class status that is contrasted with the out-of-wedlock sexual relations resulting in "outside" children that are associated with people of lower-class background. Extramarital sexual relations therefore will often be condemned not only because they may be considered "amoral," but also because they are seen to represent the "unsocialized satisfaction of needs" believed to characterize the lower classes (Alexander 1973: 307–308). "Illegitimate children," however, primarily decrease the status of women and, according to Alexander (1973: 309), men who have a well-established middle-class status may assert their position of power—for example, toward the wife—by engaging in sexual relations with other women as long as they provide support for the children (see also Douglass 1992: 191).

In the three family networks, the ideal of the nuclear family based on marriage was impressed on the cousins. Extramarital relations and outside children did not belong in the life trajectories projected by family narratives, and they therefore resulted in strong disapproval of the offending family members. Louisa thus described pregnancy out of wedlock as "very, horribly" shameful and added, "It is a very judgmental family. My generation did not have a chance just to be." Joanna, one of Louisa's cousins, felt the full brunt of the family's judgment when she visited the Gaston family in Dominica as a young single mother with a small child:

> I wasn't proud of what I had done, but mom was embarrassed. She supported me but worried about what the neighbors, cousins, aunts, uncles might say. It made me feel rebellious; it made me realize that there was too much emphasis on values like job, money, the academic, not enough on the creative. I felt creative; my accomplishments in the writing of poetry were not appreciated. All I felt was different. I associated with the Caribbean Indians, with Africa. I felt that the family did not think like me in terms of identity. I had stronger association with my African descent and Carib history. As a result, I wanted to do my own diploma in Caribbean history, and I have written a book about it.

She thus reacted to her family's rejection by seeking a new identity based on her Carib and African roots and she replaced her English first name with an African name. Joanna's preoccupation with her Carib and African roots can be interpreted in the light of the great interest in African roots, and roots in general, that emerged, in the Caribbean and in North America and Europe during the 1970s.[2] Within the context of the Gaston family, it is interesting that she chose to cultivate these roots as a form of protest against the values of the Gaston family. However, she cultivated her new identity in a very Gaston-like manner: by taking an education and writing a book, both academic pursuits that were highly valued, and strongly approved of, by the family. Despite her professed rebellion, she maintained close relations to her parents and had recently returned from a visit to Dominica when I met her.

In the Muir family, the elder generation emphasized the importance of marrying and remaining married, even when the marriage might not work out so well. Shelly, for example, remembered being told by various relatives to stay in her first marriage when she wanted to divorce, and she had to deal with remarks about being the Elizabeth Taylor of the family when she married her third husband. Several of her cousins mentioned the family's habit of keeping a lid on those problems that were perceived to challenge the family's respectable image by being silent about them, and some joked about the sudden appearance of various relatives they had never heard about who turned out to be the "outside" children of the Muir brothers. When I mentioned a relative that the person I talked with did not know, she exclaimed laughingly, "You mean they found another one?" One cousin described the Muir family as having a "light-hearted attitude toward almost everything" and added, "What they don't like, they sweep under the carpet. And it works. It is very complex." This light-hearted attitude toward "family problems" can be related to the elder Muir generation's self-image as an established (upper) middle-class family, where the men had certain sexual privileges as long as they were willing, and able, to support the children. Indeed, the "outside" children were accepted and supported by the family as long as this was requested. However, at least one of the cousins born out of wedlock, to a woman of the lower classes, seemed to have virtually disappeared from the family. His brothers had lost contact with him after he migrated, undocumented, to the United States,[3] and several of his cousins had never heard about him.

Marriage was also an important ideal in the Smith family, yet most of the children that the family home on Nevis received and reared were born out of wedlock. Debbie, one of Jean's children, remembered her early childhood in the family home on Nevis as a happy one, where all the children were treated well, but recalled that she ran into trouble when, as an adolescent, she challenged the family's authority by insisting on going out to dances and dating boys:

> Grandmother said that I would be just like my mother. She said that my mother had her children when she was young. She said that she sent my mother here [to the Virgin Islands] to get a job and to work, and then she wrote back that she was getting married, and she got children and thing. They felt that I would do the same thing.

Since Jean, Debbie's mother, never contributed much to her children's up-keep in the family home on Nevis, this gave Debbie a weak position in the home: "When certain things happened, they would say, 'Your mother doesn't have a rusty nail in this home!' Like she had nothing there; she didn't help." Debbie was told that she had to behave or move—the family home owed her nothing because her mother had never contributed to her upkeep. One year before she finished secondary school she was told to move back to her mother in the Virgin Islands. When I talked with her in the Virgin Islands a number of years later, she noted, with a certain pride, that—unlike some of her cousins—she had no out-of-wedlock children. Furthermore, she had just passed the American high-school equivalency test and was planning to take classes at the local college. Rather than bring the family down, she felt she had proved her worth as a decent person worthy of the family's respect. The case of Debbie makes clear that if children born out of wedlock were disadvantaged, this was not because they were regarded as "illegitimate" but rather because they were born in less stable unions, where the parents might have been in a difficult position to assume responsibility for child rearing and providing.

PERSONALIZED IDENTITIES

In the light of these accounts of being under pressure to live up to family expectations, and the social sanctions and marginalization they experienced if they failed, it may seem surprising that most of the cousins still identified strongly with their family origins in the Caribbean. An important reason for this is that family origins offered personalized identities rooted in an individual's own history in the Caribbean, which provided an important alternative to the ethnic, or racial, identities that were conferred on them as social identities (Jenkins 1996).

Recent research in North America and Europe has shown that black immigrants are categorized as belonging to ethnic groups associated with their country or region of origin, and that this is a mode whereby they are racialized and fit into the racial hierarchy in the receiving societies (Bashi and McDaniel 1997; Pierre 2004). Such ethnic categorization, Leith Mullings (2005: 673–74) notes in a critical review of racism, has become a primary mode of discrimination as "global expressions of racism underwent substantial reconstructions in the aftermath of World War II." Thus, "racism" is based no longer on ideas of biological inferiority but on notions of cultural differences believed to be rooted in migrants' places of origin. Within this line of understanding, people from particular places are seen to belong "naturally" to particular ethnic groups. This ethnic belonging, in turn, can then be seen as preventing them from becoming fully integrated within the receiving society, resulting in their social and economic marginalization. The discriminatory practices that in the first place led to the categorization of particular immigrants as being of another kind are thus concealed by appropriating "the concept of culture and the 'right to be different' to undergird a neoracism that essentializes cultural differences as unbridgeable" (Mullings 2005: 677). The new form of racism may thus unwittingly be supported by multicultural policies that seek to give equal rights to people with different cultural background. One of the reasons racism is so effective, Mullings adds, is that "race is always simultaneously imposed from above and experienced from below; the imposition of race inevitably creates the structural context for producing oppositional sites of resistance as well as creative spaces for the articulation of subaltern consciousness, culture, and opposition. Race thus potentially becomes a space for resistance and counter-narrative" (Mullings 2005: 682). It was apparent that the cousins who grew up in North America and Europe were subjected to ethnic, and racial, categorizations that they felt singled them out as different. The reactions to such categorization depended on the particular context in which they were categorized and the space for creating alternative identities defined by notions of race in this context. The family often represented an important resource that they drew on in this creating of other identities. When Kathy attended college during the late 1960s and early 1970s, a time when blacks sought to assert their rights in American society, she supported the black students' demands for "a black student floor and a black studies class." But when she learned that she was expected to become part of the black student body and not associate with white students, she refused, referring to her Caribbean background as one of mixing, not separation: "You had to either hate the blacks or the whites; there was no middle ground. You were either in or out. I was very good friends with white students, and part of my family was white. I could not embrace the all-or-nothing attitude."

The cousins in the Gaston family who were living in Canada found that the strong emphasis on ethnic groups fostered by the Canadian multicultural policy posed a problem of identification, because it was difficult for them to find a category that they felt matched their particular situation of being born in Canada of racially mixed middle-class migrants from a small Caribbean island.[4] Nelly's son Will noted:

> I was at a party . . . and it was full of people from the Caribbean community. All the time I was there I didn't feel black at all. I don't fit in there or in an Anglo group, either.
>
> [Do you think about not fitting in?]
>
> I think about it a fair bit. If black means you have to talk a certain way and be affected in a certain way, it is ridiculous.

Peter Gaston, who lives in Britain, also objected to being identified as "black," with all the stereotypes that this involved, because of his dark skin color, just as he objected to blacks' seeing racism everywhere: "I don't want to be stereotyped as a black person. I don't need to be part of a group to be what I want to be. People get hung up on racial issues, and they will see racism where it may not be a big issue. I have my own views."

The Smith cousins who grew up in the Caribbean neighborhood in Leeds found that the entire community of Chapeltown became stereotyped as a problem area in Leeds, and British society as such, and asked their parents to move to another neighborhood. Edwin's son Roger discovered that it was difficult to run his own business as a black man and described with ironic bitterness how it was necessary to front it with whites:

> When the customers come to the shop, they turn to the white person who is there, not me. So I said, OK, let's play the game. So I don't have anything to do with the customers. . . . If anybody turns to me, I say, "I just work here, love" and point to the woman there. This has worked very well. We make money.
>
> And when we go to people's houses to do the work, it is good to be one white and one black person. Because I am black, the first they see is a big black guy. But I speak [with] a broad Yorkshire accent, and I put them at their ease: "Yes love, cup of tea, thank you!" Then we are the best of friends. They forget the color and become customers. If I hired a black person, it would be two black persons walking up to the house, and it would be much more difficult to put them at ease.

While he was pleased about his success and proud of his ability to play the game and outwit people who discriminate against blacks, he was more cynical than happy about the solution he had found. He noted, "It is a struggle here, having people put you down." He was hoping for a better life for his children: "I don't want that for my kids. My overall aim is to go to live in a black country, where we control things. There will still be whites, but they will be in our country, and they will have to behave."

It was apparent that the cousins' categorization as "black" was based on their physical appearance. Thus, those who were light-skinned enough to pass as white found themselves classified as members of white mainstream society, and they encountered skepticism or incredulity when they tried to assert their Caribbean identity. Jane, whose mother had married a white man, found that she was not regarded as Caribbean because she looked white. She could therefore keep her family background as a private matter, explaining, "I don't want to be fitted into a group."

While the cousins' Caribbean family background led to their being subjected to racial or ethnic categorization, and the various discriminatory practices that might follow from this, it also provided a concrete community of belonging rooted in the Caribbean that enabled them to develop a more personal "Caribbean" identity that could counter the external forms of categorization. Nina, a member of the Gaston family in Canada, noted: "I don't think I look like I come from a particular place, but people assume that you are from somewhere." This expectation that she identify with a "somewhere" put her on the spot:

> I don't call myself Canadian, I always say that I was born here, and my parents are from Dominica. I don't call myself Dominican or Canadian. I don't know what to call myself. At the border I say that I am a Canadian, otherwise not. I emphasize my parents' background. It is part of my history. I have a connection there.

By establishing a personal connection to that "somewhere" else, she created a place of origin defined by personalized family relations rather than by the racial stereotyping that made people ask her where she was from in the first place.

Family history was also important to Kathy. She experienced her family tie to Jamaica as so strong that she thought of herself as a Jamaican and had to remind herself that she was an American. For her, a Jamaican identity was important because it pointed to "identifiable roots; it doesn't just blend in with some mix." In the American context, the notion of "identifiable roots" has a particular meaning, because most black Americans cannot trace their roots to a particular place of origin outside the United States but must content themselves with knowing that they are the issue of "some mix." Kathy also had mixed ancestry, but this mixing she saw as a special blend closely related to her family's past in the colored middle class in Jamaica. While she did not subscribe to the British colonial culture that had played such an important role in this class, she celebrated the particular Jamaican blend that had made her what she was. Thus, she gave her two children African names, settled in an affluent white neighborhood, decorated her home with Caribbean artwork, and displayed prominently a photograph of the Scottish forefather who moved to Jamaica.

Peter emphasized that the family identity distinguished him from other black people and gave him a unique identity in British society: "It gives a sense of belonging. I don't just belong to the immediate family. The parents are not there forever. I feel a closeness and longing to say I belong to that tribe. It is like saying you belong to the Ashanti tribe." He kept in close contact with his cousins via e-mail and explained that, when his wife had the first scan of the baby they were expecting, he sent the pictures out to all the e-mail addresses in the family, adding: "I don't want them to forget Peter is here!"

For Emmanuel, the link to Nevis, where he was reared, was still important because of the way in which he was treated in the Virgin Islands as an immigrant: "Even though I have lived most of my life here, I still have that link to Nevis. Even though I am now a citizen of the United States, I still consider myself a Nevisian. I didn't feel I was part of the setting due to the names, the stigma, and the stereotypes attached to those who were not from here." He realized, however, that it would be difficult to return to Nevis, because he had lived most of his life in the Virgin Islands and his knowledge of Nevis was limited to the village where he grew up. After the death of his grandparents, he had therefore not gone back to Nevis.

While the family network offered a community of belonging that could be drawn on to counter ethnic categorization and stereotyping, most of the cousins who were reared abroad realized that it did not offer an actual home in their Caribbean place of origin to which they realistically would be able to return. The case of Susanna, presented in the introduction, illustrates this. When Susanna, who was born and reared in Britain, tried to move to Nevis on her own as a young adult, she found it difficult to sustain a notion of home on the island. When I first met her in Nevis, she had a good job as a cook at a major hotel on the island and was enthusiastic about all the experiences she had had that she never would have enjoyed in Britain, like being asked to model, going sailing, and seeing Janet Jackson sitting on the square drinking beer. But she found it difficult to become accepted by the local population, who, she said, did not like the way she "dressed and talked" and thought that she "felt above them." Furthermore, she rarely saw her relatives, who, she thought, showed little interest in her: "I found out that when you are on holiday the family cannot do enough for you, but when you live here, they don't visit." A couple of years later, she left Nevis and decided to return to Leeds. Moving to Nevis had made her aware that she could become just a marginal member of Nevisian society and her family on Nevis, whom she knew only peripherally. In Leeds, however, she would belong to the local community of family and friends with whom she had grown up.

In the Muir and Gaston families, where most of the cousins were born and reared abroad, many were wondering whether their Caribbean place of origin would continue to have the same meaning for them when their parents died, or when there were no longer close relatives on their island of origin. Kathy explained: "I love Jamaica. It is a beautiful, wonderful place, and I have good memories of it. But a part of me realizes that when the older ones, like dad and grandmother, are gone, if there is no one there, will this close that chapter in the family? Will we just have a vague sense of roots?" For her cousin Jean in Canada, who had settled as a "white" person in a small rural community in Nova Scotia and visited Jamaica only a few times, the island had become like a tourist destination: "There is little to identify with there. Yes, I have a few relatives there. But when we go there, we are just tourists. It is hard to identify with in that sense." It may therefore be tempting to conclude that a sense of belonging in the Caribbean based on family history and personal ties will disappear in the long run as family members lose personal contact with their Caribbean place of origin. However, the life stories of the cousins' children, most of whom are third-generation migrants, painted a more complex picture.

GROWING UP IN THE FAMILY NETWORK

Approximately thirty individuals in the family networks were children or young people age twenty or younger. Due to the generational structures of the families, all but three belonged to the Muir and Gaston families. Many of them grew up in dispersed areas far from a family-based Caribbean environment. This suggests that the fragmented family network with its link to a remote Caribbean family home should be rather unimportant to these children. The life stories related by the third generation of children who were growing up in the cousins' homes both confirm and refute this suggestion. They confirm that these children in their everyday lives were strongly oriented toward the local area where they lived. At the same time, most were fascinated by their special Caribbean family connection and the ways in which this made them unique individuals. Furthermore, the children who were categorized as black, and therefore different, continued to find in their personal family history an important source of identification.

A central theme in the children's life stories was the way they developed a sense of themselves in the interplay between external forms of categorization and internal modes of identification. Laura, who lived in Toronto, explained:

> On the first day of school we had to tell where we are from and stuff. We don't do this every year, but some years. Last year, in grade four, you had to stand in front of the classroom and talk about yourself.
>
> [What did you say?]
>
> I said, "My name is Laura Lewandovski, I am eight years old. I am Canadian, I was born in . . . Hospital. My mother is English." We only do this with some teachers.
>
> [Is it important to know where people are from?]
>
> No, it is important that they are nice, that they share—their snacks and their books.

In this presentation, Laura first identified herself by stating her name and her age, an important distinguishing feature among children (Gulløv 1999). Then she noted her nationality, but this somewhat abstract nationality was then made concrete by localizing it in a particular hospital. In her local universe of school friends, being able to point to a local hospital where one was born may have presented a way of distinguishing the Canadian-born from those who were born abroad, but it also localized the Canadian-born in a particular place of birth. She then went on to claim an English origin by stating that her mother was English. This was entirely correct to the extent that her mother had been born in England and lived there during the early part of her childhood. Nevertheless, an English origin may be surprising to others, given her appearance as a person of color. She did not mention her mother's Caribbean origins—or, for that matter, her deceased father's eastern European background.

Laura's "ethnic" self-presentation as English may have been strategic. In a study of Canadian cultural politics, E. Mackey (1997: 138) notes that, despite a "mythology of pluralism, white English-speaking Canadians have economic and cultural dominance." Canadians therefore operate with three major groups in society: the "First Nations" of Native or aboriginal people; the "Founding Nations" of the English and the French; and the "ethnocultural" groups of the later immigrants. Furthermore, "white Anglophone Canadians often consider themselves simply 'Canadians' or '*Canadian*-Canadians,' whereas other groups are marked by difference from this implicit norm" (Mackey 1997: 138–39). By identifying herself as being from Britain, she thus claimed an identity associated with the dominant population group considered "real" Canadians. Her emphasis on her British origins, however, may also reflect the fact that she belonged to that branch of the Gaston network that recalled its years in Britain with great fondness. Since she grew up hearing about the wonderful country where her mother spent her early childhood, she may just have found it natural to trace her origins to that country.

Whether or not this place of origin would be accepted by the wider Canadian society is another matter. As a person of color, she would in Canada have been viewed as belonging to a "visible minority." This is an official Canadian term, introduced to refer to "persons who are non-white in colour or non-Caucasian in race, other than Aboriginal people," and who may need special protection through affirmative action (Synnott and Howes 1996: 137). Being English and therefore part of the founding nation in Canada and a dominant ethnic group thus seems irreconcilable with being "non-white in colour" and therefore part of a minority associated with the need for affirmative action. Given Laura's family background, however, being a non-white person and claiming a position of respect in society made complete sense.

While eight-year-old Laura may not have been conscious of the fact that she was challenging dominant ethnic and racial categorization, Kathy Muir's thirteen-year-old Sadia, who lived in an affluent, mostly white town outside Los Angeles, was quite aware that she presented herself in an unexpected way when she claimed a European identity. She seems to have done this to challenge conventional thinking and to find a common ground of identification with her schoolmates:

> At school, there are only three to four kids of my race; most are white. Everybody else is Scottish, Irish, and so [on]. So I say that I am Scottish, too, so that I can relate to them a little. They see my dark skin, and they think about African slaves. It is a shock to them that I am also Scottish. They only see the black part. Some who are of Scottish background say, "Oh, wow!" Whenever I see my mom's picture downstairs of the original Scotsman, I am reminded of it.

Whereas Laura and Sadia were comfortable about negotiating an identity to match a particular situation,[5] others were uncertain about how to present themselves. This was the case for one of Laura's thirteen-year-old cousins who grew up in a predominantly white suburban neighborhood north of New York City: "I don't know what I am. What am I? I am what I am. I don't care what they think. The same people asked me twice. I don't know why they ask." His eleven-year-old brother had settled on identifying himself as West Indian but worried about the connotations of the term: "Friends ask sometimes about my origin, but not often. I say that I am West Indian. I say that I am not a Native American. They may think so because of the Indian in West Indian." Their fifteen-year-old brother had also decided on a West Indian identity, but he was wondering what the meaning of his ethnic label might be:

> Close friends have asked whether I am black, like if I am from Africa or something. I don't know what to say. I say that I am West Indian. . . .
>
> [What does West Indian mean?]
>
> Being black. I know I am black. I am not sure what I am. People say they are Polish, so I say I am West Indian, just to say something. It means little.

In their study of identity among inner-city youth in the United States, S. B. Heath and M. W. McLaughlin note that "*Ethnicity* seemed, from the perspective of youths, to be more often a label assigned to them by outsiders than an indication of their real sense of self" (Heath and McLaughlin 1993b: 6). And they add: "*Ethnicity* takes on both *subjective and objective* meanings, both as an internal assignment for the self and, more often in the United States after the 1980s, as a label given by external sources" (1993b: 14). These boys were prepared to deal with ethnicity as an externally imposed identity, but they were clearly more reticent about adopting it as a personal identity. This was largely because they had little personal experience with their Caribbean background. Laura and Sadia had grown up in homes where the Caribbean family background was emphasized. Laura's grandparents had lived in the home on and off; aunts and uncles visited regularly; and she had herself vacationed in Dominica where her grandparents had returned upon their retirement. Sadia's mother, Kathy, was quite conscious of her Jamaican background, and the family had spent many holidays in Jamaica, visiting the grandfather. Both Laura and Sadia thus had personal experience with their origins—even if Laura had not been to Britain. The Gaston brothers, however, had visited Dominica only once when they were very small, and they had little recollection of doing this. Furthermore, their father, Richard, seemed to emphasize the religious aspect, rather than local Dominican aspects, of his family background, perhaps because he had ambivalent feelings about his childhood. An ethnic identity therefore meant little to them; it was just a label.

Reticence about adopting an ethnic identity was caused not only by a lack of personal experience with the Caribbean, but also by the refusal to be categorized as part of an ethnic minority when it was felt that other aspects of life should have been more important in determining their identity. Toward the end of my interview with Sarah's eighteen-year-old daughter, Nicole, who lived in a small, white-dominated town outside Toronto, I asked her how she identified herself. She replied apprehensively:

Do I have to identify myself in any particular way? I say I am a person.

[Do you ever identify with the Caribbean?]

I never say I am Caribbean.

[You prefer not to have a label?]

Yes, I am just me.

Nicole had grown up and gone to school in a small town and was well acquainted with the local community. Furthermore, her father, who was of British origin, belonged to one of the oldest families in the local community, and Nicole lived with her parents in a large, venerable wooden house in one of the better parts of town. In a small-town context dominated by a white majority, being singled out as having a particular ethnic background therefore was tantamount to being labeled as not really belonging in the local community and the national community of unmarked "*Canadian*-Canadianness" that such a white, Anglophone community represented (see Mackey 1997: 151). However, Nicole did not want to be part of this kind of Canadian community:

> It is boring, being in a small town. There is not much culture. It is the same kind of people. No culture at all. No Asians, blacks, just mostly white.
>
> [This is a problem?]
>
> Yes. It makes people narrow-minded. They are only used to one kind, they become biased; they have a small-town mentality.

Her refusal to assume an ethnic identity therefore was a critique of the "biased," "small-town mentality" of the local community, not a denial of her cultural background. Indeed, she defined multiculturalism to mean a richness, rather than a plurality, of culture, as opposed to the poverty of culture to be found in her home town, where people were all of the same kind.

Only two young people identified as "black," both of them boys in their late teens. One of them, Kathy Muir's son, did so because he wished to emphasize his tie to his father's black American family that, he felt, was not accorded as much respect in American society as was his mother's Jamaican family, even though they were much the same: "There is not much difference between my black American and my Jamaican family, except that instead of being shipped here as slaves, they were shipped there as slaves." His black identity therefore was motivated as much by family solidarity as by a feeling of black consciousness, and he still regarded Jamaica as an important part of his "heritage." The other, Laura's eldest brother, identified himself as black because, he stated, he liked the fact that American blacks had struggled for their rights, which he could identify with as a young Canadian black struggling to get through school. He saw important role models in blacks such as Martin Luther King Jr., Rosa Parks, Malcolm X, and Marcus Garvey, but also admired the poetry of Maya Angelou. He was therefore developing an identity based on a strong feeling of solidarity with people of African origins due to their shared history of suppression.

Whereas the children living in the United States and Canada were subjected to external ethnic and racial categorization, most of the children in Great Britain did not have this experience because they looked white. When I asked how she identified herself, eighteen-year-old Phyllis explained:

> If people talk, I tell them the long story about my Jamaican, English, Scottish, Norwegian background. It is quite a mix. If I fill in an application form I just put white.
>
> [English?]
>
> Yes, I think so. Before, if I said that I was partly Jamaican, I was told that I don't look that way.

Like their "black" relatives, they were therefore not able to choose the part of their background they wished to identity with but had to adopt an identity that suited their appearance. Nevertheless, several of the "white" children liked to refer to their non-British background to make themselves more interesting, to stand out in the crowd of ordinary Britishness. A seventeen-year-old girl living in a southern English village explained: "It is nice to have family all over the place—to have not just a normal English family with an auntie two miles down the road and another auntie, and another auntie, and that is what you've got. I couldn't bear that." A cousin of the same age similarly found that her ethnic background made her unusual: "It is more interesting; you have more to talk about when you meet somebody. You don't just come from Portsmouth." She was of both German and Jamaican background but preferred her Jamaican origins, she explained, "because of Hitler." For these young people, their multiple places of origin therefore offered additional sources of belonging and identification that they could draw on when they wanted to create their own identity among friends, but that they could ignore when they wished to be part of the white majority in the wider society.

For all of the children—whether they looked white or black—visiting the Caribbean gave an opportunity to experience their family's island of origin and the people and places connected with it. When Jeanette visited her grandfather in Jamaica, the family legacy of belonging to a respected family of high status was confirmed: "I love to go there. It is awesome, because grandpa Bill knows everybody. He is the rich guy there. All know him, and he introduces us. It is a nice island." Others described being overwhelmed by the feeling of being related to everybody when they visited their island of origin:

> My grandparents and my grandmother's family, almost the entire island is re-
> lated. . . . I didn't realize there were so many before I went there and spent the
> summer with my grandparents. Wherever I went, I had to explain whose grand-
> child I was. It was nice. I felt totally welcomed by everyone. Everybody has
> something for you—fresh mangoes, lunch. We knew we had relatives there but not
> really that there were so many. It was funny.

The place of origin in the Caribbean thus presented a close-knit society where the children experienced fitting into the social order by virtue of their family relations rather than their ethnic category. It was also a place where they, and their family, had a clear social identity and, in some cases, a high status in the local social system. This experience of the Caribbean, however, depended on the presence of relatives on the island of origin who were seen as representing a family network and giving it a name in local society.

CONCLUSION

The life stories related by the cousins and their children show that they had highly varied experiences in relation to their engagement with their family's network and its place of origin in the Caribbean. Nevertheless, most of them regarded this engagement as providing an important context in their life. They associated their family network with specific social norms and cultural values that they felt had an important impact on their lives. While some saw the family as a great source of inspiration and motivation, helping to make them the people they became, others were critical of aspects of the family network and resisted incorporation in various ways. Critical or not, however, most realized that their lives, and their understanding of themselves as individuals, were shaped by their family network, just as they, in turn, had contributed to reshaping this network.

The family network was also important because it offered a concrete link with the Caribbean that gave individuals a personal identity rooted in the family's place of origin. Their experiences with the family network, and their knowledge of the family's Caribbean origins, thereby provided them with a personal source of identification different from the ethnic or racial categories with which they tended to be associated in the societies where they lived. By distancing themselves from categories of people who were accorded a position in the bottom of the racially based hierarchies of the receiving societies, the family members showed a strong awareness of racially and ethnically based hierarchies and the forms of discrimination that they involved. Furthermore, they ended up lending support to these hierarchies. Their emphasis on personal family relations rather than ethnic collectivities should not be reduced to a tactic of the weak (de Certeau 1984) to navigate a dominant system of inequality in the way most advantageous to them. It must also be seen as caused by a deep-seated desire to have a personal identity for themselves rather than being part of an anonymous mass with no identity of its own. This points to the need to take ideas of selfhood, or individuality, into account when examining the importance of collectivities for identify formation. As Anthony Cohen (1994: 178) notes, it is easy to jump to the conclusion that people assert their identity through collective categories based on, for example, nationality or ethnicity because of the "ease with which individuals could locate themselves in them." Instead, he suggests that the relationship is inverse, and that "people read collectivities through their experience as individuals" (Cohen 1994: 178).

The narratives examined in this chapter show that people do not just read but also construct collectivities through their experience as individuals. Thus, when family members talked about their connection with the Caribbean and their Caribbean identity, they did not speak of it in terms of an ethnic identity or a cultural heritage connected with a distant country of origin. They actively defined their Caribbean heritage and identity through their knowledge of family stories that grounded them in the Caribbean, their relations with the people who belonged to the family, and their own visits to the Caribbean. The family networks therefore allowed individuals to develop a personal Caribbean identity rooted in collective family relations, as well as in their parents' upbringing and their individual life experiences.

The family-based identities were in some ways more spacious than ethnically based collective identities, because they incorporated people of varying racial, ethnic, social, and economic background and thus allowed for more personalized identities and communities of belonging. At the same time, these family identities were constraining, because they involved adherence to particular social norms and cultural values associated with social and economic mobility in the place of origin. For this reason, those who failed to live up to the family's social expectations risked exclusion from the family. Furthermore, while the three families were well known in their place of origin and within the immigrant communities in the migration destinations, they were little known in the national community of the society to which they had immigrated. The family-based identities therefore were more important at the individual level of intimate relations than in the public arena. This does not mean that such identities are insignificant. On the contrary: They can be of vital importance to the individuals who make them their own, not just within the intimate sphere of family relations, but also in terms of how they interpret and act in relation to the wider society. These identities are only meaningful, however, as long as they are situated within living family networks that can give meaning and purpose to individuals' lives.

Identity has been a major topic of investigation in migration research, largely because changes in the social and cultural orientation of migrants and their descendants have been regarded as an important measure of immigrants' integration into a new nation-state. Many migration studies therefore have analyzed individuals' and their immediate families' integration in terms of generational stages of incorporation, where each new generation of children is expected to display progressively more successful forms of integration into a receiving country. This is reflected, among other ways, in their internalization of the culture of the receiving society and their adoption of a new national identity.[6] This generational model, however, has been criticized in recent years for being based on the assumptions that the culture of the receiving society is homogeneous and that adopting an identity associated with the culture of the receiving society accords higher social status than maintaining an identity tied to the place of origin (Waters 1999a: 194–95). Both assumptions have been shown to be wrong.

In her study of West Indian immigrants in New York, Mary Waters (1999a) found that for black immigrants, the only possible form of integration was incorporation into a black American subculture associated with low status in society. Because "assimilation to black America was downward mobility," many therefore distanced themselves from black Americans and held on to their Caribbean immigrant identity (Waters 1999a: 65).[7] Such distancing, Jemima Pierre has emphasized, must be seen as a reaction to wider "processes of racialization and the incorporation of racially distinct immigrants" in the United States. This form of "cultural assertion" is thus "a product of racialization, not the cause" (Pierre 2004: 156). The particular racialization processes that took place in Britain, where there was little native black population occupying the lowest ranks of society, thus led many Caribbean immigrants to adopt an identity as "black British" that represents their shared position of struggle against oppression from which people of color from the Commonwealth have experienced migration to British society.[8] More recently, it has been suggested that Caribbean migrants also construct hybrid, diasporic identities that reflect their historical experience of displacement and rupture, which has continued into the present (Chamberlain 1998; Gilroy 1987, 1993; Hall 1990). In the Canadian context, the remaking of identities among Caribbean migrants and their descendants in the face of racial discrimination has also been debated (Henry 1994).

It is reasonable to argue, following the various theories of identity construction among Caribbean immigrants, that the identities of the cousins and their children have been created in response to the negative categorization, and related discrimination, that they have experienced in the migration destinations. Indeed, it was quite apparent that those family members who were "unmarked," largely because they were perceived as white, were generally content to become "invisible"—that is, adopt a local identity and merge with mainstream society. Those who were marked as different, however, did not have this choice; they had to develop some sort of identity to deal with the social identity as members of a racialized ethnic group they were given by the majority society. This involved various strategies, depending on the racial and ethnic structures of the society where they lived. The varying identities in the three family networks, however, cannot merely be analyzed as reactive identities developed in response to various conditions of stereotyping and dis-crimination in a migration destination or to a continuous history of rupture and exile. The cousins and their children did not just react. Within the "space for resistance and counter-narrative" created by the notion of "race" (Mull-ings 2005: 682), they actively created their identities as part of the family networks that connected them with the Caribbean. These family networks shared not only common roots in a Caribbean place of origin but a notion of relatedness involving moral values and social expectations. These identities therefore were under constant transformation as individuals negotiated places for themselves in society, given their particular experience as people of Ca-ribbean origin. This points to the importance of examining identities in relation to the individuality of their makers as well as in relation to the communities of belonging with which individuals are associated as immi-grants of a particular ethnic or racial background.

............................RELATING REGIONAL, FAMILY,

...........AND INDIVIDUAL HISTORIES OF MIGRATION

Toward the end of the twentieth century, notions of "diaspora," "home-land," and "transnational systems" became prominent in migration stud-ies. They emerged in an era with increasing awareness of the mobility, fluid-ity, and interconnectedness on a global scale that characterize modern life. With this awareness has come a new focus on the significance of locality and place, not as naturally existing local frameworks of existence, but as sites of identification and belonging that are constructed within wider global con-texts of life. Within migration studies, this has led to a growing interest in experiences of border crossing and the transnational sociocultural systems and diasporic identities grounded in distant homelands to which such experi-ences may lead.

The concern with the notions of diasporic identities and transnational relations today signals a concern with attachment to place of origin that is new within migration research. Until recent decades, the field of migration research emphasized such aspects of the migration process as the push–pull factors that induce people to leave for various migration destinations and the processes of incorporation that migrants undergo in their new place of resi-dence. This focus on the receiving countries is illustrated by a special collec-tion of articles in the winter 1997 issue of *International Migration Review* devoted specifically to reexamining the continued relevance of the integration paradigm in North American migration studies. In their concluding discussion of the articles presented in the issue, Josh DeWind and Philip Kasinitz (1997) make the point that the contributors are not primarily concerned with the phenomenon of migration as such. Instead, they address such questions as "how immigrants and their children are being incorporated into the fabric of American life. What sort of Americans will they be, and what sort of America is being created in the interaction of immigrants and natives?" (DeWind and Kasinitz 1997: 1096).

As many migration studies have begun to shift focus during the past two decades, they no longer concentrate on examining integration processes in the receiving country and what kind of local citizens immigrants will become. They conceptualize migrants in terms of wider, translocal networks of relationships defined in terms of their country of origin. Such ties are not just interpreted as signs of migrants' continued ties to family and friends in a place of origin or their feelings of loyalty toward a distant "homeland." They are seen to reflect migrants' desire to resist suppression in the migration destination and to negotiate better social and economic conditions for themselves. In her study of migration from St. Vincent and Grenada to New York, for example, Linda Basch writes that, while transnational networks involve the difficult physical separation of close relatives, they also empower the families. The networks thereby enable families "to resist specific state policies aimed at controlling and exploiting their labor and also to challenge the terms of their subordinated insertion into structures of global capital" and to be "less dependent on any single national economy" (Basch et al. 1994: 83). Thus, by maintaining, and further developing, ties with their country of origin, the migrants are seen to retain a certain measure of independence in relation to the external structures that set the conditions for their position as labor migrants. As Sarah Mahler (1998: 68) notes in her discussion of the transnational approach, much of the literature has conceptualized "transnational processes" in terms of "creole identities and agencies that challenge multiple levels of structural control: local, regional, national, and global."

The traditional, integrationist approach and the new, resistance-oriented approach to migration lead to dissimilar interpretations. The former perceives migration as a more or less one-way movement from a country of origin to a new country that sets in motion a process of social, economic, and cultural integration that is complete only when the migrants have become fully incorporated as new citizens in the receiving society. The latter views migration within the context of increasing mobility and interconnectedness on a global scale. This globalization places people in systems of inequality at the same time that it allows them to transgress the sociocultural, economic, political, and legal constraints posed by local contexts of life, particularly in relation to nation-states. This situation, where a field of research is characterized by two interpretive frameworks that represent a minority population in terms of its desire, or need, to either integrate or resist, finds a parallel in Edward Bruner's analysis of anthropological studies of "American Indians" (Bruner 1986).

Bruner argues that most ethnographies are constructed around a dominant narrative structure that, in turn, constitutes and interprets the people we study in a certain mode. In the case of American Indians, the dominant narrative for many years was one that described a proud people with a rich cultural heritage who, upon American colonization, experienced a loss of cultural traditions so that they had no choice but to become assimilated into North American society. Since the 1960s, a new narrative has emerged in North American society in which American Indians are represented as having had a past of oppression and exploitation, followed by a future of resistance to cultural denigration. While the narrative of assimilation tends to conceal the oppression to which Indians have been exposed, the narrative of resistance serves as a justification for the Native American population's demand to reclaim lost rights. Furthermore, whereas the assimilation narrative renders the Indians inarticulate and mute, the resistance narrative invites the people to speak out for themselves. After a period of confrontation between the two narratives, the narrative of resistance has become dominant, and the narrative of assimilation is no longer significant in ethnographic writing on Native Americans, as they are termed in contemporary ethnography.

It is possible to see the disparate approaches to migration research as representing two different narratives—one of assimilation, or integration, and one of resistance—that are at present competing for a dominant position. This approach clearly represents a simplification of the complexity of migration research. Nevertheless, it does help clarify trends in the perception of migration that can be contrasted to the approach taken in this study. According to this line of analysis, the integration narrative can be seen to describe immigrants as pushed out of their old countries of origin, which are rich in cultural traditions but poor in terms of social and economic resources, and pulled toward migration destinations that promise a better life. This narrative will view integration into the new land of opportunity as the only viable future for the migrant. With its focus on statistics of population movements and integration processes, however, this narrative risks treating migrants as inarticulate and mute, as unable to speak for themselves. Indeed, such criticism has been leveled against integration-focused migration research (Tilly 1990; Yans-McLaughlin 1990; see also Hvidt 1975; Olwig and Sørensen 2002). The resistance narrative, by contrast, will depict migrants as people who travel to other countries to escape social and economic problems caused by many years of colonial and neocolonial exploitation of their countries of origin but who refuse to subordinate themselves to the various forms of oppression that they encounter in receiving countries. They will therefore maintain and further develop transnational relations to their countries of origin while taking advantage of the opportunities in migration destinations. Due to its concern with migrants' ties to their homelands and the extralocal identities that they involve, this narrative can be seen as allowing migrants to speak for themselves.

I am not convinced that the narrative of resistance fully represents the migrants' point of view. It seems, rather, to be part of a larger narrative of resistance that points to the emergence of new transgressive identities and associated forms of cultural consciousness. This is apparent in Michael Kearney's suggestion that an important aspect of "transnationalized identities" is their ability to "escape the either–or categorization" inherent in national identities. The concept of the transnational, he states, therefore "calls attention to the cultural and political projects of nation-states as they vie for hegemony in relations with other nation-states, with their citizens and 'aliens'" (Kearney 1995:548, 558). The focus on identity issues in relation to migrants' places of origin has led to a certain merging of the notions of transnationalism and diaspora so that "social formations spanning borders" have become known as "ethnic diasporas" (Vertovec 1999: 449; see also Cohen 1998). An important topic of study here, according to Steven Vertovec, has been the "diasporic consciousness" developing among people who hold "dual or multiple identifications" (Vertovec 1999: 450).

What began as an interest in transnational sociocultural systems has become a concern with "ethnic diasporas." This is not without problems, as several authors have noted. The editor of the American journal *Diaspora*, Khachig Tölölyan, has expressed both surprise and concern over the widespread use of the term "diaspora" by intellectuals today. He finds that "diasporic identity has become an occasion for the celebration of multiplicity and mobility—and a figure of our discontent with our being in a world apparently still dominated by nation-states" (Tölölyan 1996: 28), the "our" here referring to intellectual scholars, many of them of immigrant background like himself. This leads Tölölyan to point to the danger of intellectuals' projecting their own personal projects into studies of transnational and diasporic phenomena, thereby causing these phenomena to become infused with intentions related to the identity politics of particular intellectual strata (see also Schnapper 1999). Mahler has made a somewhat similar point, stating that studies of the sociocultural aspects of transnationalism have provided "detailed information on a limited set of activities and practices [related primarily to identity politics], and not a clear picture of the breadth of the social field, nor of the demography or intensity of players' participation in all the activities people engage in" (Mahler 1998: 82). This has led her to question whether "transnationalism" is in fact as "empowering, democratic, and liberating" as much of the literature suggests. She calls for careful testing of the "subaltern image" projected in the literature that has resulted from the overwhelming interest in identity issues (Mahler 1998: 92).

Because research on sociocultural aspects of transnationalism has been preoccupied with identity issues, it has focused on investigating the range of cultural phenomena that Arjun Appadurai (1996) has termed "marked culture" and left unexamined the much wider range of "unmarked culture" on which "marked culture" draws. Whereas unmarked culture, according to Appadurai (1996: 13–14), refers to "the plethora of differences that characterize the world today, differences at various levels, with various valences, and with greater and lesser degrees of social consequences," marked culture only includes "the subset of these differences that has been mobilized to articulate the boundary of difference" or "that constitutes the diacritics of group identity." By focusing on marked culture among migrants, in other words, migration scholars have investigated a highly select subset of differences and left unexamined the "virtually open-ended archive of differences" presented by migrants' unmarked culture (Appardurai 1996: 13–14).[1] Furthermore, the transnational approach has tended to lead migration researchers to concentrate on those aspects of marked culture that are mobilized in connection with migrants' identification with differing nations and to neglect investigating those dimensions that may be associated with other aspects of migrants' lives (Olwig 2003b).

This focus on marked culture is too narrow. I am especially concerned about the tendency within some migration research to perceive migrants' "marked" culture in terms of counter-national identities as they are understood and evoked in receiving countries. In studies of transnational migration, the receiving countries overwhelmingly have been North American and European. Research on the sociocultural dimensions of transnational migration therefore tends to become narrowed to studies of identity constructions that resist hegemonic nation-states and associated identities of the migration destinations. For this reason, the resistance narratives that guide this body of research arguably say relatively little about the migrants and their concerns, and they therefore would seem to "mute" migrants rather than empower them with a framework for self-expression.

HISTORICAL CONTEXTS OF MIGRATION

According to Bruner (1986: 139), implicit narrative structures do not just guide the ethnographies that we write. They also influence how we conduct our research, because we "choose those informants whose narratives are most compatible with our own" (Bruner 1986: 151). For this reason, Bruner argues, it is naïve to believe that ethnographic field research will lead to the emergence of new narratives: "New narratives do not arise from anthropological field research, as we sometimes tell our graduate students, but from history, from world conditions" (Bruner 1986: 152). The ethnographic studies of migration seem to bear out Bruner's analysis.

Migration is a broad phenomenon. It has been identified with movements from the countryside to the towns in Europe; from tribal place of birth to mining districts in Africa; from poor, racist Southern states to northern industrial regions less marked by racial discrimination in the United States; and, of course, between various countries (Olwig and Sørensen 2002; see also Sanjek 2003). Migration studies, however, emerged primarily as a distinct field of investigation in close association with research on the massive European migration to North America during the nineteenth century (Gmelch 1980: 135). This was a historical context in which migration was perceived to be a final act; where people left their home in the old world for good to create another home in the new world and where they helped build the new North American nation-states (Conway 1989: 17). For this reason, an implicit narrative guiding this field of research has concerned nation building. Indeed, nation building and migration are so closely connected in North America, according to the American sociologist Mary Waters, that the study of immigration and the integration of immigrants into society has been a major focus in American sociology (Waters 1999b: 1264).

The connection between migration and international population movements has been consolidated by the introduction in the course of the twentieth century of immigration regulations by nation-states that attempt to control ever more comprehensive and widespread population movements. In the nineteenth century, there was little control over migration from Europe to North America. At the beginning of the twentieth century, however, restrictions were passed in North America to limit the flow of mass immigration that by then had begun to include people from countries outside Europe. Despite these restrictions, and the instituting of intensive patrolling of political borders, mass immigration to North America has continued, much of it illegally. Various European countries have similarly introduced restrictions, since they, too, have become important migration destinations. At the same time that the regulation of population movements over political borders has been tightened, increasing attention has been paid to the cultural aspects of migration. Migration has come to be defined as the study of people who leave the nation-state where they belong not only legally and administratively, but also culturally.

In the historical era of nation building, research on migration largely took the form of integration narratives—at least, as far as migration to North America is concerned. When the historical context changed to one of global movement and interconnectedness, however, researchers began to question the continued role of the nation-state and reconceptualized migration in terms of narratives of resistance. However, the people who depart for various destinations are not just immigrants who become part of the historical narrative of the receiving society, whether as new citizens eager to become integrated into the society or as the more recalcitrant residents who resist such

4

integration. They are also individuals with their own personal histories of movement and emplacement. By exploring such histories, and the narratives that they embody, anthropologists can locate other, perhaps more useful methodological and analytical frameworks of research. This, I suggest, is a fruitful strategy when studying migration that, by implication, involves movements between different places with different histories and related narrative structures. This is the approach that I have adopted in my research on three dispersed families of Caribbean origin.

FAMILY HISTORIES OF MOVEMENT AND EMPLACEMENT

Nation-states have a rather brief history in the English-speaking Caribbean islands of Nevis, Jamaica, and Dominica, the places of origin of the three families I have studied. The Caribbean islands were still British territories, and the inhabitants British citizens, when the family members migrated in the period from the 1940s to the '70s. When the individuals I interviewed described their family's background in the Caribbean and the family's relocation in a migration destination, they therefore did not represent themselves as belonging to, or changing affiliation in relation to, a particular people or ethnic group grounded in a specific nation-state. The historical context of the individual life stories and the narratives of origin that various family members related was that of differing British colonial societies. They did not consist of stable local communities inhabited by people with a long past of rootedness in the ancestral soil, but were relatively open, populated by people with origins in widely different parts of the world. After the abolition of slavery, these Caribbean societies were characterized by significant internal population movements as the former slaves and indentured laborers sought to establish independent communities outside the European plantations. These movements constituted the historical framework for the family narratives related here. The different ways in which individuals described and interpreted their movements were constitutive of the place of origin that they envisioned for themselves in the Caribbean.

In the Smith family, narratives revolved around a family home located on land that the siblings' parents purchased around 1940. This family descended mainly from African slaves brought to Nevis to labor in the plantation fields. Colonized in 1628, Nevis represents one of the oldest British plantation

societies, where planters early on established a firm grip on the island society
that they did not loosen until the plantation system collapsed in the beginning of the 1900s (Frucht 1966; Olwig 1993b). The Smith family's narratives
had their focus on a home located in one of the large independent African
Caribbean villages that emerged when estate land was finally sold to the local
population in the first half of the twentieth century. When they described
how the siblings' parents had toiled on their land and struggled to maintain
the family and keep the children in school, they were also explaining why it
became necessary for them to migrate for wage employment. These migratory moves did not constitute an abandonment of the home in the Nevisian
village that the family members left behind. They entailed a commitment to
support this home and the way of life that it embodied, mainly in the form of
remittances.

The Muir family also traced its roots to an African Caribbean village on its
island of origin, Jamaica. This much larger Caribbean island was established
as a plantation society a few decades after Nevis and became an important
center of sugar production and a major colony in the British empire. In
Jamaica, however, independent African Caribbean villages emerged soon
after emancipation of the slaves, as part of the free-village movement that
developed with the aid of nonconformist British missionaries (Besson 2002).
The mother in the Muir family was born in Refuge, one of the oldest free
villages, as the daughter of a second-generation Portuguese immigrant father
and an Afro-Jamaican mother from a local family. She left this village behind,
geographically as well as mentally, when she moved to the nearby town of
Falmouth, where she married into a family of fairly recent immigrants from
Scotland who made a comfortable living in the shipping industry. This move
constituted an important step of upward social and economic mobility, and in
their life stories Muir family members identified strongly with their urban
background in a prosperous commercial center where the family belonged to
the colored middle class. They hardly acknowledged their roots in the old
free village of Refuge. When they emigrated, they saw their journey as a
continuation of the family tradition of moving for upward mobility.

Unlike Nevis and Jamaica, Dominica never developed into a full-fledged
plantation society, but had a long history of settlement by peasant proprietors
of French origin who, at various points in the family's history, mixed with the
African slaves as well as with the local population of Caribs (Honychurch

1995; Trouillot 1988). This was the background of the Gaston family, who originated in one of the oldest French Creole villages on the island. The family moved beyond the peasant way of life when the father left his natal village to train as a schoolteacher and eventually head his own school in another French creole village. While members of the Gaston family talked a great deal about the family's background in a remote Dominican village, where it had been part of the local community, they were also quite conscious of the fact that their family had assumed a position of leadership as educators active in the socioeconomic development of the community. When the members of this family moved away from the village, they did so in pursuit of further education that would equip them better for such positions of leadership and enlightenment. Within this family, migration was therefore described as a way to heed the call, instilled in the children by their father, to seek self-improvement in order to serve the community.

While all the three families shared common roots in the African Caribbean past of plantation slavery, they had a past of quite different movements within the Caribbean as they sought to improve their social and economic condition in their particular island society of origin. From a Caribbean point of view, they can be described as participating in the long historical journey that, in the course of several generations, took Caribbean people from slave labor in the fields on the large sugar plantations to the free villages of small farmers and fishermen; to the colonial centers of middle-class occupations in education, commerce, and administration; and, finally, to various metropolitan centers abroad, with wider social and economic opportunities. For the Muir and Gaston families, migrating from the Caribbean to a metropolitan center seemed to come as a logical next step in the sequence of moves that they had already begun within the local society. For the Smith family, the direct migratory move from the small African Caribbean village to urban centers in Great Britain or the Virgin Islands involved a more drastic change of environment. This difference between the families is reflected in their responses to their moves. During the first many years of settlement abroad, members of the Smith families chose to settle among, and socialize with, migrants of similar background from the small Leeward Islands with whom they felt comfortable. Members of the Muir and Gaston families, by contrast, sought out members of middle-class society like themselves, whether they were inhabitants of a southern English village, fellow students, educated professionals in the New York area, or residents in an established middle-class neighborhood in Toronto.

Just as individuals narrated their emigration and settlement within the framework of their family's movements in a Caribbean historical context, they related their (eventual) return to their island of origin in terms of their family's place in Caribbean history and society. Members of the Smith family generally perceived their home in the Caribbean in relation to their village of origin, but they wanted to bring the material comforts of modern life to this village, primarily in the shape of a large house with all the modern conveniences, but also in the form of a secure means of livelihood. Since both of these goals were difficult to meet, their narratives explained, they had to spend a long working life abroad until they had earned sufficient funds to acquire the house and qualified for old-age pensions, the only dependable income they could hope for on Nevis.

In the Muir family's narratives, the Caribbean home was closely tied to the family's position in the respectable layers of colonial society in the commercial center of Falmouth. This class lost economic ground with the decrease of the commercial and business activities associated with the sugar industry. Furthermore, with the declaration of the independent nation-state of Jamaica, the relatively high status of the old colored middle class, which had been tied to the hierarchical structure of the colonial society, became less secure. There was therefore no ready place for this family in the modern, racially aware nation-state that, at least officially, favors a black, African, non-colonial identity. In their narratives, most of the members of the Muir family therefore did not see a return to Jamaica as desirable but, rather, emphasized that they maintained the good qualities of their Jamaican middle-class culture in the lives they had established abroad.

The Gaston family, where many succeeded in obtaining higher education abroad, found that there was a great need for their knowledge and skills in the new nation-state of Dominica. Their narratives therefore emphasized the desirability of returning to serve the country as members of the new middle class of professionals. This return was not directed toward the family's village of origin, which was located in a remote area of the island state, but toward the island's capital and administrative seat. While the village was not important as a concrete place to which family members might return, it became of central significance as a symbolic place of origin that legitimized their identity as members of the new nation-state. This claim was particularly effective at a time when a new national identity was being established based on the country's long history as an island of independent villages.

By examining life stories related within the three families in the light of the larger historical contexts within which they are grounded in the Caribbean, it is possible to see the migratory moves as guided by quite another logic from that embodied by the historical contexts of the receiving societies. Thus, family members did not migrate to gain a new national identity in a specific country, whether Britain, Canada, or the United States. Nor were they concerned with challenging the international order of nation-states that these countries represent. They moved to pursue objectives that gave sense and purpose in relation to their family's history of movements and the Caribbean place identity this history had generated. While it is possible to interpret migratory moves as guided by dominant family narratives of socioeconomic mobility related within the larger framework of the history of the British Caribbean region, the families also displayed a great deal of variation. Individual life trajectories unfold in complex ways that reflect the varying experiences of individuals and the special choices that these experiences have led them to make.

INTIMATE CONTEXTS OF MIGRATION

Families not only provide a link to a distant place of origin; they also constitute a context of intimate interpersonal relations where life experiences are shared, discussed, and interpreted—and reinterpreted in the light of actually lived lives. The family sphere of intimate relations therefore provides an important context within which individuals make decisions at critical moments in their lives. Jennifer Johnson-Hanks (2002) argues that human beings do not necessarily follow well-ordered life stages. The social, economic, and personal conditions of life are uncertain, and individuals therefore cannot count on having a well-thought-out future of successive life stages. They will encounter a series of "vital conjunctures," or potentially transformative periods in which "structured expectations" intersect with "uncertain futures" (Johnson-Hanks 2002: 871–72). As a result, life trajectories may move along, or shift between, several concurrent paths associated with different life stages as individuals opt for the particular opportunities that present themselves. In a migration context, this means that individuals' migratory trajectories do not necessarily follow well-defined stages such as those of movement, permanent settlement, and integration or movement, temporary settlement, and return. Life trajectories may involve movements in different directions and between a number of different places that entail the sustaining of several communities of belonging tied to these various places as individuals negotiate the contingencies of life and make decisions in relation to the various vital conjunctures that they face.

The life trajectories of the family members I interviewed offered many examples of moves that do not fit into the expected pattern of migration processes, and related life stages, in the three families. There were planned departures that never materialized, multiple and multidirectional transnational or transcontinental moves, incomplete integration processes, and unexpected or delayed returns. In their life stories, some family members accounted for these moves in terms of specific decisions made at "vital conjunctures" where they had to carefully consider a "nexus of potential social futures" (Johnson-Hanks 2002: 871). When Edith accounted for why she decided to move back to Nevis after sixteen years on the Dutch island of St. Martin, despite the fact that her economic basis for returning was very limited, she explained that her return to Nevis was caused by her mother's sudden illness, which made her realize that she was more helpful caring for her mother on Nevis than working on St. Martin to send economic support to the family there. To her, it was no coincidence that she was the one who decided to care for her mother. As the last child, she had been especially close to her parents, she explained, and this made it mandatory for her to be with her mother when she was in need of help. When Mark talked about his decision to re-migrate to Britain, even though he had returned to Dominica dedicated to work for his country, he stated that, after being involved in an unsuccessful political campaign, he realized that his strong political engagement was getting out of hand and that it was ruining his family life and his profession. His social and economic responsibility to his family therefore overrode his desire to serve the country. He related his desire to solve his family problems to his childhood experiences that had taught him that the family will suffer if the father neglects his family. And when Henry described his move to Britain, he noted that his application for a visa to travel to the United States had drawn out so long that he gave up on it and instead decided to join the Royal Air Force. The failed departure for the United States meant that he ended up living in Britain, far away from most of the family and under difficult material conditions. Yet he emphasized that the move was a serendipitous one because it allowed him to continue the good British way of life that he and his siblings enjoyed during their colonial childhood in Jamaica, whereas his more affluent siblings had been forced to adopt what he saw as the foreign, superficial mode of life in the United States.

Whereas some moves were accounted for as the outcome of individuals' decisions made at what were perceived to be vital conjunctures in their lives, other moves were hardly accounted for. In some cases, individuals simply offered little in the way of an explanation for a move; in other cases, they presented themselves as victims of developments beyond their control, or they chose to ignore problematic moves altogether in their life stores. It is highly likely that Anna and her husband moved to Canada at least partly because of the racial hostility their children said the family encountered in Britain. Anna, however, did not say anything about this aspect of the family's decision to leave Britain. She merely noted that her sister had encouraged them to join her in Canada, where better economic opportunities were being offered. It was obvious that Claudette's many years as an undocumented immigrant in the U.S. Virgin Islands had been traumatic, both because she feared that she would be deported and because she was not able to visit her family on Nevis. Yet she did not describe her change from legal to illegal status as a major turning point. She merely noted that this was something that just more or less happened to her because she attempted to secure higher wages and better working conditions at a time when the exploitative labor-certification system became increasingly restrictive. It became clear that Benjamin, who had returned to Dominica to serve his country as a well-educated professional, had applied for an American green card at a certain point in his life. With an American visa he could have advanced his career considerably. He mentioned this application for a visa only parenthetically, however, and added that he dropped the idea when he learned that the Dominican immigration quota would be full for many years to come.

These examples show that the lives of the family members were full of occurrences that individuals could have turned into major turning points in their life stories but chose to downplay or ignore entirely. They did this, I suggest, because these events could not easily be incorporated into the narrative order that they were establishing in their life stories. Thus, the racial problems in Britain encountered by Anna's family did not fit into Anna's narrative of her happy years in Britain, where the family enjoyed the British way of life and her husband's practice was doing well—a period in her life that was put in contrast to the more difficult time the family experienced in Canada. Claudette's life story of a quiet life devoted to the family could not easily incorporate the dramatic story of the problems she faced as an undocumented migrant. Benjamin's plans to leave Dominica did not match his image as a person who had spent his life serving his country. Individuals therefore remolded their life experiences to fit the family narrative in which they wished to inscribe themselves.

Not all of the family members attempted to fit their lives into a dominant family narrative. Some developed their own narratives that fit their particular situation. An example is John, who grew up with his grandparents on Nevis while his parents worked abroad. Since he was the only boy in the home, he was expected to help his grandfather with the animals in the bush. Because of these work demands, he hardly attended school, but he developed great skills in rearing animals and liked being with animals. As a young adult, he joined his mother on St. Martin, but he returned to Nevis after only nine months. When I talked with him, he was living with his wife and child in a small wooden house that he had built on the outskirts of the village where he had grown up. He explained that he realized that he could not live the kind of life with animals that he liked in "another man's country":

> My life is simple. From when I was small I was around a lot of animals. I raised and cared for them. I still do it; it is a constant thing. I don't intend to give it up. Right now, I do mason work. . . . I do work for people, and they like that. I like to be around people, and they like that. I have nothing else to say, my life is very simple.

By emphasizing the value of the simple life close to the land, John identified with the traditional African Caribbean culture of small-scale farming, in contrast to the modern culture of the Western world that the other family members had sought through migration abroad. He thereby rejected the whole idea of migration and the social and economic improvements that it might bring.[2]

John was not the only one who preferred the simple local life to the "potential futures" that might emerge abroad with migration. The oldest brother in the Muir family, Hubert, apparently left for the United States when he was a young man. According to his mother, he returned after a short while, announcing: "The U.S. is for the birds." When he died, he was living in the family home, where he engaged in a variety of economic activities that included raising pigs, keeping chickens, and selling animal feed while maintaining a respectable government position. This story of the good, simple life in the Caribbean also figures in Benjamin's life story. When I asked him to elaborate on why he had decided not to pursue a professional career in the United States, he not only emphasized that he wanted to stay and serve his country, but he also noted that he just liked living in Dominica, where he could be in his garden every day and go fishing when he felt like it—something that would be much more difficult in the United States. These accounts of relatively modest, but contented and respectable lives, in the Caribbean constituted important counter-narratives to the narratives of migration for social and economic opportunities in the outside world. They were often related by those who opted to live in the newly independent Caribbean nation-states to point to the value of local ways of life and criticize Caribbean people's propensity to look for better pastures abroad.

RELATED LIVES

By investigating life stories related by individuals in dispersed family networks, one can explore the complexity of the movements and interconnectedness, rupture, and continuity that has been described as such a central feature of the modern age of globalization. The life stories related by migrants and their descendants will describe departures, arrivals, and life trajectories that span different areas of the world. They will also depict the complicated ways in which individual lives have been influenced by wider social, economic, political, and legal structures that have presented individuals with various opportunities and constraints. Life stories, however, are not just "a window to the past" (Peacock and Holland 1993: 369) that offer the empirical data needed to write a history of Caribbean migration and analyze the various factors that have had an impact on migrants' performance in various destinations. They represent lives lived by real people and they are therefore related in such a way that they give meaning and purpose to the narrators.

Life stories therefore offer important insights into how migratory moves are experienced and given meaning by those most affected by them.

In this work, I have studied the families of three groups of siblings who grew up in family homes on three different islands in the English-speaking Caribbean and who, from the mid-twentieth century on, became dispersed through migration to North America, Europe, and various part of the Caribbean. Through life-story interviews with the family members, I have investigated how they describe themselves both as individuals living varying lives in different parts of the world and as members of a family network that can trace its origins to a particular place in the Caribbean. I have therefore sought to create a framework of study that allowed individuals to represent themselves both as people with their own life experiences encountered in different times and places, and as part of a collectivity that links them with a specific place of origin in the Caribbean. As individuals related their life stories and accounted for their life trajectory, they therefore did so with reference to their origins in the family home in the Caribbean and the cultural values and social expectations that this had given them. In the process of doing so, they both confirm and further develop the notions of relatedness that define these family relations. By asking people to relate their life stories, wherever they are, we may therefore obtain data on the sociocultural order that these people establish in their life stories and their own particular understanding of themselves in this order—in other words, the kinds of communities of belonging and sentiment within which they inscribe themselves from their particular social, economic, geographic, and personal vantage points.

Migration studies necessarily comprise a variety of factors, ranging from push–pull economic and social forces to national and transnational identities. It is important, however, not to lose sight of the key role played by the ways that family relatedness drives people to be both pushed and pulled, but also to push and pull, just as it drives them to take on both national and transnational identities and to transgress these identities.

INTRODUCTION

1. For a critical discussion of the role of nation-states in migration as well as in studies of migration, see Wimmer and Schiller 2003.

2. Further issues that have received relatively little attention are thus the unequal power relationships these networks often involve and the conflicts to which they may give rise. It is also important to examine the creating of new ties, and the resultant reconfiguring of individuals' networks (cf. Levitt and Glick Schiller 2004; Menjívar 2000: 23–36).

3. The cultural construction of place has been an important topic of interest in anthropology since the late 1980s, when several works began to critically appraise the ways in which notions of place have informed theory and method within the discipline (see, e.g., Appadurai 1988; Augé (1995 [1992]); Fardon 1990; Gupta and Ferguson 1992, 1997; Olwig and Hastrup 1997; Rosaldo 1988). This created an awareness of the importance of distinguishing between the ethnographic sites of investigation and analysis that emerged in anthropological research and the notions of place nourished and sustained by the subjects of anthropological investigation. See, for example, Steven Feld's and Keith Basso's edited volume of ethnographic studies of "native constructions of particular localities" that analyze how people in different parts of the world perceive and experience place (Feld and Basso 1996: 6).

4. In a critical reexamination of the concept of community, Vered Amit (2002a: 3) argues that a shift has occurred in the meaning of the term. Whereas formerly the notion of community was used to designate concrete contexts of social relations, today it is employed mainly to refer to collective identities believed to be associated with categories of people. As a result, "community is read as peoplehood and people-

hood is treated as independent of actual ongoing social relations" (Amit 2002a: 9–10). This, she concludes, puts the researcher in the predicament of having to interpret communities as either intentional constructs, established for various manipulative purposes, or primordial entities that continue to exist and have meaning whether or not they are grounded in any social practice (Amit 2002a: 10).

5. For examples of such narrative theory, see Bruner 1986; White 1973, 1981. In the context of migration research, Mary Chamberlain (1997, 2004, 2005) has employed such a narrative approach.

6. The idea that individuals can become "appropriated by" certain categories derives from McDermott 1993.

7. Mary Chamberlain's most recent book, *Family Love in the Diaspora: Migration and the Anglo-Caribbean Experience*, was published in 2006, after I had finished this book manuscript. It offers an important, complementary perspective on the role of family relations in Caribbean migration processes.

8. For Caribbean examples of such studies, see Basch et al. 1994; Cohen 1993; Nunley 1988; Olwig 1993a, 1993b; Scher 2003; Sutton and Chaney 1987. While these studies have offered valuable insights into important aspects of migration, they have tended to be confined to examining those contexts of life that have been pre-defined as central to immigrant groups. They have thus focused on local communities of immigrants that have provided, for their members, a sense of purpose and belonging grounded in their home country. The limitations of this view, I suggest, become apparent when the focus is shifted to individuals who may share a particular background in a place of origin but whose lives are not necessarily grounded in local immigrant communities.

9. In his autobiographical depiction of a middle-class migrant's move from China to England, and then to the United States, the geographer Yi-Fu Tuan writes that the struggles of lower-class migrants for a better life have provided the stuff that goes into a good migration story. The stories of middle-class migrants, by constrast, do not have "the attractive and highly marketable theme of struggle and heroic climb." "What," he asks rhetorically, "is more boring than a story of unqualified success—from good student to well-paid engineer?" (Tuan 1999:10).

1. LEARNING TO MIX IN SOCIETY

1. Baptist ministers helped establish free villages by purchasing large tracts of land with the help of loans obtained in Great Britain and reselling the land in smaller lots of typically two to four acres to the families of the emancipated slaves (Besson 2002: 104–105). For other accounts of the development of the post-emancipation period in

Jamaica and the development of free villages, see Austin-Broos 1997: 34–42; Mintz 1974: 146–79.

2. A cognatic descent group consists of all of the descendants, through both men and women, of a common ancestor—in this case, a former slave.

3. For a comparison with Methodist missionizing, see Olwig 1990, 1993b.

4. For a brief account of the history of Falmouth, see Besson 2002, esp. 73–80. According to Marcus Binney and colleagues, Falmouth enjoyed only a brief forty-year period of economic prosperity, from approximately 1790 to 1830 (Binney et al. 1991: 13).

5. There are several reasons for this. Among them can be mentioned the town's poor harbor facilities for the steamers that replaced the sailboats and the general decline in the sugar industry.

6. In Jamaica, poor women have always been an essential part of the workforce, and they have long played a central role in the internal marketing system as higglers selling agricultural produce, grown first in the slaves' provision grounds and later on peasant farms (Mintz 1974). Since the eighteenth century, Falmouth has had a market where women have come to sell their goods (Besson 2002: 206).

7. This would have been during the late 1930s, when James's business was declining and before Emma had opened her store. Sylvia, the eldest daughter, probably did not attend a private secondary school but was trained as a nurse.

8. Wolmer attempted as early as the 1850s to introduce a secondary-school curriculum that included "Greek, Latin, mathematics, Spanish, French, English, history and sacred teaching, as well as the elementary subjects, reading, writing, spelling, grammar, arithmetic, general knowledge and geography." Due to objections from the white population, the school was forced to give up its advanced program in the late 1860s (Miller 1990: 54–55). While Wolmer began as a school for white students, it had shifted to being a school primarily for "colored" students by 1830, when it had 88 white students and 194 colored students (Smith 1996: 155). For other works on the role of education in Jamaican society, see Foner 1973; Gordon 1987, 1988; Kuper 1976; Whyte 1983 (1977).

2. SEEKING IMPROVEMENT BEYOND JAMAICA

1. As noted, Hubert died in the early 1980s. I therefore was not able to ascertain exactly what had motivated him to stay in Jamaica.

2. She died a year before I began my research. Her migration experiences therefore are not well illuminated. This is unfortunate, because Sylvia seems to have played a central role in family relations in New York. Her husband was too ill to interview when I was in New York.

3. While migration to the United States was largely unrestricted until 1924, it was heavily dominated by Europeans, especially Italians and Eastern European Jews, during the late nineteenth century and early twentieth century. The number of Caribbean immigrants would have been relatively small (Foner 2000:6).

4. According to Nancy Foner, 15,300 West Indians were reported to be living in Britain in 1951. Two decades later, the figure had increased to 446,200. About half of these immigrants were Jamaicans: "By 1966, an estimated 188,100 Jamaican immigrants lived in Britain, and the total Jamaican population in Britain at that time, including those of Jamaican descent born in Britain, was 273,800" (Foner 1979: 13).

5. Anancy, or Anancie, is a spider trickster figure known for his cunning. He is a hero in folk tales throughout the Caribbean and is believed to have derived from West African mythology.

3. THE VILLAGE ORIGINS

1. He is referring to his father's eldest child, born to another women before the father married the younger children's mother.

2. I did not interview the last sibling, Vera, who was mentally disabled.

3. Only Dominica has a sizable indigenous population of Carib Indians (Baker 1994; Honychurch 1982, 1995).

4. According to Cecilia Green (1999: 65), the "enrolment figure had risen to three-quarters of all primary school-age children" by 1950; see also Gordon 1963: 33. In his study of Wesley, one of the few English-speaking villages in Dominica, Michel-Rolph Trouillot argues that the traditionally good educational record of these villagers is caused by the fact that these children understood the English language of instruction much better than did other Dominican rural children (Trouillot 1988: 188).

5. Even as late as the 1980s, when Trouillot did fieldwork in Dominica, he noted that the expression "patois people foolish" was often heard (Trouillot 1988:280).

6. In a study of language use in Dominica published in the 1980s, Pauline Christie found that more than two hundred years after the institution of English as the formal language, French creole was still widely spoken in many villages. Furthermore, in fairly isolated communities, such as Sainte-Anne, it was still the dominant language, and some people were monolingual patois speakers (Christie 1982: 41, 46).

7. The use of physical discipline in Caribbean child-rearing practices has been noted especially in Caribbean migration destinations in Great Britain and North America, where it has been seen as a major problem (see, e.g., Goulborne 2001: 28; Waters 1999a: 225).

8. For an analysis of the importance of children's labor power in the peasant economy of Dominica, see Trouillot 1988: 243–55.

9. Green (1999) notes that Dominican women have always played a central economic role, but that their contribution has often been trivialized and viewed as subordinate to the male household head.

10. See, e.g., Baker 1994; Eguchi 1984; Trouillot 1988; Wylie 1982, 1993.

11. According to Honychurch (1995: 207), vanilla production became of major importance in Dominica in the late 1930s. The vanilla was cultivated by peasants: "Because the plants needed a great amount of personal care and each flower had to be pollinated by hand, this prevented it from becoming a large-scale estate crop. Beans were sold to local merchants or to the Vanilla Growers Association who cured and packed the product for export to North America." Vanilla production broke down in Dominica in 1945 when a fire ruined a warehouse that stored 50,000 pounds of vanilla beans owned by the Vanilla Growers Association. Vanilla continued to be cultivated on the island at a lower level until 1959, when it could no longer compete with cheap, artificially produced vanilla. Spencer Gaston seems to have dried and cured the vanilla beans independently of the Vanilla Growers Association.

12. In his analysis, Jonathan Wylie is drawing on fieldwork conducted by Jonathan Wouk in Dominica in the mid-1960s. It resulted in an undergraduate honors thesis at Harvard University. Unfortunately, I have not had access to it.

4. IN PURSUIT OF A PROPER LIVELIHOOD

1. Acording to Robert Amory Myers (1976:36), until a few years before he did his fieldwork in Dominica, "the most common form of transportation was by launch, small boat, or schooner from one village or estate to another. Overland, wealthier planters and merchants rode horses, while others walked along paths and wagon trails from one point to another."

2. Honychurch (1995: 188) notes that construction of a highway between this area and Roseau was not completed before 1972. Myers (1976:171) described the road as still unpaved in large sections in 1976, so that it was "a slow, rough journey of one and one-half hours to cover less than twenty miles." Riva Berleant-Schiller and William Maurer (1993) have argued that because travel is so difficul in Dominica, important networks of communication have developed among people who travel on the island.

3. It even led one newspaper columnist to write "scathingly about 'square legs in round holes,' according to Honychurch (1995: 236).

4. Most of the secondary schools were located in Roseau when the Gaston siblings

went to school. The grammar school for boys and the Catholic convent high school for girls were established in Dominica during the nineteenth century. By the 1940s, the Catholic St. Mary's Academy for boys and the Methodist Wesley High School for girls had also come into existence (Baker 1994:187; Honychurch 1995:201).

5. This preference, of course, may not just have been caused by color. Alan, however, referred to it as if his father's choice was based on color prejudice.

6. The West Indian governments instituted the highly competitive island scholarships for university education in the late nineteenth century (Gordon 1963: 239). I do not know when the island scholarship was established in Dominica, one of the poorer Windward Islands. It seems that when Benjamin won the island scholarship in Dominica, it was only awarded on a biennial basis.

7. In her history of secondary education in the West Indies, Shirley Gordon refers rather scathingly to "the exaggerated importance given to the small number of university scholarships available for the best pupils of the year so that they could go away, about half of them not to return, mainly to train in English medicine and law" (Gordon 1963: 3–4).

8. In a review of the literature on return migration, George Gmelch has proposed that the return be regarded as constituting a final closure of the migration movement in the sense that it involves the "movement of emigrants back to their homelands to resettle" (Gmelch 1980: 136). Returning is not just a matter of traveling back to a place of origin, however, because most migrants leave to achieve a specific goal and do not want to return before they have succeeded. See also King 2000.

9. For further discussion of the Canadian domestic scheme, see Barber 1991; Douglas 1968; Henry 1968.

10. In a study of Caribbean women who were employed as domestic workers in New York City, Shellee Colen (1989a, 1989b, 1990) argues that they often find themselves in a precarious situation of providing essential parental services to children but being treated as alien elements in the family because they disrupt normal parent–child relations in the nuclear family. Nelly made no reference to such problems.

11. Until 1962, Canadian legislation favored European immigrants, and there were severe restrictions on immigration from other parts of the world. According to Elisabeth Thomas-Hope, Canada changed its immigration legislation in 1962 and in 1965 in response to changes in labor demands (Thomas-Hope 1998: 195). Many of those who arrived early on the scheme had a fair amount of education, and some of them were even trained as nurses and teachers (Barber 1991: 213–24; Henry 1994: 121).

12. In the new legislation, migrants to Canada are required to pass a "points test" where "fifty out of 100 points based on a number of educational, employment, linguistic, and other criteria have to be earned to qualify for entry into the country"

(Henry 1994: 27). This law favors English-speaking Caribbeans, many of whom are relatively well educated. In the period from 1967 to 1992, Dwaine Plaza (1998: 248) states, about 300,000 Caribbean immigrants entered Canada, the vast majority settling in Toronto, where many migrants already had family and friends. According to Frances Henry (1994: 28), the census in 1991 listed a population of 269,705 born in the former British and present French and Dutch Caribbean. The breakdown by main country in official statistics from 1992 was Jamaica, 102,440 (37.9 percent); Guyana, 66,055 (24.4 percent); Trinidad and Tobago, 49,385 (18.3 percent); Barbados, 14,820 (5.4 percent); all other, 37,005 (13.7 percent). Dominicans are a small population group compared with those from the larger Caribbean countries. Apparently, the Caribana began when the Canadian federal government invited a Caribbean group to participate in the parade at the Canadian Centennial celebrations. When John Nunley studied the Caribana festivals in 1985 and 1986, the Dominica Association of Ontario was one of the main organizations participating in the event. At that time, Caribana attracted approximately half a million people (Nunley 1988: 174–75). In 1992, an estimated million people participated in the festival (Henry 1994: 178).

5. A FAMILY HOME

    1. Carol, born after Jean, died as a young woman.

    2. For a discussion of some of the other social aspects of using children to run errands, see Olwig 2002d.

6. TO BETTER OUR CONDITION

    1. Among students in the highest grades of the secondary school and the A-level college in Charlestown, about half wanted to emigrate (Olwig 1987:159).

    2. For works on Nevisian migratory movements through time, see Frucht 1966; Olwig 1993b; Richardson 1983.

    3. In her work on migration from Nevis to Britain, Margaret Byron also notes that most Nevisians migrate with the expectation that they will return (Byron 1994: esp. 168–97; 1999). See also King 2000; Philpott 1968: 468, 474.

    4. Edwin's younger sister Carol, who died in the early 1960s, may already have moved to St. Kitts when Edwin left for England. St. Kitts is located a few miles from Nevis, and a trip to St. Kitts would involve a fairly short boat ride. It would therefore not have been regarded as a major migratory move.

    5. These three islands were an administrative unit at the time and became an associated state in 1966. In 1967, Anguilla withdrew from the state (Lowenthal 1972: 10–11).

6. These experiences resonate with those recounted by other Caribbean migrants in Britain (see Chamberlain 1997; see also chapter 4 on the Gaston family).

7. Chapeltown is one of the areas in Britain with the heaviest concentration of a Caribbean ethnic population. In 1991, the "indices of segregation of the Caribbean ethnic population at enumeration district level"—using a scale from 0 (no segregation) to 100 (total segregation)—were 43 in Leicester, 49 in London, 68 in Liverpool, and 72 in Leeds. In comparison, the level of segregation "for African Americans in cities in the United States is about 80" (Peach 1998: 207).

8. West Indian migration to the U.S. Virgin Islands has been documented in a number of works. See, e.g., Green 1972; Lewis 1972; Olwig 1985.

9. See the chapters on the Muir and Gaston families.

10. The annual permanent immigration quota was two hundred for the British dependency of St. Kitts, Nevis, and Anguilla. Most of these visas would have been issued to close relatives (spouses, parents, children) of immigrants with permanent visas or citizenship.

11. By saying that she was "on his time," she indicates that her husband sponsored her labor certificate. This would have been a highly unusual procedure, so I assume that she meant that she was dependent on her husband for her legal status in the Virgin Islands.

12. According to Lito Valls (1981: 48), there are different theories concerning the etymology of the term: "The most plausible seems to be the theory that down-islanders referred to Antiguans as garrots. In turn, the native Virgin Islands lumped them all together as garrats. Although it is sometimes accepted jocularly for the most part, it carries pejorative connotations of crudeness, stupidness and bad manners."

7. THE FIRST GENERATION

1. It has been shown that families muster the economic means necessary to travel, to help find work and a place to stay in the migration destination, and to look after migrants' children and family home in the place of origin (see, e.g., Basch et al. 1994; Garrison and Weiss 1979; Olwig 1993b; Philpott 1973).

2. Chamberlain (2005: 182) notes that, because the family is an important context within which cultural values are transmitted, it "has become a statement of cultural and ethnic identity."

3. For a further comparative analysis of Henry and Edwin, see Olwig 2002b.

4. In a review of migration studies in a broader global context, Aiwa Ong (1999: 8–34) discusses three major approaches to migration research: (1) U.S.-centered migration studies; (2) cultural globalization; and (3) diasporas and cosmopolitanisms.

8. GENERATIONAL PERSPECTIVES

1. I interviewed sixty-one cousins, as well as a number of their spouses.

2. Alex Haley's *Roots* (1976), published in the United States shortly before the Gaston family returned to England, created huge interest in African roots on the part of people of African descent in North America and Europe.

3. As noted, he was not sponsored by members of the Muir family living in the United States. I do not know whether or not he requested this.

4. Multiculturalism has been subjected to critical discussion in anthropology and related fields. See, e.g., Amit 2002a: 254–58; Amit-Talai 1995; Amit-Talai and Knowles 1996; Baumann 1996, 1997, 1999; Turner 1993; Verdery 1994; Werbner and Modood 1997.

5. This flexible approach to ethnicity was also apparent among the children of British Greek parents studied by Michael Anderson (1999). He found that the children of these mixed marriages identified themselves as Greek or British, depending on the social context in which they found themselves. As was the case with the children of British and Greek parents, the children I interviewed had a mixed ethnic background, and it was therefore difficult to settle on one particular ethnic identity. See also Ackroyd and Pilkington 1999; Amit 2002a: 22.

6. This approach has been particularly influential in North American migration research, where Warner's and Srole's three-generational integration model was prevalent (Waters 1999a: 194).

7. For a further discussion of the issue of race in an American context, see also Foner 2000: 167; Scales-Trent 1995: 136–37.

8. For a critical discussion of the category "black" in a British context, see Amit 2002b: 18–20.

9. RELATING HISTORIES OF MIGRATION

1. A similar point has been brought out by Peggy Levitt and Nina Glick Schiller (2004: 1010), who call for the need to distinguish between "ways of being" and "ways of belonging."

2. For a further discussion of this point, as well as John's life story, see Olwig 1999a; see also Olwig 1993b.

Abrahams, Roger. 1983. *The Man-of-Words in the West Indies*. Baltimore: Johns Hopkins University Press.

Ackroy, J., and A. Pilkington. 1999. "Childhood and the Construction of Ethnic Identities in a Global Age: A Dramatic Encounter." *Childhood* 6, no. 4: 443–54.

Alexander, Henry Jacob [Jack]. 1973. "The Culture of Middle-Class Family Life in Kingston, Jamaica." Ph.D. diss, University of Chicago.

———. 1977. "The Culture of Race in Middle-Class Kingston, Jamaica." *American Ethnologist* 4, no. 3: 413–35.

———. 1984. "Love, Race, Slavery, and Sexuality in Jamaican Images of the Family." Pp. 147–80 in *Kinship Ideology and Practice in Latin America*, ed. Raymond T. Smith. Chapel Hill: University of North Carolina Press.

Alleyne, Brian W. 2005. "Cultural Politics in Personal Narratives of Caribbean Heritage in Britain." Pp. 263–79 in *Caribbean Narratives of Belonging: Fields of Relations, Sites of Identity*, ed. Jean Besson and Karen Fog Olwig. Oxford: Macmillan.

Amit, Vered. 2002a. "An Anthropology without Community?" Pp. 11–70 in Vered Amit and Nigel Rapport, *The Trouble with Community*. London: Pluto Press.

———. 2002b. "Reconceptualizing Community." Pp. 1–20 in *Realizing Community: Concepts, Social Relationships and Sentiments*, ed. Vered Amit. London: Routledge.

Amit-Talai, Vered. 1995. "Anthropology, Multiculturalism, and the Concept of Culture." *Folk* 37: 125–33.

Amit-Talai, Vered, and Caroline Knowles, eds. 1996. *Re-Situating Identities: The Politics of Race, Ethnicity and Culture*. Peterborough, Ont.: Broadview Press.

Anderson, Benedict. 1991 (1983). *Imagined Communities: Reflections on the Origins and Spread of Nationalism*. London: Verso.

Anderson, Michael. 1999. "Children In-Between: Constructing Identities in the Bicultural Family." *Journal of the Royal Anthropological Institute* 5, no. 1: 13–26.

Anderson-Levy, Lisa M. 2001. "Colliding/Colluding Identities: Race, Class, and Gender in Jamaican Family Systems." Pp. 185–203 in *New Directions in Anthropological Kinship*, ed. Linda Stone. Lanham, Md.: Rowman and Littlefield.

Appadurai, Arjun. 1988. "Putting Hierarchy in Its Place." *Cultural Anthropology* 3, no. 1: 36–49.

——. 1996. *Modernity at Large: Cultural Dimensions of Globalization*. Minneapolis: University of Minnesota Press.

Augé, Marc. 1995 (1992). *Non-Places: Introduction to an Anthropology of Supermodernity*. London: Verso.

Austin, Diane J. 1983. "Culture and Ideology in the English-Speaking Caribbean: A View from Jamaica." *American Ethnologist* 4, no. 3: 223–40.

Austin-Broos, Diane J. 1994a. "Race/Class: Jamaica's Discourse of Heritable Identity." *Nieuwe West-Indische Gids* 68, nos. 3–4: 213–33.

——. 1994b. "Talking Race: The Violence of Words and Silences in a Jamaican Discourse." Paper presented at the panel "The Violence of Words and Silences," American Anthropological Association Meetings, Atlanta.

——. 1997. *Jamaica Genesis: Religion and the Politics of Moral Orders*. Chicago: University of Chicago Press.

Baker, Patrick L. 1994. *Centring the Periphery: Chaos, Order, and the Ethnohistory of Dominica*. Kingston: University of the West Indies Press.

Barber, Marilyn. 1991. *Immigrant Domestic Servants in Canada*. Booklet No. 16. Ottawa: Canadian Historical Association.

Barnes, John A. 1969. "Networks and Political Process." Pp. 51–76 in *Social Networks in Urban Situations*, ed. J. Clyde Mitchell. Manchester: Manchester University Press.

Barth, Fredrik. 1969. *Ethnic Groups and Boundaries*. Boston: Little, Brown.

Basch, Linda, Nina Glick Schiller, and Cristina Szanton Blanc. 1994. *Nations Unbound: Transnational Projects, Postcolonial Predicaments and Deterritorialized Nation-States*. Langhorne, Pa.: Gordon and Breach.

Bashi, Vilna, and Antonio McDaniel. 1997. "A Theory of Immigration and Racial Stratification." *Journal of Black Studies* 27, no. 5: 668–82.

Baud, Michiel. 1994. "Families and Migration: Towards an Historical Analysis of Family Networks." *Economic and Social History in the Netherlands* 5: 83–107.

Baumann, Gerd. 1996. *Contesting Culture: Discourses of Identity in Multi-ethnic London*. Cambridge: Cambridge University Press.

——. 1997. "Dominant and Demotic Discourses of Culture: Their Relevance to

Multi-ethnic Alliances." Pp. 209–25 in *Debating Cultural Hybridity: Multi-Cultural Identities and the Politics of Anti-Racism*, ed. Pnina Werbner and Tariq Modood. London: Zed Books.

———. 1999. *The Multicultural Riddle: Rethinking National, Ethnic and Religious Identities*. London: Routledge.

Berleant-Schiller, Riva, and William M. Maurer. 1993. "Women's Place Is Every Place: Merging Domains and Women's Roles in Barbuda and Dominica." Pp. 65–79 in *Women and Change in the Caribbean*, ed. Janet Momsen. London: James Currey.

Besson, Jean. 2002. *Martha Brae's Two Histories: European Expansion and Caribbean Culture-Building in Jamaica*. Chapel Hill: University of North Carolina Press.

———. 2005. "Sacred Sites, Shifting Histories: Narratives of Belonging, Land and Globalization in the Cockpit Country, Jamaica." Pp. 17–43 in *Caribbean Narratives of Belonging: Fields of Relations, Sites of Identity*, ed. Jean Besson and Karen Fog Olwig. Oxford: Macmillan.

Binney, Marcus, John Harris, and Kit Martin. 1991. *Jamaica's Heritage, an Untapped Resource: A Preservation Proposal by Tourism Action Plan Limited in Collaboration with the Jamaica National Heritage Trust*. Kingston: Mill Press.

Blake, Judith. 1961. *Family Structure in Jamaica*. New York: Free Press of Glencoe.

Boissevain, Jeremy. 1974. *Friends of Friends*. Oxford: Basil Blackwell.

Brettell, Caroline. 2000. "Theorizing Migration in Anthropology." Pp. 97–136 in *Migration Theory: Talking across Disciplines*, ed. Caroline B. Brettell and James F. Hollified. New York: Routledge.

———. 2003. *Anthropology and Migration. Essays on Transnationalism, Ethnicity, and Identity*. Walnut Creek, Calif.: AltaMira Press.

Brown, Jacqueline Nassy. 2005. *Dropping Anchor, Setting Sail: Geographies of Race in Black Liverpool*. Princeton: Princeton University Press.

Bruner, Edward M. 1986. "Ethnography as Narrative." Pp. 139–55 in *The Anthropology of Experience*, ed. Victor W. Turner and Edward M. Bruner. Urbana: University of Illinois Press.

Bruner, Jerome. 1987. "Life as Narrative." *Social Research* 54, no. 1: 11–32.

Bryceson, Deborah Fahy, and Ulla Vuorela. 2002. "Transnational Families in the Twenty-First Century." Pp. 3–30 in *The Transnational Family: New European Frontiers and Global Networks*, ed. Deborah Fahy Bryceson and Ulla Vuorela. Oxford: Berg.

Byron, Margaret. 1994. *Post-War Caribbean Migration to Britain: The Unfinished Cycle*. Avebury: Aldershot.

———. 1999. "The Caribbean-Born Population in 1990s Britain: Who Will Return?" *Journal of Ethnic and Migration Studies* 25, no. 2: 247–62.

———. 2000. "Return Migration to the Eastern Caribbean: Comparative Experiences and Policy Implications." *Social and Economic Studies* 49, no. 4: 155–88.

Campbell, John R., and Alan Rew. 1999. "Preface." Pp. ix–xi in *Identity and Affect: Experiences of Identity in a Globalising World*, ed. John R. Campbell and Alan Rew. London: Pluto Press.

Carnegie, Charles V. 1987. "A Social Psychology of Caribbean Migrations: Strategic Flexibility in the West Indies." Pp. 32–43 in *The Caribbean Exodus*, ed. Barry B. Levine. New York: Praeger.

Carsten, J. 1991. "Children In-Between: Fostering and the Process of Kinship on Pulau Langkawi, Malaysia." *Man* 26, no. 3: 425–43.

———. 2000. "Introduction: Cultures of Relatedness." Pp. 1–36 in *Cultures of Relatedness: New Approaches to the Study of Kinship*, ed. J. Carsten. Cambridge: Cambridge University Press.

Chamberlain, Mary. 1997. *Narratives of Exile and Return*. New York: St. Martin's Press.

———. 1998. "Introduction." Pp. 1–17 in *Caribbean Migration: Globalised Identities*, ed. Mary Chamberlain. London: Routledge.

———. 2004. "Transnational Families: Memories and Narratives." *Global Networks* 4, no. 3: 227–41.

———. 2005. "Language, Identity and Caribbean Families: Transnational Narratives." Pp.171–88 in *Caribbean Narratives of Belonging: Fields of Relations, Sites of Identity*, ed. Jean Besson and Karen Fog Olwig. Oxford: Macmillan.

———. 2006. *Family Love in the Diaspora: Migration and the Anglo-Caribbean Experience*. New Brunswick, N.J.: Transactions Publishers.

Christie, Pauline. 1982. "Language Maintenance and Language Shift in Dominica." *Caribbean Quarterly* 28, no. 4: 41–51.

Clarke, Edith. 1970 (1957). *My Mother Who Fathered Me*. London: George Allen and Unwin.

Cohen, Abner. 1993. *Masquerade Politics*. Oxford: Berg Publishers.

Cohen, Anthony. 1994. *Self Consciousness: An Alternative Anthropology of Identity*. London: Routledge.

———. 1996. "Personal Nationalism: A Scottish View of Some Rites, Rights and Wrongs." *American Ethnologist* 23, no. 4: 802–15.

Cohen, Robin. 1998. "Cultural Diaspora: The Caribbean Case." Pp.21–35 in *Caribbean Migration: Globalised Identities*, ed. Mary Chamberlain. London: Routledge.

Colen, Shellee. 1989a. "'Just a Little Respect': West Indian Domestic Workers in New York City." Pp. 171–94 in *Muchachas No More: Household Workers in Latin America and the Caribbean*, ed. Elsa M. Chaney and Mary Garcia Castro. Philadelphia: Temple University Press.

———. 1989b. " 'Like a Mother to Them': Stratified Reproduction and West Indian Childcare Workers and Employers in New York." Pp. 78–102 in *Conceiving the New World Order: The Global Politics of Reproduction*, ed. Faye D. Ginsburg and Rayna Rapp. Berkeley: University of California Press.

———. 1990. " 'Housekeeping' for the Green Card: West Indian Household Workers, the State, and Stratified Reproduction in New York." Pp. 89–118 in *At Work in Homes: Household Workers in World Perspective*, ed. Roger Sanjek and Shellee Colen. American Ethnological Society Monograph Series, no. 3. Arlington, Va.: American Anthropological Association.

Conway, Denis. 1989. "Caribbean International Mobility Traditions." *Boletin de Estudios Latinoamericanos y del Caribe* 46: 17–47.

Conway, Denis, and Ualthan Bigby. 1987. "Residential Differentiation among an Overlooked Black Minority: New Immigrant West Indians in New York." Pp. 74–83 in *Caribbean Life in New York City*, ed. Constance R. Sutton and Elsa M. Chaney. New York: Center for Migration Studies.

Davis-Palmer, Yvonne. 2005. "Narratives and the Cultural Construction of Belonging in Sligoville, Jamaica's First Free Village." Pp. 44–62 in *Caribbean Narratives of Belonging: Fields of Relations, Sites of Identity*, ed. Jean Besson and Karen Fog Olwig. Oxford: Macmillan.

de Certeau, Michel. 1984. *The Practice of Everyday Life*. Berkeley: University of California Press.

Des Chene, Mary. 1997. "Locating the Past." Pp. 66–85 in *Anthropological Locations: Boundaries and Grounds of a Field Science*, ed. Akhil Gupta and James Ferguson. Berkeley: University of California Press.

DeWind, Josh, and Philip Kasinitz. 1997. "Everything Old Is New Again? Processes and Theories of Immigrant Incorporation." *International Migration Review* 31, no. 4: 1096–1111.

Douglas, E. M. K. 1968. "West Indians in Canada: The Household-Help Scheme." *Social and Economic Studies* 17, no. 2: 215–17.

Douglass, Lisa. 1992. *The Power of Sentiment: Love, Hierarchy, and the Jamaican Family Elite*. Boulder, Colo.: Westview Press.

Edwards, J., and M. Strathern. 2000. "Including Our Own." Pp. 149–66 in *Cultures of Relatedness: New Approaches to the Study of Kinship*, ed. Janet Carsten. Cambridge: Cambridge University Press.

Eguchi, Nobukiyo. 1984. "Relative Wealth and Adaptive Strategy among Peasants in a Small Village Community of Dominica, West Indies." Ph.D. diss., University of North Carolina, Chapel Hill.

Epstein, A. L. 1969. "The Network and Urban Social Organization." Pp.77–116 in

Social Networks in Urban Situations: Analyses of Personal Relationships in Central African Towns, ed. J. Clyde Mitchell. Manchester: Manchester University Press.

Fardon, Richard. 1990. "Localizing Strategies: The Regionalization of Ethnographic Accounts." Pp. 1–35 in *Localizing Strategies: Regional Traditions of Ethnographic Writing*, ed. Richard Fardon. Edinburgh: Scottish Academic Press.

Feld, Steven, and Keith H. Basso. 1996. "Introduction." Pp. 3–11 in *Senses of Place*, ed. Steven Feld and Keith H. Basso. Santa Fe, N.M.: School of American Research Advanced Seminar Series.

Fleming, W. G. 1964. *Secondary and Adult Education in Dominica*. Toronto: Ontario College of Education, University of Toronto.

Foner, Nancy. 1973. *Status and Power in Rural Jamaica: A Study of Educational and Political Change*. New York: Teachers College Press.

———. 1979. *Jamaica Farewell: Jamaican Immigrants in London*. London: Routledge and Kegan Paul.

———. 2000. *From Ellis Island to JFK: New York's Two Great Waves of Immigration*. Chelsea, Mich.: Russell Sage Foundation.

Freeman, Carla. 1993. "Designing Women: Corporate Discipline and Barbados's Off-Shore Pink-Collar Sector." *Cultural Anthropology* 8, no. 2: 169–86.

———. 2000. *High Tech and High Heels in the Global Economy: Women, Work and Pink Collar Identities in the Caribbean*. Durham: Duke University Press.

Frucht, Richard. 1966. "Community and Context in a Colonial Society: Social and Economic Change in Nevis, British West Indies." Ph.D. diss., Brandeis University, Waltham, Mass.

Garrison, Vivian, and Carol I. Weiss. 1979. "Dominican Family Networks and United States Immigration Policy: A Case Study." *International Migration Review* 13, no. 2: 264–83.

Geertz, Clifford. 1973. *The Interpretation of Cultures*. New York: Basic Books.

Gilroy, Paul. 1987. *"There Ain't No Black in the Union Jack": The Cultural Politics of Race and Nation*. London: Hutchinson.

———. 1993. *The Black Atlantic: Modernity and Double Consciousness*. London: Verso.

Glick Schiller, Nina, and Georges Eugene Fouron. 2001. *George Woke Up Laughing: Long-Distance Nationalism and the Search for Home*. Durham: Duke University Press.

Gluckman, Max. 1963 (1961). "Anthropological Problems Arising from the African Industrial Revolution." Pp. 67–82 in *Social Change in Modern Africa*, ed. Aidan Southal. London: Oxford University Press.

Gmelch, George. 1980. "Return Migration." *Annual Review of Anthropology* 9: 135–59.

Gordon, Derek. 1987. *Class, Status and Social Mobility in Jamaica*. Mona, Jamaica: Institute of Social and Economic Research, University of the West Indies.

———. 1988. "Race, Class and Social Mobility in Jamaica." Pp. 264–82 in *Garvey: His Work and Impact*, ed. Rupert Lewis and Patrick Byran. Mona, Jamaica: Institute of Social and Economic Research, University of the West Indies.

Gordon, Shirley. 1963. *A Century of West Indian Education*. London: Longmans, Green.

Goulbourne, Harry. 2001. "The Socio-Political Context of Caribbean Families in the Atlantic World. Pp. 12–31 in *Caribbean Families in Britain and the Trans-Atlantic World*, ed. Harry Goulbourne and Mary Chamberlain. London: Macmillan.

Green, Cecilia. 1999. "A Recalcitrant Plantation Colony: Dominica, 1880–1946." *Nieuwe West-Indische Gids* 73, nos. 3–4: 43–71.

Green, James W. 1972. "Social Networks in St. Croix, United States Virgin Islands." Ph.D. diss., University of Washington, Seattle.

Gulløv, Eva. 1999. *Betydningsdannelse blandt børn*. Copenhagen: Gyldendal, Social-pædagogiske Bibliotek.

Gupta, Akhil, and James Ferguson. 1992. "Beyond 'Culture': Space, Identity, and the Politics of Difference." *Cultural Anthropology* 7: 6–23.

———. 1997. "Discipline and Practice: 'The Field' as Site, Method, and Location in Anthropology." Pp. 1–46 in *Anthropological Locations: Boundaries and Grounds of a Field Science*, ed. Akhil Gupta and James Ferguson. Berkeley: University of California Press.

Haley, Alex. 1976. *Roots: The Saga of an American Family*. New York: Dell.

Hall, Douglas. 1971. *Five of the Leewards 1834–1870*. St. Laurence, Barbados: Caribbean Universities Press.

Hall, Stuart. 1990. "Cultural Identity and Diaspora." Pp. 222–37 in *Identity, Community, Culture, Difference*, ed. Jonathan Rutherford. London: Lawrence and Wishard.

Heath, Shirley Brice, and Milbrey W. McLaughlin. 1993a. "Ethnicity and Gender in Theory and Practice: The Youth Perspective." Pp. 13–35 in *Identity and Inner-City Youth: Beyond Ethnicity and Gender*, ed. Shirley Brice Heath and Milbrey W. McLaughlin. New York: Teachers College Press.

———. 1993b. "Introduction: Building Identities for Inner-City Youth." Pp. 1–12 in *Identity and Inner-City Youth: Beyond Ethnicity and Gender*, ed. Shirley Brice Heath and Milbrey W. McLaughlin. New York: Teachers College Press.

Hendricks, Glenn. 1974. *The Dominican Diaspora: From the Dominican Republic to New York City—Villagers in Transition*. New York: Teachers College Press.

Henry, Frances. 1968. "The West Indian Domestic Scheme in Canada." *Social and Economic Studies* 17, no. 1: 83–91.

———. 1994. *The Caribbean Diaspora in Toronto: Learning to Live with Racism*. Toronto: University of Toronto Press.

Heuman, Gad. 1981. *Between Black and White*. Westport, Conn.: Greenwood Press.

Honychurch, Lennox. 1982. *Our Island Culture*. Roseau: Dominica Cultural Council.

———. 1995. *The Dominica Story: A History of the Island*. London: Macmillan.

Hvidt, Kristian. 1975. *Flight to America: The Social Background of 300,000 Danish Emigrants*. New York: Academic Press.

Jenkins, Richard. 1996. *Social Identity*. London: Routledge.

Johnson-Hanks, Jennifer. 2002. "On the Limits of Life Stages in Ethnography: Toward a Theory of Vital Conjunctures." *American Anthropologist* 104, no. 3: 865–80.

Kahn, Miriam. 1996. "Your Place and Mine: Sharing Emotional Landscapes in Wamira, New Guinea." Pp. 167–96 in *Senses of Place*, ed. Steven Feld and Keith H. Basso. Santa Fe, N.M.: School of American Research Advanced Seminar Series.

Kasinitz, Philip. 1992. *Caribbean New York: Black Immigrants and the Politics of Race*. Ithaca, N.Y.: Cornell University Press.

Kearney, Michael. 1995. "The Local and the Global: The Anthropology of Globalization and Transnationalism." *Annual Review of Anthropology* 24: 547–65.

Khan, Aisha. 2004. *Callaloo Nation: Metaphors of Race and Religious Identity among South Asians in Trinidad*. Durham: Duke University Press.

King, Russell. 2000. "Generalizations from the History of Return Migration." Pp. 7–55 in *Return Migration: Journey of Hope or Despair?* ed. Bimal Ghosh. Geneva: International Organization for Migration and the United Nations.

Kuper, Adam. 1976. *Changing Jamaica*. London: Routledge and Kegan Paul.

Langness, Lewis, and Gelya Frank. 1981. *Lives: An Anthropological Approach to Biography*. Novato, Calif.: Chandler and Sharp.

Levitt, Peggy, and Nina Glick Schiller. 2004. "Transnational Perspectives on Migration: Conceptualizing Simultaneity." *International Migration Review* 38, no. 3: 1002–39.

Lewis, Gordon K. 1972. *The Virgin Islands*. Evanston, Ill.: Northwestern University Press.

Linde, Charlotte. 1993. *Life Stories: The Creation of Coherence*. New York: Oxford University Press.

Löfgren, Orvar. 1989. "Learning to Remember and Learning to Forget: Class and Memory in Modern Sweden." Pp. 145–61 in *Erinnern und Vergessen*, ed. Brigitte Bönisch-Brednish et al. Beiträge zur Volkskunde in Niedersachsen, no. 5. Göttingen: V. Schmese.

Lowenthal, David. 1972. *West Indian Societies*. London: Oxford University Press.

Mackey, E. 1997. "The Cultural Politics of Populism: Celebrating Canadian National Identity." Pp. 136–64 in *Anthropology of Policy: Critical Perspectives on Governance and Power*, ed. Chris Shore and Susan Wright. London: Routledge.

Mahler, Sarah. 1998. "Theoretical and Empirical Contributions: Toward a Research

Agenda for Transnationalism." Pp. 64–100 in *Transnationalism from Below*, ed. Michael Peter Smith and Luis Eduardo Guarnizo. New Brunswick, N.J.: Transaction.

Manning, Frank E. 1981. "Celebrating Cricket: The Symbolic Construction of Caribbean Politics." *American Ethnologist* 8, no. 3: 616–32.

Marcus, George. 1995. "Ethnography in/of the World System: The Emergence of Multi-Sited Ethnography." *Annual Review of Anthropology* 24: 95–117.

McDermott, Ray P. 1993. "The Acquisition of a Child by a Learning Disability." Pp. 269–305 in *Understanding Practice: Perspectives on Activity and Context*, ed. Seth Chaiklin and Jean Lave. Cambridge: Cambridge University Press.

Menjívar, Cecilia. 2000. *Fragmented Ties: Salvadorean Immigrant Networks in America*. Berkeley: University of California Press.

Merrill, Gordon C. 1958. *The Historical Geography of St. Kitts and Nevis, the West Indies*. Mexico City: Instituto Panamericano de Geografía e Historia.

Miller, Daniel. 1994. *Modernity: An Ethnographic Approach*. Oxford: Berg.

Miller, Errol. 1990. *Jamaican Society and High Schooling*. Mona: Institute of Social and Economic Research, University of the West Indies.

Mintz, Sidney. 1974. *Caribbean Transformations*. Chicago: Aldine.

Mullings, Leith. 2005. "Interrogating Racism: Towards an Antiracist Anthropology." *Annual Review of Anthropology* 34: 667–93.

Myers, Robert Amory. 1976. " 'I Love My Home Bad, but . . .': The Historical and Contemporary Contexts of Migration on Dominica, West Indies." Ph.D. diss., University of North Carolina, Chapel Hill.

Nunley, John. 1988. "Festival Diffusion into the Metropole." Pp. 165–82 in *Caribbean Festival Arts*, ed. John W. Nunley and Judith Bettelheim. Seattle: Saint Louis Art Museum and University of Washington Press.

Ochs, Elinor, and Lisa Capps. 1996. "Narrating the Self." *Annual Review in Anthropology* 23: 19–43.

Olwig, Karen Fog. 1985. *Cultural Adaptation and Resistance on St. John: Three Centuries of Afro-Caribbean Life*. Gainesville: University of Florida Press.

———. 1987. "Children's Attitudes to the Island Community: The Effects of Outmigration on Nation Building in the Caribbean." Pp. 153–70 in *Land and Development in the Caribbean*, ed. Jean Besson and Janet Momsen. London: Macmillan.

———. 1990. "The Struggle for Respectability: Methodism and Afro-Caribbean Culture on 19th Century Nevis." *Nieuwe West-Indische Gids* 64, nos. 3–4: 93–114.

———. 1993a. "Defining the National in the Transnational: Cultural Identity in the Afro-Caribbean Diaspora." *Ethnos* 58, nos. 3–4: 361–76.

———. 1993b. *Global Culture, Island Identity: Continuity and Change in the Afro-Caribbean Community of Nevis*. Reading: Harwood Academic Publishers.

———. 1995. "Cultural Complexity after Freedom: Nevis and Beyond." Pp. 100–20 in *Small Islands, Large Questions*, ed. Karen Fog Olwig. London: Frank Cass.

———. 1997. "Cultural Sites: Sustaining a Home in a Deterritorialized World." Pp. 17–38 in *Siting Culture: The Shifting Anthropological Object*, ed. Karen Fog Olwig and Kirsten Hastrup. London: Routledge.

———. 1999a. "Narratives of the Children Left Behind: Home and Identity in Globalised Caribbean Families." *Journal of Ethnic and Migration Studies* 25, no. 2: 267–84.

———. 1999b. "Travelling Makes a Home: Mobility and Identity among West Indians." Pp. 73–83 in *Ideal Homes? Social Change and Domestic Life*, ed. Tony Chapman and Jenny Hockey. London: Routledge.

———. 2001. "New York as a Locality in a Global Family Network." Pp. 142–60 in *Islands in the City: West Indian Migration to New York*, ed. Nancy Foner. Berkeley: University of California Press.

———. 2002a. "A Wedding in the Family: Home Making in a Global Kin Network." *Global Communities* 2, no. 3: 205–18.

———. 2002b. "The Ethnographic Field Revisited: Towards a Study of Common and Not So Common Fields of Belonging." Pp.124–45 in *Realizing Community: Concepts, Social Relationships and Sentiments*, ed. Vered Amit. London: Routledge.

———. 2002c. "A 'Respectable' Livelihood: Mobility and Identity in a Caribbean Family." Pp. 85–105 in *Work and Migration: Life and Livelihood in a Globalizing World*, ed. Ninna Nyberg Sørensen and Karen Fog Olwig. London: Routledge.

———. 2002d. "'Displaced' Children? Risks and Opportunities in a Caribbean Urban Environment." Pp. 46–65 in *Children in the City: Home, Neighbourhood and Community*, ed. Margaret O'Brien and Pia Havdrup Christensen. London: Falmer Press.

———. 2003a. "Children's Places of Belonging in Immigrant Families of Caribbean Background." Pp. 217–35 in *Children's Places: Cross Cultural Perspectives*, ed. Karen Fog Olwig and Eva Gulløv. London: Routledge.

———. 2003b. "'Transnational' Socio-Cultural Systems and Ethnographic Research: Views from an Extended Field Site." *International Migration Review* 37, no. 3: 692–716.

———. 2004. "Place, Movement and Identity: Processes of Inclusion and Exclusion in a 'Caribbean' Family." Pp. 53–71 in *Diaspora, Identity and Religion: New Directions in Theory and Research*, ed. Waltraud Kokot, Khachig Tölölyan, and Carolin Alfonso. London: Routledge.

———. 2005. "Narratives of Home: Visions of 'Betterment' and Belonging in a Dispersed Family." Pp. 198–205 in *Caribbean Narratives of Belonging: Fields of Relations, Sites of Identity*, ed. Jean Besson and Karen Fog Olwig. London: Macmillan.

Olwig, Karen Fog, and Kirsten Hastrup, eds. 1997. *Siting Culture: The Shifting Anthropological Object*. London: Routledge.

Olwig, Karen Fog, and Ninna Nyberg Sørensen. 2002. "Mobile Livelihoods: Making a Living in the World." Pp. 1–19 in *Work and Migration: Life and Livelihoods in a Globalizing World*, ed. Ninna Nyberg Sørensen and Karen Fog Olwig. London: Routledge.

Ong, Aiwa. 1999. *Flexible Citizenship: The Cultural Logics of Transnationality*. Durham: Duke University Press.

——. 2003. *Buddha Is Hiding: Refugees, Citizenship, the New America*. Berkeley: University of California Press.

Patterson, Orlando. 1982. *Slavery and Social Death*. Cambridge, Mass.: Harvard University Press.

Peach, Ceri. 1998. "Trends in Levels of Caribbean Segregation, Great Britain, 1961–91." Pp. 203–16 in *Caribbean Migration: Globalised Identities*, ed. Mary Chamberlain. London: Routledge.

Peacock, James L., and Dorothy C. Holland. 1993. "The Narrated Self: Life Stories in Process." *Ethos* 21, no. 4: 367–83.

Pierre, Jemima. 2004. "Black Immigrants in the United States and the 'Cultural Narratives' of Ethnicity." *Identities* 11, no. 2: 141–70.

Philpott, Stuart B. 1968. "Remittance Obligations, Social Networks and Choice among Montserratian Migrants in Britain." *Man* 3, no. 3: 465–76.

——. 1973. *West Indian Migration*. London: University of London Press.

Plaza, Dwaine. 1998. "Strategies and Strategizing: The Struggle for Upward Mobility among University-Educated Black Caribbean-Born Men in Canada." Pp. 248–66 in *Caribbean Migration: Globalised Identities*, ed. Mary Chamberlain. London: Routledge.

Richardson, Bonham. 1983. *Caribbean Migrants: Environment and Human Survival on St. Kitts and Nevis*. Knoxville: University of Tennessee Press.

Rosaldo, Renato. 1988. "Ideology, Place, and People without Culture." *Cultural Anthropology* 3, no. 1: 77–87.

Rosenwald, George C., and Richard L. Ochberg. 1992. "Introduction: Life Stories, Cultural Politics, and Self-Understanding." Pp. 1–18 in *Storied Lives: The Cultural Politics of Self-Understanding*, ed. George C. Rosenwald and Richard L. Ochberg. New Haven, Conn.: Yale University Press.

Rubenstein, Hymie. 1987. *Coping with Poverty: Adaptive Strategies in a Caribbean Village*. Boulder, Colo.: Westview Press.

Sanjek, Roger. 2003. "Rethinking Migration, Ancient to Future." *Global Networks* 3, no. 3: 315–36.

Scales-Trent, Judy. 1995. *Notes of a White Black Woman: Race, Color, Community*. University Park: Pennsylvania State University Press.

Scher, Philip W. 2003. *Carnival and the Formation of a Caribbean Transnation.* Gainesville: University Press of Florida.

Schnapper, Dominique. 1999. "From the Nation-State to the Transnational World: On the Meaning and Usefulness of Diaspora as a Concept." *Diaspora* 8, no. 3: 225–54.

Scott, Stephen Kingsley. 2002. "Through the Diameter of Respectability: The Politics of Historical Representation in Postemancipation Colonial Trinidad." *Nieuwe West-Indische Gids* 76, nos. 3–4: 271–304.

Smith, M. G. 1962. *Kinship and Community in Carriacou.* New Haven, Conn.: Yale University Press.

Smith, Raymond T. 1982. "Family, Social Change and Social Policy in the West Indies." *Nieuwe West-Indische Gids* 56, nos. 3–4: 111–42.

———. 1988. *Kinship and Class in the West Indies.* Cambridge: Cambridge University Press.

———. 1996. *The Matrifocal Family: Power, Pluralism and Politics.* New York: Routledge.

Somers, Margaret. 1994. "The Narrative Constitution of Identity: A Relational and Network Approach." *Theory and Society* 23: 605–49.

Strathern, Marilyn. 1992. *Reproducing the Future: Essays on Anthropology, Kinship and the New Reproductive Technologies.* Manchester: Manchester University Press.

Sutton, Constance R., and Elsa M. Chaney, eds. 1987. *Caribbean Life in New York City: Sociocultural Dimensions.* New York: Center for Migration Studies.

Synnott, Anthony, and David Howes. 1996. "Canada's Visible Minorities: Identity and Representation." Pp. 137–60 in *Re-Situating Identities: The Politics of Race, Ethnicity, and Culture,* ed. Vered Amit-Talai and Caroline Knowles. Peterborough, Ont.: Broadview Press.

Thomas, Deborah A. 2004. *Modern Blackness: Nationalism, Globalization, and the Politics of Culture in Jamaica.* Durham: Duke University Press.

Thomas-Hope, Elizabeth. 1978. "The Establishment of a Migration Tradition." Pp. 66–81 in *Caribbean Social Relations,* ed. Colin G. Clarke. Monograph Series no. 8, Centre for Latin-American Studies, University of Liverpool.

———. 1992. *Explanation in Caribbean Migration: Perception and the Image—Jamaica, Barbados and St. Vincent.* London: Macmillan.

———. 1998. "Globalization and the Development of a Caribbean Migration Culture." Pp. 188–99 in *Caribbean Migration: Globalised Identities,* ed. Mary Chamberlain. London: Routledge.

Tilly, Charles. 1990. "Transplanted Networks." Pp.79–95 in *Immigration Reconsidered: History, Sociology, and Politics,* ed. Virginia Yans-McLaughlin. New York: Oxford University Press.

Tölölyan, Khachig. 1996. "Rethinking Diaspora(s): Stateless Power in the Transnational Moment." *Diaspora* 5, no. 1: 3–36.

Trouillot, Michel-Rolph. 1988. *Peasants and Capital: Dominica in the World Economy*. Baltimore: Johns Hopkins University Press.

Tuan, Yi-Fu. 1974. "Space and Place: Humanistic Perspectives." *Progress in Geography* 6: 211–52.

———. 1980. "Rootedness versus Sense of Place." *Landscape* 24: 3–8.

———. 1999. *Who Am I? An Autobiography of Emotion, Mind, and Spirit*. Madison: University of Wisconsin Press.

Turner, Terrence. 1993. "Anthropology and Multiculturalism: What Is Anthropology That Multiculturalists Should Be Mindful of It?" *Cultural Anthropology* 8, no. 4: 411–29.

Valls, Lito. 1981. *What a Pistarckle! A Dictionary of Virgin Islands English Creole*. St. John, U.S. Virgin Islands: Prestige Press.

Verdery, Kathrine. 1994. "Ethnicity, Nationalism and State-Making: Ethnic Groups and Boundaries. Past and Future." Pp. 33–58 in *The Anthropology of Ethnicity: Beyond "Ethnic Groups and Boundaries,"* ed. Hans Vermeulen and Coral Grovers. Amsterdam: Het Spinhuis Publishers.

Vertovec, Steven. 1999. "Conceiving and Researching Transnationalism." *Ethnic and Racial Studies* 22, no. 2: 447–62.

Wallman, Sandra. 1979. "Introduction." Pp.1–24 in *Social Anthropology of Work*, ed. Sandra Wallman. ASA Monograph 19. London: Academic Press.

Warner, Oswald S. 2006. "Encountering Canadian Racism: Afro-Trini Immigrants in the Greater Toronto Area, Canada." *Wadabagei* 9, no. 1: 4–37.

Waters, Mary C. 1999a. *Black Identities: West Indian Immigrant Dreams and American Realities*. Cambridge, Mass.: Harvard University Press.

———. 1999b. "Sociology and the Study of Immigration." *American Behavioral Scientist* 42, no. 9: 1264–67.

Werbner, Pnina, and Tariq Modood, eds. 1997. *Debating Cultural Hybridity: Multicultural Identities and the Politics of Anti-Racism*. London: Zed.

White, Hayden. 1973, *Metahistory: The Historical Imagination in Nineteenth-Century Europe*. Baltimore: Johns Hopkins University Press.

———. 1981. "The Value of Narrativity in the Representation of Reality." Pp. 1–23 in *On Narrative*, ed. W. J. T. Mitchell. Chicago: University of Chicago Press.

Whyte, Millicent. 1983 (1977). *A Short History of Education in Jamaica*. London: Hodder and Stoughton.

Whyte, Susan R., and Michael A. Whyte. 2004. "Children's Children: Time and Relatedness in East Uganda." *Africa* 74, no. 1: 76–94.

Wilson, Peter. 1969. "Reputation and Respectability: A Suggestion for Caribbean Ethnology." *Man* 4, no. 1: 70–84.

———. 1973. *Crab Antics: The Social Anthropology of English Speaking Negro Societies of the Caribbean.* New Haven, Conn.: Yale University Press.

———. 1992 (1974). *Oscar: An Inquiry into the Nature of Sanity?* Prospect Heights, Ill.: Waveland Press.

Wilson, Tamar Diana. 1994. "What Determines Where Transnational Labor Migrants Go? Modifications in Migration Theories." *Human Organization* 53, no. 3: 269–78.

Wimmer, Andreas, and Nina Glick Schiller. 2003. "Methodological Nationalism, the Social Sciences, and the Study of Migration: An Essay in Historical Epistemology." *International Migration Review* 37, no. 3: 576–610.

Wylie, Jonathan. 1982. "Sense of Time, the Social Construction of Reality, and the Foundations of Nationhood in Dominica and the Faroe Islands." *Comparative Study of Society and History* 24, no. 3: 438–66.

———. 1993. "Too Much of a Good Thing: Crises of Glut in the Faroe Islands and Dominica." *Comparative Study of Society and History* 35, no. 2: 352–89.

Yans-McLaughlin, Virginia. 1990. "Metaphors of Self in History: Subjectivity, Oral Narrative, and Immigration Studies." Pp. 254–90 in *Immigration Reconsidered: History, Sociology, and Politics,* ed. Virginia Yans-McLaughlin. New York: Oxford University Press.

KAREN FOG OLWIG is professor in the Department of Anthropology at the University of Copenhagen. She is the author of *Global Culture, Island Identity: Continuity and Change in the Afro-Caribbean Community of Nevis* (1993); and *Cultural Adaptation and Resistance in St. John: Three Centuries of Afro-Caribbean Life* (1985). She edited *Small Islands, Large Questions: Society, Culture and Resistance in the Post Emancipation Caribbean* (1995) and coedited, with Eva Gulløv, *Children's Places: Cross-Cultural Perspectives* (2003); with Ninna Nyberg Sørensen, *Work and Migration: Life and Livelihoods in a Globalizing World* (2002); with Kirsten Hastrup, *Siting Culture: The Shifting Anthropological Object* (1997); and, with Jean Besson, *Caribbean Narratives of Belonging: Fields of Relations, Sites of Identity* (2005).

Library of Congress Cataloging-in-Publication Data
Olwig, Karen Fog
Caribbean journeys : an ethnography of migration and home
in three family networks / Karen Fog Olwig.
p. cm.   Includes bibliographical references and index.
ISBN 978-0-8223-3977-9 (cloth : alk. paper)
ISBN 978-0-8223-3994-6 (pbk. : alk. paper)
1. Ethnology—Caribbean Area. 2. Family—Caribbean Area.
3. Work and family—Caribbean Area. 4. Caribbean Area—Social conditions.
5. Caribbean Area—Economic conditions. 6. Caribbean Area—Emigration
and immigration. I. Title. GN564.C370S9 2007
306.09729—dc22   2006101129